GEORGE JOA~~CHIM GOSCHE~~N

THE TRANSF~~ORMATION OF A~~ VICTORI~~AN LIBERAL~~

THOMAS J. SPINNER, JR.

UNIVERSITY OF VERMONT

CAMBRIDGE
AT THE UNIVERSITY PRESS
1973

Published by the Syndics of the Cambridge University Press
Bentley House, 200 Euston Road, London NW1 2DB
American Branch: 32 East 57th Street, New York, N.Y. 10022

Library of Congress Catalogue Card Number: 73-77263

ISBN 0 521 20210 8

Printed in Great Britain
by Western Printing Services Ltd, Bristol

TO MY MOTHER AND FATHER

CONTENTS

PREFACE

The life of George Joachim Goschen helps to explain how one element of nineteenth-century liberalism became a significant part of twentieth-century conservatism. In his portrait of Victorian England, G. M. Young observed: 'Of all decades in our history, a wise man would choose the eighteen-fifties to be young in.' At the time of the Crystal Palace exhibition in 1851, Goschen was twenty years of age. When he entered the House of Commons in 1863, he was a member of the Liberal party. At the time of his death in 1907, he had joined the Conservative party, even though his principles and general outlook had changed very little.

British conservatism has never been dominated by reactionaries; conservatives are often caught in the dilemma of having to administer programmes which they, at one time, opposed. An innovation accepted over a period of time soon becomes a part of tradition and the conservative may find himself arguing that it is wise to conserve what he previously thought so destructive to the social fabric. The situation is equally difficult for the young reformer or liberal who sees his ideas accepted but does not wish to go beyond them. It is only logical that he will begin to find a greater community of interest with those who are now willing to preserve the reforms for which the reformer had previously fought. This helps to explain how Toryism and a satisfied *laissez-faire* liberalism eventually combined to form the modern Conservative party of Great Britain. Though the Tory was much more willing to employ the state for social purposes than the *laissez-faire* liberal, both could agree that society should remain hierarchical and divided into classes.

The British middle class succeeded in transforming the aristocratic state and sought to replace it with a *laissez-faire* market society. But the middle class soon came to fear the demands of

ix

the working class for Parliamentary regulation, the welfare state and socialism. The central conflict of contemporary history was apparent: the struggle between those with much wealth and property and those with little or none.

Goschen had been in the vanguard of the struggle to destroy aristocratic privilege and to create in its place a liberal state in which each individual would have equality of opportunity and all careers would be open to talent. His belief in a self-regulating market and free trade forced him to reject most proposals for social legislation.

Goschen's 'financial liberalism' was soon overshadowed by his 'liberal realism'. He was repelled by the idea of democracy, for he had no faith in the ability of the lower classes to govern the country and expected to be plundered when they obtained the vote. Democracy, he feared, would lead to equality and equality would destroy the liberty for which the middle class had fought.

It is unfortunate that Goschen is usually 'remembered' – if at all – because of Lord Randolph Churchill's 'forgetfulness'. His career is really of much greater importance: son of an immigrant, youthful merchant banker, member of the House of Commons for over thirty-five years, Cabinet member for sixteen years, Egyptian delegate of the Council of Foreign Bondholders, Special Ambassador to the Ottoman Empire, and organizer of the Liberal Unionist party. It illuminates many of the problems confronted by the British in the late nineteenth century. It also demonstrates why one nineteenth-century Liberal entered the twentieth century as a Conservative.

It is a pleasure to record the kindness and assistance which I received while conducting my research in the United Kingdom. One year in Putney and one year in Hampstead have provided memories which my wife and I shall always cherish. Space prohibits me from listing all of the many people who aided me but special thanks are due to several organizations and libraries: the Royal Archives at Windsor, the Institute of Historical Research, the Public Record Office, the National Register of Archives, the British Museum, the Bodleian Library, the India Office Library, the Kent Archives Office, the Ipswich and East Suffolk Record Office, the Public Record Office of Northern Ireland, the libraries of the universities of Birmingham, Cambridge, Durham and London, and the libraries of New College and Christ Church, Oxford, and the London School of Economics.

I would like to record my indebtedness to Her Majesty the Queen for her gracious permission to use material from the Royal Archives at Windsor. Thanks are also due to the following individuals who allowed me to work on their family papers and to quote extracts from them: the Duke of Devonshire, the Marquess of Salisbury, the Honourable David Smith, the Earl of Cranbrook, Earl St Aldwyn, Earl Spencer, Viscount Chilston and Hubert Elliot. I would also like to thank the present Lord Goschen and other members of his family for their assistance. Mr D. C. Goschen of Rusape, Rhodesia was especially helpful in providing several bundles of interesting letters. The Warden and Fellows of New College, Oxford have kindly permitted me to quote from the Milner Papers.

My work on Goschen began while I was a graduate student at the University of Rochester. I am very grateful to Dr Willson H. Coates, the supervisor of my doctoral thesis, and to the other members of the Department of History at that university. The University of Vermont provided me with a summer grant in 1968 and a magnificent sabbatical in 1969–70. Professor Peter Stansky of Stanford University, the editor of this series, read several drafts of this study and provided me with invaluable advice and assistance. The faults and flaws are, of course, my own. This is the first biography of Goschen to appear since the authorized study prepared by his friend and political associate, Arthur R. D. Elliot, in 1911.

My deepest debt is to my wife and children. My wife has typed and retyped numerous drafts over the past few years as we tried to bring Goschen to the light of day. And in the midst of it all, two children were born. While the book might have been completed much sooner without the appearance of Carolyn and Tommy, it would not have been half so much fun.

THOMAS J. SPINNER, JR.

ABBREVIATIONS

BP: Earl of Balfour Papers
ChP: Joseph Chamberlain Papers
CrP: Earl of Cromer Papers
DP: Devonshire Papers
F.O.: Foreign Office
GP: William E. Gladstone Papers
HP: Sir Edward Hamilton Papers
K.A.O.: Kent Archives Office
MP: Milner Papers
P.R.O.: Public Record Office
RA: Royal Archives at Windsor
SP: Marquess of Salisbury Papers

Elliot: Arthur R. D. Elliot,
Life of George Joachim Goschen
(London, 1911)

RUGBY, OXFORD — AND AMBALEMA

George Joachim Goschen was distinguished throughout his career by a vigorous patriotism, perhaps partially explained by his being the son of an immigrant.[1] He was also a proud member of the Church of England and reacted strenuously – though with out any sign of bigotry – to taunts by his political opponents that he was a product of Jewish forebears.[2] These innuendos may have furnished just the spur necessary to bring a twenty-year, intermittently-pursued, project to an end. This was a biography of Goschen's grandfather and it provided an excellent opportunity to explore his genealogy. Rejecting family mythology about the romantic origins of his progenitors, Goschen concluded that the oldest verifiable ancestor whom he could discover had been a Lutheran minister in the principality of Merseburg in 1609 who was called by the Latinized name of Joachimus Gosenius.[3]

After a destitute childhood Goschen's grandfather – Georg Joachim Goschen – became a very successful publisher and printer in the city of Leipzig in the kingdom of Saxony. But the unsettled era of the Napoleonic wars brought him close to economic disaster. Early in 1814 when his two eldest sons had already joined the struggle against Bonaparte he wrote to a friend that his third son, William Henry, then twenty years of age, was in London. Instead of joining the army, he had entered into a

---

[1] See the comment by Goschen's Oxford contemporary and friend of many years, J. Franck Bright, later Master of University College, Oxford, in *A History of England* (London, 1904), vol. 5, p. 268. It is also stressed by Goschen's protégé, Viscount Alfred Milner, in 'George Joachim Goschen: Obituary', *Proceedings of the British Academy 1907–1908*, 359–64.

[2] James W. Lowther (Viscount Ullswater), *A Speaker's Commentaries* (London, 1925), vol. 2, pp. 44–5; Robert Farquharson, *In and Out of Parliament* (London, 1911), pp. 259–60. See also Sir Sidney Lee, *King Edward VII* (New York, 1925–7), vol. 2, pp. 618–19, for Kaiser William II's grumbling comment on the appointment of Sir Edward Goschen – George Joachim Goschen's youngest brother – as Ambassador to Germany in 1908.

[3] George Joachim Goschen, *The Life and Times of Georg Joachim Goschen, Publisher and Printer of Leipzig, 1752–1828* (London, 1903), vol. 1, p. 3.

partnership with a wealthy Bremen merchant by the name of
Fruhling.[1]

William Henry Goschen was George Joachim Goschen's
father. In writing of this phase of his family history, George
Goschen noted that Fruhling had not been rich but 'he was a man
of some means and of good standing'.[2] The firm of Fruhling and
Goschen, primarily merchant bankers, prospered after some years
of difficulties and in 1829 William Henry Goschen took an
English wife. Ten of their twelve children grew to maturity.[3]
Their first son was born in 1831 and was named after the publisher of Leipzig who had died three years before. Three other
sons, Henry, Charles Hermann and Alexander Heun, eventually
became senior partners of the firm while the youngest, William
Edward, entered the diplomatic service. Two sisters married
British clergymen and two others married brothers, Baron
Gustav and Baron George von Metzsch-Reichenbach of Ger-
many.

The years immediately following the Congress of Vienna were
difficult for many inhabitants of the British Isles. But they were
also a time of astonishing expansion and of great opportunity for
forceful merchants such as William Henry Goschen. Honest but
determined to show a profit, aggressive but rational, a Christian
but not aspiring to imitate the path of Jesus, he never ceased to
believe that by being a worldly success and accumulating wealth
he was glorifying his God.

And accumulate he certainly did. So much so that the opportunities open to his children were continually expanded. Assuming that young George would enter the firm, his father had him
educated at home until he was nine. He then attended the Black-
heath Proprietary School near the family residence at Eltham,
about 10 miles distant from the City of London. At the age of
eleven he was sent off to Saxe-Meiningen to continue his education. For the next three years he lived what he later called 'a

[1] *Ibid.*, vol. 2, pp. 387–88. Fruhling married a sister of his young partner and
died in 1841.
[2] *Ibid.*, vol. 2, p. 388.
[3] Elliot, vol. 1, pp. 4–5. This account of Goschen's early life is largely based upon
Chapter I of Elliot's biography.

rather Spartan life' since it was often so cold in the dormitories that 'we had to break the ice in our basins with our boots'.

Recognizing his son's great ability, the elder Goschen decided to bring him back to England and in August 1845 George became a pupil at Rugby. In later years George recalled that his 'father's ambition for me, at all times, was indeed almost a passion'. Goschen's arrival at Rugby occurred three years after the death of the school's most famous headmaster, Dr Arnold. Along with improvements in the curriculum Arnold emphasized freedom, responsibility, self-government and plenty of exercise. The public school boy was expected to be 'manly' – an everrecurring word in Victorian England – and to have acquired the character of a 'gentleman'. Friends and acquaintances made at public school and college were often indispensable in later life. The public schools – as in Goschen's case – also succeeded in bringing together the children of the new aristocracy of industrial, financial and commercial wealth created by the Industrial Revolution and the children of the ancient landed aristocracy which had governed England for so many centuries.

The young English boy with the German name and German accent had some difficulties with Britain's future leaders during his first year and could see 'that the *elite* hardly considered me as one of their number'. This had 'mortified' him and caused 'unpleasant feelings'. But this soon changed and he reported to his father that he finally seemed 'quite to belong to all the rest of the preposters'.

While one of Goschen's schoolmates remembered him as 'slow but persistent' in sports, he was not at all sluggish in his academic work. He won a number of scholastic awards at Rugby including the English Prize Poem, earned by Matthew Arnold a few years before. Both young poets borrowed a line from Byron's *Childe Harold* as their source of inspiration. Goschen's poem was called 'The Celts' and viewed the Celtic soul as the embodiment of 'deathless liberty'. The French, the Irish and the Highlanders were characterized by a 'restlessness' and an 'abhorrence of tyranny'.

3

Goschen was soon thoroughly at home at Rugby and so completely a part of the system that he was prepared to lead a rebellion against his own house master, Bonamy Price – later Professor of Political Economy at Oxford and a strong defender of *laissez-faire* – when it appeared that an attempt was being made to whittle away the authority and 'privileges' of the sixth form. After some extreme remarks by the youthful rebels an amicable understanding was achieved and Rugby's headmaster, Dr A. C. Tait, later Archbishop of Canterbury, was able to report to William Henry Goschen in 1850 that his son had been 'one of the best heads of the school that I have known during my Headmastership'.

In the summer of 1850 young George travelled to the Continent with his sister Henrietta in order to visit relatives and to rest before beginning his Oxford career. After some amusing encounters and several flirtations which caused concern at home, Goschen returned to England and wondered: 'Here is the last evening before my college life, a momentous moment, treated, however, with improper levity by me. Persiflage. Shall I like Oxford? Will Oxford like me?'

Failing to win a scholarship at University or Trinity Colleges, Goschen began as a commoner at Oriel. He had great success as a debater at the Union and was elected president in 1853 but he remained troubled at not having won a scholarship. One examiner had called him 'the cleverest man' in the competition but with a 'deficiency in scholarship'. This led Goschen to write to his father that he could not 'bear to be beaten – either by men or subjects, and I have been beaten by both'. Shortly thereafter he was encouraged by winning an Exhibition at Oriel and his father rewarded him with bonds worth £2,000.

J. Franck Bright and Frederic Harrison, the future champion of Positivism, provide glimpses of Goschen at Oxford. Bright recalled that Goschen's room had been an excellent example of the 'intellectual side of Oxford Undergraduate life'. The conversation of Goschen and his friends 'invariably touched on serious and important matters'. Goschen was devoid of all 'priggishness' and had a fine sense of humour. 'He was what the slang of the day calls thoroughly "human", and he enjoyed to the full the lighter side of college life.' Frederic Harrison looked back 'with gratitude' to the Essay Society which had been founded by Goschen and some of his contemporaries at Oxford. 'The papers read and debated and the discussions and general meetings were continued long after we had quitted the University.'[1]

At the Oxford Union, Goschen spoke in defence of Shelley and against papal aggression. He supported Tennyson as 'the poet' of the nineteenth century and while approving the state endowment of the Roman Catholic Maynooth Seminary in Dublin, he opposed the admission of Jews to Parliament. He rejected a motion demanding 'a remedy against the concentration of large masses of capital in the hands of a few individuals' as well as one which stated that 'the increasing power of the great towns is opposed to the idea of the English constitution and inconsistent with the national prosperity'. In November 1851 Goschen moved that the French Revolution had 'conferred the greatest benefits on mankind' and in 1852 he denounced the Derby ministry and defended Gladstone and the Peelites against the charge of betraying their party. 'Consistency' could be 'dangerous' if it led men 'to continue in error after they have discovered it'.

In an autobiographical letter which he wrote to a friend during these years at Oxford he commented that he was somewhat 'different from other people' because of his 'two nationalities, the grafting of English sentiments and feelings upon German blood, and one continual change that has been going on in me is the gradual passing from the German to the English'. Goschen's father was a Whig and a Free Trader and young George acquired the same general political orientation. His happy days at Oxford came to an end in 1853 after a distinguished academic career.

Goschen hoped to marry Lucy Dalley but his father objected: not so much to the young lady as to the comparative youth of a son who had not yet proved himself in the business world. No doubt the senior Goschen remembered that both he and his father had deferred marriage until their mid-thirties when they

---

[1] Frederic Harrison, *Autobiographic Memoirs* (London, 1911), vol. I, p. 93.

were financially independent. There were some trying moments between father and son until they decided to postpone the 'marriage question'. George would first fulfill an apprenticeship overseeing the investments of Fruhling and Goschen in South America. Goschen's father – reflecting upon his own experiences – urged his son 'to become a great merchant – a little one is but a poor beast'. Ambition – though not an excessive amount – was a good thing and would not militate 'against thoughts on eternity. It is one of the motives planted in the human breast on purpose to work out what is beneficial.'

In the autumn of 1854 Goschen left for New Granada (now Colombia), and the change must have been a startling one for a young gentleman from Oxford. Though Bogotá was pleasant, most of Goschen's time was spent supervising investments in tobacco, sugar, rice and cochineal in Ambalema, a small tropical town on the Magdalena River. Here he lived a life of primitive simplicity for more than a year and despite a very varied climate he seemed to thrive. But he longed for Miss Dalley and 'to return once more to the great world'.

The letters which passed between George and his father provide a fascinating view of the activities of a merchant banker in the 1850s.[1] The profits could be immense but so too were the investments and the risks involved. Britain's entry into the Crimean War in early 1854 caused new complications. On 31 October 1854 – in one of his first letters – Goschen's father was 'glad to say that no sinister events have occurred in business, no failures have happened which interest us, indeed there has been nothing of the sort, but things do not look well'. He was particularly worried about their India accounts but noted that all the markets in London were 'weak' with the exception of sugar and rice.

The elder Goschen sent advice and information to his son at two-week intervals. But George soon 'alarmed' his father with demands for larger sums than anticipated at Ambalema. On 16 May 1855 the elder Goschen thundered his misgivings over

---

[1] The letters written by Mr Goschen to George and Charles and by Mrs Goschen to Charles were made available by Mr D. C. Goschen of Rusape, Rhodesia.

6

George's speculations in the quinine-producing cinchona bark. George had admitted that he 'undertook the matter with fear' and that he 'foresaw . . . dissatisfaction'. His father wondered why he had done it. 'I assure you that had I been at Bogotá and felt convinced of the displeasure of my partner, I should not have done the thing: much less should you have done it knowing that Wallroth would be furious.'[1] George's impetuous actions meant that Fruhling and Goschen had so much money tied up at Ambalema that they would have to 'abstain from business, be it ever so profitable, which requires cash advances'.

By the autumn of 1856 George Goschen had returned to the 'great world' of London though father and son continued to worry about the political turmoil in New Granada. By the early 1860s their investment exceeded £300,000 and profits were becoming 'very nice'. Fruhling and Goschen kept the Ambalema complex and as late as 1890 George Joachim Goschen still maintained an investment of £23,000 through the firm, which brought him a yearly return of £1200.

Unfortunately, Goschen's father was still not reconciled to accepting Miss Dalley as his daughter-in-law. Entertainment was made difficult for the family as the elder Goschen would not permit Lucy to be present. Mrs Goschen regretted her husband's attitude but found it impossible to reason with him. But George was as determined as his father and refused to put off the wedding. To the joy of his family, Mr Goschen finally agreed – at the last moment – to be present in September 1857 when the marriage took place.

The newlyweds still had one major obstacle to hurdle. What would the senior Goschen do when they arrived for their first visit? Mrs Goschen described the scene. The train was nearly an hour late and the family was 'getting anxious' when

at last the sound of carriage wheels announced their approach and the juveniles rushed to the Hall door! I followed and was the first to receive them, and then to my great delight Papa appeared, gave Lucy a kiss and we heard the word 'welcome' which sounded gracefully on our listening ears.

[1] Charles Wallroth became a partner in Fruhling and Goschen in 1834. The senior Goschen had a somewhat uneasy relationship with him.

Poor thing! She was nervous and too agitated to speak – it was a trying moment for her to come amongst us for the first time after our 3 years painful estrangement. However Papa's one kind word reassured her, and set her at ease and it was so late we hurried in to dinner and Papa and George talked away at a great rate, and very cheerfully.

William Henry Goschen had capitulated to his son and all indications are that the family once again became the close-knit unit it had been before. A week later (29 October 1857) Mrs Goschen observed that 'it becomes quite natural now to have George and Lucy with us'. Lucy Goschen will not be heard of much in this biography but she will always be in the background – a strong support for her husband. It would seem to have been an extremely happy and successful marriage.

George Goschen now concentrated his energies upon becoming a successful merchant banker and he graduallly took more and more of the company's operations under his personal direction. Wallroth died in 1857 – worth £160,000 – and his father was happy to play a slightly less active role. But the elder Goschen's energy did not diminish until the day of his death in 1866; he maintained a paternal, and often very active, supervision over the firm to which he had dedicated his life. He made numerous visits to the continent for rest, to visit his German relatives and to further the interests of Fruhling and Goschen.

Much of the senior Goschen's time was spent in Saxony where he moved in the highest social circles; his letters refer to many balls which he had given or attended with Saxony's ranking dignitaries. But he never forgot that he was a merchant banker, and once he realized that George was definitely embarked on a public career with his election to the House of Commons in 1863, the elder Goschen began to pour advice into the ears of Charles, now marked out as George's successor. On 16 October 1864 he wrote; 'Deal with young men for the purpose of helping them forward in the world, of obliging family and friends, act from sentiment and – you are done always . . . Is not it sad that we merchants cannot be amiable?' He had great doubts about committing the firm too heavily in the field of Egyptian government bonds though he acknowledged that large profits might be made. But George and

Charles apparently insisted upon going ahead and the father congratulated George on 18 November 1864 for the successful completion of an 'audacious enterprise'.

In early 1866, however, William Henry Goschen was deeply worried over a new Egyptian loan. The risks involved seemed much too great. Fruhling and Goschen had already floated sizable Egyptian government bonds in 1862 and 1864. In 1866 they contracted to handle yet another £3 million's worth.[1] On 22 January 1866, the elder Goschen roared his disapproval. Charles had informed him that £1 million had already been taken but what of the other £2 million? The reports which Charles had sent to Saxony were much too vague and he had admitted that the money market did not look too strong. 'To me the whole affair is awful. If those 1½ or two millions are *not* placed — and is that an alternative not to be thought of at all — Fruhling and Goschen will fail. The thought is too horrible; it must have occupied your mind.' He wondered how they could 'have played such a hazardous game' at that particular moment. 'Great Heavens How would George [he had just entered the Russell Cabinet] appear on his pinnacle of glory.' He was sure there 'must be some safety valve, some way to escape, someone, or rather some association to fall back upon. I shall not have a moment's rest, till I am assured upon this point.' Still it would be necessary for him to continue his social activities in Saxony 'miserable' though he was and 'whilst I should like to bury my head in the ground, I have to go through scenes which require my best appearance to-night at Court, where the King is sure to congratulate me on George's promotion'. Within a short time, however, Mr Goschen could smile again, for the loan turned out to be another success.

The Goschen family had its origins in Saxony and not in Prussia and thus had mixed feelings over the brutal way in which Bismarck achieved German unity. In 1864 William Henry Goschen wrote that Beust, Saxony's chief minister, was not very

---

[1] See Leland H. Jenks, *The Migration of British Capital to 1875* (New York, 1927), pp. 419–24. See also David S. Landes, *Bankers and Pashas* (London, 1968).

popular. 'But Bismarck is a beast, and it seems as if Beast and Beust love to tease each other.' On 2 May 1866 – just before the outbreak of the Austro-Prussian War – he wrote to Charles in bitter terms about Prussia's alliance with Italy. 'It is perfectly awful to contemplate that Germans, if Prussians may be called so, are getting up Foreigners to attack other Germans, to assist in humbling Austria because they have made up their mind at any price to have undivided sway over all Germany.' As war became inevitable the senior Goschen decided to return to London. But he died on the way at Ghent, on 28 July 1866. His will provided for every member of the family and indicated just how successful he had been. A trust fund of £85,000 was established for his wife. It was concluded that Fruhling and Goschen was worth about £1 million.

George Joachim Goschen had been quickly accepted by the English financial elite. In 1858, while only twenty-seven years of age, he was selected as one of the directors of the Bank of England and became known in the City of London as the 'Fortunate Youth'.[1] Walter Bagehot, in his classic study of the Bank of England, wrote that a new director was expected to be 'a well-conducted young man who seems likely to be fairly efficient twenty years later'.[2] A few years later Goschen published *The Theory of the Foreign Exchanges*.[3] He believed that his daily contact with a great variety of international transactions enabled him to test a number of theories which had been advanced with respect to the Foreign Exchanges. While hoping to interest both the theoretical economist and the general reader, he wrote primarily for those who were acquainted with the international money market but had not 'systematized their experiences or drawn any conclusion from the facts which they have observed'. Goschen later conceded that his knowledge of political economy

[1] Elliot, vol. 1, p. 46. Goschen ended his service as a director of the Bank of England in 1865.
[2] Walter Bagehot, *Lombard Street* (London, 1910), p. 211 (first published in 1873).
[3] (London, 1861). The book was partially revised in 1863 and again in 1864. It subsequently went through a number of printings and was translated into many languages. All references to the book are from the 1886 edition.

had been limited to Aristotle and John Stuart Mill when he wrote his book and he admitted that he had 'never been a regular student of the literature of the science'. His views were based upon 'individual study, observation and analysis'.[1]

The book was based upon the idea of a self-regulating market which should not be interfered with by any of the national states involved in international commerce. To Goschen there was nothing difficult about the way in which foreign exchanges functioned. Supply and demand working 'naturally' and without interference would determine interest rates and thus regulate the flow of capital around the world. His analysis accepted the business cycle as a natural part of economic life. It also accepted implicitly the existence of a pool of labourers who would be employed in good times and unemployed during a time of economic depression.

In his book Goschen did recommend – and his advice seems to have been followed – that when the Bank of England decided to change its interest rate as a 'natural' reaction to economic fluctuations, it must do so by increments of 1 per cent rather than of $\frac{1}{2}$ per cent in order to have any immediate significant effect upon the exchanges.[2] Some doctrinaire members of the *laissez-faire* school thought that this modest proposal was designed to give the bank excessive authority to regulate the market. Goschen hastened to deny this intention in the second edition of his book in 1863. He agreed with his critics 'that the action of banks or individuals' could not, and should not, 'accomplish that which must really be determined by supply and demand'.

In early 1865 George Goschen had no difficulty in explaining an interest rate at the Bank of England of 7 per cent while in January 1868 it was just as 'natural' for him to accept an interest

---

[1] George Joachim Goschen, *Essays and Addresses on Economic Questions, 1865–1893* (London, 1905), p. viii. This book contains nine essays which were written over the thirty years from 1865. Each of the essays contains a brief introduction in which Goschen comments upon his earlier writings.

[2] Goschen, *Foreign Exchanges*, pp. 132–46. Bagehot thought this was a wise proposal. See also Sir John H. Clapham, *The Bank of England* (Cambridge, 1944), vol. 2, pp. 258–9.

rate of 2 per cent.[1] The high rate of interest in 1865 was absolutely necessary to keep gold from going abroad. England and
France were sending the banking techniques of capitalism 'on a
crusading tour throughout the world'. But too much British gold
had been invested abroad. The Bank of England reacted by
raising the interest rate and Goschen saw 'no alternative between
this remedy, painful as it is for the moment, and an inconvertible
currency, which is not only painful but absolutely ruinous'.
Governmental intervention was not warranted since 'money
becomes scarce and dear from natural causes and not from
legislation'. He warned: 'You may legislate as you will, but you
cannot legislate for panics.' Measures designed to 'artificially'
lower the interest rate would 'disturb the free play of supply and
demand'. Forty years later he affirmed that 'The main principles
which I defended then I still hold today.'

Between 1865 and 1868 there had been a financial panic and the
interest rate collapsed to 2 per cent. Gold was piling up in Paris
and London but no one wanted to borrow; 1867 could be summarized as 'one long financial, commercial, industrial, and railway
crisis'. The mind of the public had been transformed 'from an
excess of confidence to exaggerated despondency'. Confidence
had withered away and people were hoarding money or putting
it into banks and not into speculative ventures. The low interest
rate came not 'from the abundance, but from the disgust of
capital'. Capital was 'on strike' and had 'retired to its tents'. And
nothing could be done. When confidence revived, the machinery
was in proper order to function again but until then it was
necessary to accept a situation which could only be made worse
by unnatural interference. 'Come what may, contracts must be
fulfilled, credits be honoured, goods be paid for, and the loss
endured.' Many years later he still agreed with his original assessment but he granted that 'the changes in the currency laws of our
neighbours have made watchful caution as to our gold reserves
more imperative than ever.'

[1] Both essays are reprinted in *Essays and Addresses* and quotations are made from
this source. 'Seven Per Cent' originally appeared in the *Edinburgh Review* of
January 1865 and 'Two Per Cent' in the *Edinburgh Review* of January 1868.

In a primitive way Goschen had seen what John Maynard Keynes would later develop with such brilliance, though Goschen would never have accepted the Keynesian solution. It was possible for the economy to come to a halt at the bottom of the business cycle and to remain there for a considerable length of time before public confidence revived and private investment began the long process of recovery. Keynes advocated governmental investment in order to 'prime the pump' and thereby restore confidence and encourage investment from the private sector of the economy. Goschen could see the problem but his solution was to do nothing until 'natural causes' eventually got the economy moving once again in the direction of prosperity and full employment. He was not, however, a rigid doctrinaire and was prepared to accept a very limited amount of state intervention if it was designed to create those conditions in which the self-regulating market might be able to work more efficiently. This attitude was acceptable in an aristocratic–bourgeois society but it would be intolerable to a mass democracy. By the time these articles were published, Goschen had been elected to Parliament and was now in a position to apply his ideas to a much wider range of problems.

Blessed with a rugged constitution, a sturdy physique and excellent health, the thirty-one-year-old Goschen could look back over a pleasant and secure life. His youth and young manhood had provided him with the broad philosophical attitudes and general political views from which he deviated only imperceptibly during the next forty-five years. The attention to detail and hard work which had enabled his father to become a great success had convinced Goschen that 'freedom' and 'liberty' would provide the atmosphere in which every citizen could achieve his full potential.

All restrictions on the right of the individual to pursue his own self-interest must be removed. The influence of Adam Smith's *laissez-faire* ideas and Jeremy Bentham's utilitarianism is clear. But Goschen never fully grasped the distinction between Smith's 'natural' harmony of interests and Bentham's 'artificial' harmony of interests. Goschen was prepared to plan for a *laissez-faire* utopia, believing that this would lead to the greatest amount of happiness for the greatest number of people. Many would disagree, however, and urge that planning be done for other purposes and ends because *laissez-faire* seemed to provide too much happiness for the few and too much unhappiness for the many.

CHAPTER 2

THE 'FORTUNATE YOUTH'
ENTERS POLITICS

In the elections of 1859, which had been won by the supporters of Lord Palmerston and Lord John Russell, the City of London returned four Liberal members for its four seats. The change in political orientation of the City of London demonstrates the changing outlook of the British financial community. Liberal in the period of Palmerston, the City moved gradually into the Conservative fold until it was considered a stronghold of Conservatism in 1880.

Looking back upon his entry into active politics Goschen recalled that two colleagues from the Bank of England, Robert Crawford and Kirkman Hodgson, came to his office in 1863 to request that he contest a by-election for the City of London. He remembered that Westminster had been his goal since youth but he 'had never dreamt' that the opening would come so soon, or in so brilliant a form'.[1] At a meeting of the London Liberals, Goschen was preferred to two other candidates and was elected without opposition, as the Conservatives failed to provide a nominee. Goschen's main problem came from a whispering campaign which expressed indignation over the choice of a candidate with such an un-English name.[2] His election address which he later called a bit too 'rhetorical and academical' advocated local self-government while respecting the ancient rights of the Corporation of the City of London, the secret ballot, parliamentary reform, the ending of all religious disabilities and the abolition of church rates.

The Parliament to which George Goschen was elected had already been sitting for four years. Palmerston, the aged but still powerful Liberal Prime Minister, had almost as many minor differences of opinion with his colleagues, Gladstone and Lord

[1] Elliot, vol. 1, pp. 47–8.
[2] At this time he still used an umlaut in the spelling of his last name: Göschen.

John Russell, as he did with the Conservative opposition, led by the fourteenth Earl of Derby and Benjamin Disraeli. The tendency of the country and of most parliamentarians was to forget the relatively small disagreements which existed and to enjoy the fruits of mid-Victorian prosperity. The old and respected Prime Minister embodied and reflected the interests and desires of both the aristocracy and the middle classes.

Goschen quickly emerged as a leader in the fight to remove certain religious disabilities (such as subscription to the Thirty-nine Articles) which still existed at Oxford and Cambridge. These requirements prevented Nonconformists from obtaining advanced degrees and excluded them from many positions at the ancient universities. Goschen's campaign for their abolition indicates his genuine desire to remove all old restrictions on the right of the individual to pursue his interests and his career to the limit of his abilities. In his maiden speech Goschen stated that he spoke as a member of the Church of England and as a graduate of Oxford but he could see no danger to either if religious tests were abolished. It was necessary to have every type of opinion at a university and 'he was ready to assert that it would be unfortunate if repose were the chief characteristic of our Universities'.[1] Despite valiant efforts by Goschen and his friends in the following years, the major remaining religious disabilities at Oxford and Cambridge were not abolished until 1871.

Goschen's views on government interference with industry and trade were quickly stated. While prepared to admit that the government should maintain 'a watchful eye' over the anchors and chains of passenger ships, Goschen reminded the House that 'the ships did not belong to them, but to the shipowners; and, if Government was to interfere in such matters there would be no end to their interference, and great injury would be done to the free course of trade.'[2] During the session of 1863 he also spoke in support of limited liability in partnership arrangements. 'There ought to be as full and perfect freedom of contract as was consistent with the interests of commerce and morality.'[3] Some years

[1] *Hansard's Parliamentary Debates*, CLXXI (24 June 1863), 1385–97.
[2] *Hansard*, CLXXII (8 July 1863), 407.   [3] *Hansard*, CLXXII (15 July 1863), 834–6.

later when he re-read his first speeches in the Commons he noted that he had 'already struck the note of that objection to the encroachments of Government interference on the freedom of individual action which, for good or for evil, has coloured to a certain extent my political opinions throughout my career'.[1]

The purpose of the House of Commons, Goschen contended, was neither to 'prevent' nor to 'stimulate enterprise or speculation' but rather 'to clear the field so that individuals might take their own course'.[2] He did qualify his opposition to government intervention when he supported a measure designed to protect the invested savings of the working class. It would provide 'that absolute security and honesty' which 'every man who made a painful sacrifice of the present for the sake of the future – for such it was to the working man – was entitled'. Nothing was being forced on the working classes but without 'interfering with their liberty of action in any way, it gave them help to be self-helpful'.[3]

It seemed clear that Goschen had made a favourable impression upon the leaders of the Liberal party when he was invited by Lord Palmerston to second the address in reply to the speech from the throne at the opening of the 1864 session of Parliament. Palmerston instructed him on the topics to be discussed. The emphasis was to be upon foreign policy. Goschen asked if he should not say something about domestic legislation. The Prime Minister replied – perhaps playfully – that there was 'really nothing to be done' as they could not 'go on adding to the Statute Book *ad infinitum*'. But Goschen decided to discuss both domestic and foreign affairs in 'a bold throw for success'. Looking back upon this 'memorable incident' forty years later, he conceded that he might have been regarded as 'presumptuous and possibly ridiculous'. Fortunately, it turned out to be 'extremely successful'.[4]

---

[1] Elliot, vol. 1, p. 60.
[2] *Hansard*, CLXXIV (3 May 1864), 2126.
[3] *Hansard*, CLXXIV (17 March 1864), 242–7.
[4] Elliot, vol. 1, pp. 65–6. See also Herbert C. F. Bell, *Lord Palmerston* (London, 1936), vol. 2, pp. 370–1 and Donald Southgate, '*The Most English Minister . . .*' (London, 1966), pp. 527–8.

Although the Southern insurrection had not yet been extinguished in the United States the main diplomatic problem which confronted the European world at that time was Schleswig-Holstein. Palmerston and Russell were inclined, under certain conditions, to aid the Danes against Prussian and Austrian aggression. Goschen agreed and wanted to indicate in his speech that the 'Manchester School with its strong inclination to non-intervention, and its too absolute devotion in my judgment, to peace at any price' did not control the Liberal party. With respect to domestic matters he wished to show that 'the attitude of some of the extreme Radicals towards the upper classes and their alleged indictment against the latter for their indifference to the poor, had jarred upon me, and in this respect, too, I thought it right to show that one wing of the Liberal party repudiated such an attitude'. Goschen believed that this speech, though delivered early in his parliamentary life, gave 'the key of my general attitude both towards foreign and domestic questions during my whole career'.[1]

The Times of the following day thought Goschen's speech showed 'germs of unusual promise' but John Bright was not pleased. 'This Oxford "young man of great promise" has, I suppose, already found out the way to please the Aristocratic Order. It shows a disposition which does not promise honesty or generosity in his Liberalism. The future will prove what he is.'[2] Two days later Goschen received a letter from Bright's ally, Richard Cobden. Was it wise, Cobden queried, for Goschen to attack the Radicals when it appeared that they would often be voting together? He warned Goschen that 'there is nothing more seductive to a new member than an eager hearing which a many-sided criticism is sure to command for him'.

Goschen replied that there were many issues upon which he could agree with Bright and Cobden. But this made it imperative for him to demonstrate that there was no total accord. There was a 'great difference' between them 'on the foreign policy of the country, and on the language to be held with regard to the rela-

---

[1] Elliot, vol. 1, p. 67. See *Hansard*, CLXXIII (4 February 1864), 80–6.
[2] Walling, R. A. J. (ed.), *The Diaries of John Bright* (London, 1930), p. 267.

tions between different classes in this country'. Bright's views on 'the motives and intentions of the governing classes' were a 'libel' and 'most dangerous'.[1]

The General Election of 1865 resulted in a victory for Goschen and the supporters of Palmerston but before the new Parliament met, the old statesman was dead. John Russell – in the House of Lords since 1861 – formed a new ministry. Gladstone retained the Exchequer but was also designated Leader of the House of Commons and thus clearly marked out as Russell's heir. Just before his death Palmerston had given some thought to moving Goschen into a minor office. It was his hope to expand the responsibilities of the Civil Lord of the Admiralty and thus justify an increase in the pay of this official. Palmerston suspected, however, that Goschen was 'largely engaged in commercial Pursuits which he would not give up for office, unless it were . . . of some prominent political character'. Gladstone agreed that the post would not be satisfactory for Goschen.[2]

When news of Palmerston's death reached Gladstone, he assured Russell of his support but warned that 'any Government now to be formed cannot be wholly a continuation, it must be in some degree a new commencement'.[3] Speculation was rife as to what changes and new appointments Russell would make.[4] His decision to move Lord Clarendon from the Duchy of Lancaster to the Foreign Office meant that a new Chancellor for the Duchy was required. There were also many minor posts to be filled.

Goschen's father cautioned his son about accepting a ministerial position so early in his career. The life-expectancy of Russell's government did not seem promising. He was sure that George would be in the Cabinet in the future and reminded his son that that would mean 'an end of money making. What you have got, you may keep and that is all; whilst on the other hand

---

[1] Elliot, vol. 1, pp. 71–6.
[2] Philip Guedalla (ed.), *Gladstone and Palmerston* (London, 1928), pp. 343–4.
[3] Spencer Walpole, *The Life of Lord John Russell* (London, 1891), vol. 2, p. 422, Gladstone to Russell, 18 October 1865.
[4] Russell's thoughts and actions about the reconstruction of the government can be followed in the Russell Papers, P.R.O. 30/22/15*f*, 15*g*, 15*h* and 16*a*.

your rank may be raised.' This was not idle speculation but a realistic appraisal and it followed, according to William Henry Goschen, that his son should wait until he had 'enough money for a peerage'.[1]

Despite his father's warning Goschen accepted the post of Vice-President of the Board of Trade (without a seat in the Cabinet) when it was offered by Russell in early November 1865. The appointment was greeted with a chorus of approval: he seemed ideally suited for such a position on the basis of his business and commercial experience.

Political speculation and gossip continued to revolve around possible additions to the Cabinet and a general feeling prevailed that the individual appointed to the Duchy of Lancaster would be in the Cabinet. This ancient office carried with it little in the nature of specific duties but it provided the Cabinet with an individual who could be assigned specific tasks as the need arose. Robert Lowe was considered the individual best qualified for the Cabinet but his opposition to the extension of the suffrage made his entry impossible. Hoping to alienate as few people as possible, Russell suddenly decided to promote Goschen to the Duchy of Lancaster and the Cabinet in early January 1866. There was both surprise and indignation in the ranks of the Liberal party. It seemed a much too rapid promotion for a young member of Parliament. Those who were passed over, particularly Hartington, Layard and Stansfeld, could point to the fact that Goschen had been in the Commons for less than three years and had almost no ministerial experience. Sir George Grey, the Home Secretary, had urged the appointment of Goschen to the Duchy but he had not advocated his immediate admission to the Cabinet.[2] Russell and Grey had calculated that Goschen might be able to help Gladstone with his Treasury work but the Chancellor of the Exchequer was not happy with the new appointment. Gladstone believed that Goschen ought to have proved

[1] Elliot, vol. 1, pp. 80–1.
[2] Russell Papers, Grey to Russell, 6 January 1866, P.R.O. 30/22/16a and G. P. Gooch (ed.), *The Later Correspondence of Lord John Russell 1840–1878* (London, 1925), vol. 2, pp. 342–3.

himself in office before being elevated to the Cabinet.[1]
The Manchester Guardian thought Goschen's appointment
'odd, after the long delay' and somewhat strange since he seemed
to be 'fitly placed' at the Board of Trade.[2] Gladstone described
the affair to his wife on 11 January 1866: 'All that I heard last
night and to-day shows me more and more the extreme and
gratuitous folly of Lord R's proceedings about Goschen. It is a
serious political error, without the smallest excuse of any kind and
committed in the teeth of remonstrance.'[3] Henry Brand, the Chief
Whip of the Liberal party, regarded Russell's precipitate decision
as a 'mistake'. The 'old hands' were offended and Layard was
threatening to resign.[4] The Secretary of State for War, Lord de
Grey, reported that the Goschen promotion had been a 'surprise'
to most of the Cabinet. The 'future stability' of the government
might have been jeopardized.[5]

The queen had approved of Goschen's appointment but was
dubious about giving him a seat in the Cabinet until a year or so
had passed. She feared there might be 'much jealousy'. Russell
granted that some members of the Cabinet had acquiesced 'rather
unwillingly' but argued that 'a Chancellor of the Duchy of Lancaster is of great use in the Cabinet, and of no use at all out of the
Cabinet'.[6] Russell formally offered Goschen a seat in the Cabinet
on 11 January 1866 and a delighted Goschen accepted with
enthusiasm on the same day.[7]

The astute political commentator, T. Wemyss Reid, editor of
The Leeds Mercury, provided a perceptive analysis of Russell's
reasoning. Goschen's appointment was due to his lack of 'political encumbrances'. There was no opposition to him as there was
to Lowe or Bright. It was true that he 'did not belong to any of

---

[1] Russell Papers, P.R.O. 30/22/16a. See also John Morley, *Life of William E.
Gladstone* (New York, 1903), vol. 2, p. 156, note 1 and Elliot, vol. 1, p. 82.
[2] *The Manchester Guardian* (10 January 1866), 1.
[3] A. Tilney Bassett (ed.), *Gladstone to his Wife* (London, 1936), pp. 170–1.
[4] Herbert Maxwell, *Life of the 4th Earl of Clarendon* (London, 1913), vol. 2,
p. 306.
[5] *Ibid.*, vol. 2, pp. 306–7.
[6] George E. Buckle (ed.), *Letters of Queen Victoria* (New York, 1907–32), 2nd
series, vol. 1, pp, 294–5.
[7] Russell Papers, P.R.O. 30/22/16a.

the great governing families of the country, he could not boast of the enormous wealth of the Rothschilds and he was not even a specially eloquent or powerful speaker'. But he was 'an accomplished man of affairs' and it struck Reid that Russell found Goschen 'a man after his own heart'. The new Cabinet member had strong 'Liberal sympathies' but he was 'the reverse of an adventurous or extravagant politician. Cool-headed, far-seeing, cautious, more anxious to go safely than swiftly, there can be no doubt that in the eyes of the veteran Whig Chief he was a much more acceptable personage than most of the young politicians of that day.'[1]

Goschen's first term as a Cabinet member did not last long. The Cabinet decided upon resignation in June of the same year when Lord Dunkellin carried a motion to substitute rateable for rental value in the proposed Electoral Reform Bill of 1866. Gladstone's measure was being resolutely opposed by the Conservatives and a section of the Liberals led by Lowe. Russell disliked seeing his career come to an end and the queen was distressed that there should be political instability at the very moment hostilities had broken out between Austria and Prussia. Gladstone insisted, however, that it would be dishonourable to remain in office after losing a major vote. He later regretted that he had not fought harder for a dissolution but he absolutely opposed the idea of asking for a general vote of confidence.[2] After a week of evaluating the alternatives, the Cabinet finally resigned. On the following day (27 June) Goschen praised Gladstone for his 'gallant stand' against the proposal for a general vote of confidence and concluded: 'I can assure you that I feel personally indebted to you for having carried your point.'[3]

Goschen's arguments in support of the defeated Reform Bill are important in the light of his subsequent refusal to see the vote extended to the agricultural labourers in the counties. The main provision of the Russell–Gladstone bill had been to lower the voting qualification for householders in the boroughs from a £10

[1] Sir T. Wemyss Reid, *Politicians of Today* (London, 1880), pp. 234–9.
[2] Morley, *Life of Gladstone*, vol. 2, p. 207.
[3] GP, Add. Mss 44161, f. 145.

rental to a £7 rental. Lowe contended that Britain would soon be a democracy and subject to the same abuses which characterized political life in the United States and Australia. The mob and the caucus would govern rather than those best qualified by education and training. Goschen challenged Lowe's comparison of Britain with the United States and Australia and went on from his criticism of a fellow Liberal to a general assault upon the Conservative opposition. It seemed to him that the British working classes were anti-democratic and giving them the vote 'would not turn them into democrats in a country like this, where the circumstances were entirely different from those in Australia'. Only about 400,000 voters in the boroughs were to be added to the electoral rolls and this was hardly a revolutionary number. Was it really possible to say that the Commons represented the entire nation? 'It is true that we all represent the interests of the working classes as well as we can. We represented them paternally; but we really cannot be called, in the strict sense of the word, a representation of the working classes.'[1]

After the Cabinet's decision to resign, Goschen found himself sitting on the opposition side of the House for the first time in his short career. His brief service in the Cabinet also entitled him to sit on the opposition front bench. While recognized as an effective and knowledgeable debater, Goschen's delivery remained mediocre throughout his career. Part of his problem came from poor eyesight which grew progressively worse and made it almost impossible for him to see his notes. Even if he had been able to see them he may well not have been able to read them; his handwriting was atrocious and grew worse with age. One friend urged him to 'make style as style, and elocution as elocution, your study for *the next few years* . . . It is that *one thing*, and that *only, which separates you from the first orators of the day and places you in the third rank.*'[2]

This well-intentioned advice was never taken and a political associate writing at the time of Goschen's death remarked that he

[1] *Hansard*, CLXXXII (23 April 1866), 1959–71. See also his speech of 30 May 1866 in which he opposed an educational test as a requirement for voting in *Hansard*, CLXXXIII, 1497–9.

[2] Bernard Cracroft to Goschen, 8 October 1868, Elliot, vol. i, pp. 104–5.

had been 'one of the ablest and most popular platform speakers of the day' which was surprising 'for he suffered from a husky enunciation, excessively short sight' and 'an ungainly deportment'. The public however had always been impressed by Goschen's 'singular independence and honesty of purpose, and the skill with which he could retort on interrupters. In fact, he rather courted interruptions and enjoyed it.'[1]

The great event of 1867 was the introduction of a new Reform Bill by the Conservative Prime Minister, Lord Derby, and his Leader in the Commons, Benjamin Disraeli. The Conservatives had brought down Russell but now found themselves supporting a measure of reform which would enfranchise approximately twice as many voters as the abortive Reform Bill of 1866. A number of moderates from both parties were scandalized but Lord Derby had gradually become convinced that household suffrage in the boroughs was inevitable and he saw no reason why the Conservatives should not receive credit for it. After twenty years of leading a minority party he was prepared for a 'leap in the dark'. Disraeli agreed with his chief. Armed with his fantasies about Tory democracy, Disraeli was willing to gamble on obtaining a Conservative majority from among the new working-class voters in the boroughs. Three resignations from the Cabinet did not deter them. The third reading of the bill failed to bring a division; the Lords' amendments were quickly dealt with; and the bill became law.

The Conservative leaders had been influenced by both public and parliamentary opinion. Liberals and Conservatives shuddered at the thought of yet another Reform Bill in 1868 if this one was rejected. The necessities of finding and maintaining a working parliamentary majority had led to the introduction of abortive Reform Bills in 1852, 1854, 1859, 1860 and 1866. By 1867 the vast majority of the Members of Parliament yearned to hear no more about this topic. How delightful to solve the suffrage question – perhaps for the remainder of the century – and silence John

[1] Lowther, *Commentaries*, vol. 2, pp. 44–5. See also George W. E. Russell, *Collections and Recollections* (London, 1904), pp. 170–2 and Lord George Hamilton, *Parliamentary Reminiscences and Reflections* (London, 1916–22), vol. 1, pp. 36–9.

Bright's relentless diatribes at the same time. Public opinion was insistent, the parliamentarians weary – the bill became law.

Goschen's support of the moderate but unsuccessful Reform Bill of 1866 and his qualified acceptance of the more radical one of 1867 were now tempered by apprehension about the demands which the new voters would make. More than willing to enfranchise the aristocracy of the working class since they had a real 'stake in society', he worried about the lower part of the workers in the boroughs who had now received the vote. He shuddered when he contemplated the demand which was bound to be made by the agricultural labourers: that household suffrage be extended to the counties. These views were expressed in two articles which he wrote in late 1867 for Anthony Trollope's new journal of opinion, *St. Paul's Magazine*.[1] Goschen was astonished that Disraeli expected to find a large number of Conservatives among the newly enfranchised. What disturbed Goschen even more was the fact that 'the probable effects of the Reform Bill . . . were scarcely discussed till the Bill was on the point of passing into a law of the realm'. It seemed as though the great majority in the Commons wanted to pass a bill, any bill, in order to get Reform out of the way. This lack of concern for 'future political consequences' was 'remarkable'. Usually a revolution was required to produce such a massive 'transfer of power'. But now England's governing classes, which had 'taken care, to say the least, not to govern in a manner hostile to their own interests' were convinced that parliamentary reform was 'not likely to be followed by any great changes of policy of a nature to affect their interests, their comforts, or even their practical supremacy'. The upper classes demonstrated 'their faith in the deep-rooted stability of our institutions and their belief that all Englishmen are very much alike'.

Goschen observed that there had been no great issues before the Commons which excited the public since the repeal of the

[1] Elliot, vol. 1, pp. 159–62. The articles were published anonymously but, according to Elliot, it was well known that Goschen was the author. 'The Leap in the Dark', *St. Paul's Magazine*, I (October 1867), 8–22, and 'The New Electors; or Probable Effects of the Reform Bill on the Strength of Parties' (November 1867), 148–62.

Corn Laws. Unfortunately, there were growing demands 'for more central and drastic actions by Parliament'. Until recently 'compulsory legislation' aimed at limiting 'the free action of individuals' had been very limited. But the English people often forgot the 'supreme power in every department of life' which Parliament could exert. In recent years, Parliament had been mainly concerned with approving a Budget, levying taxes, and then spending the money which had been raised. This had enforced the idea that 'political power shall stand in some relation to tax-paying' and that 'those who paid little ought not to be allowed to outnumber in the polling book those who paid much'. But now this was all to be changed.

In his second article, Goschen donned the mantle of prophet. He agreed with the Conservatives that the new electors would be loyal to the throne and the existing form of government but doubted that this would mean Conservative votes. Many new questions would be raised in the next Parliament and it was not too difficult to deduce the type of subjects the Radicals would introduce. The poorer classes would be more attracted to warlike tactics than the representatives of middle-class Liberalism but he could not believe they would accept 'the more professional military spirit which is so often somewhat ostentatiously exhibited on the conservative benches of the House of Commons'. The new electors could certainly not be enthusiastic over Tory support of the game laws. This question was not even a class question since the Conservative farmer suffered much more from the game laws than the Radical artisan. The Conservatives had much more confidence in the 'residuum' of the towns than in the unenfranchised 'residuum' they had nearby in the counties.

Goschen had no doubt that the Liberal party would be 'greatly invigorated by the accession of the new electors, not from the point of view of any probable increase to the nominal majority of liberal members, but from the likelihood of a stronger and broader character being imparted to the creed which they will be called upon to hold'. While admitting that there might be occasional alliances between landlord and worker, he expected that 'on the vast majority of political subjects there will be more identity of interest and sympathy of feeling between the different classes of borough voters amongst themselves, than between the poorest class of borough electors and territorial lords'. The new electors would surely not support the Conservative programme on taxes, primogeniture and entails. Disraeli's programme which was now partially designed to gain him the support of the new voters might very well cause him to lose his own party.

Goschen predicted his own future career when he wrote;

There may be sore trials in store for that large number of men who have been honest Liberals all their lives, friends to Reform, keen for religious liberty, true to the backbone on most matters which have hitherto constituted the test of political loyalty, but who may yet be unable to fall in with the broader tone which already has begun to mark the temper and opinions, and will soon begin to mark the measures of the great liberal party.

The major new phenomenon which Goschen saw was 'sentiment'. 'Sentimental grievances' still received some ridicule but by and large they were given a much greater hearing than before. 'Conspicuous amongst sentimental grievances are some of the Irish questions.' Sentimental reasons were also advanced to end flogging in the army and to limit capital punishment. These were questions

which, if we might use a very dangerous phrase, Frenchmen would analyse as connected with 'the dignity of man'. It appears to us that the new electors will impart a stimulus to this whole class of subjects, and that by their aid 'sentiment', with its virtues and its faults, will make considerable progress in extruding cynicism from the very commanding position which it still occupies in politics.

The lower classes even wanted the state 'to assist them in raising themselves by passing compulsory laws which might lessen their temptations and protect them against themselves'. Whether 'for good or evil' the new electors were going to increase the strength of the sentimental section in the Commons and 'their influence will materially lessen the stringency with which the doctrines of "*laissez-faire*" will be applied'.

Goschen judged that the new electors would 'throw most of their weight onto the most liberal side of the liberal party' and thus an 'immense responsibility will rest on those Liberals whose strength the Reform Bill has most tended to increase'. They would have 'to direct the new forces into useful channels, while preventing them from overflowing the banks'. He concluded on an optimistic note:

But we firmly believe that the accession of vigour and new blood, the appreciation of the wants and feelings of our fellow-subjects, the revelations on matters of which the majority of present electors are necessarily ignorant, the extension of sympathy with our forms of government which must result from the admission of many hundred thousands of voters belonging to a class which had hitherto few accredited channels for making its wishes known, will vastly increase the usefulness and the authority of Parliament, while the classes who have hitherto exclusively wielded political power will still retain ample strength to prevent their being overwhelmed by numbers on any question where they have right and justice on their side.

It was in early 1868 that Gladstone brought in his motions advocating the disestablishment of the Church of Ireland. Disraeli, now Prime Minister, was defeated several times but did not resign as the new electoral registers had not been completed. Later in the year the new voters were given an opportunity to determine whether they preferred Disraeli and the Conservatives or the Liberal party, now led by Gladstone. Goschen prepared to fight his first election under the new conditions imposed by the extension of the suffrage.

CHAPTER 3

PAUPERS AND ADMIRALS 1868—1874

The elections of late 1868 gave the Liberals a majority of about 120. Disraeli decided not to meet Parliament and resigned office. While chopping down a tree Gladstone received word that he was to become Prime Minister for the first time. The middle class, it appeared, was determined to curtail further aristocratic and ecclesiastical privilege. While some of the wealthier and more established members of the commercial, financial and industrial elite were already moving toward the Conservative party, the vast majority were still committed to the Liberal party as the embodiment of the spirit of reform and progress.[1]

Religious tests were abolished at Oxford and Cambridge, the purchase of commissions in the army was revoked by royal warrant and most posts in the Civil Service were thrown open to merit. Anglican and Nonconformist, landlord and capitalist, the upper classes in general, decided they had better compromise as best they could on matters of religion and agree to a system of national primary education. Their 'new masters' had to be educated. Despite these important reforms no great break with the past occurred: Gladstone and his colleagues had an outlook similar to Peel and Cobden and were carrying out reforms which had been advocated by John Bright for twenty years. The economic prosperity which lasted into the late 1870s prevented any demand for the fundamental transformation of the structure of society from being heard. But British politics were now more neatly polarized behind two charismatic leaders representing two major groupings of opinion. Political parties in the modern sense were slowly being created.

Gladstone hastened to designate his Cabinet. Much surprise was generated by the inclusion of Robert Lowe at the Exchequer,

---

[1] See John R. Vincent, *The Formation of the Liberal Party, 1857–1868* (London, 1966), pp. 257–8 and Trygve R. Tholfsen, 'The Transition to Democracy in Victorian England', *International Review of Social History*, VI, pt. 2 (1961), 226–48.

while his most vehement opponent in the Adullamite debates, John Bright, became President of the Board of Trade. Gladstone's 'umbrella' had begun the difficult task of attempting to cover Whigs and Radicals, Reformers and anti-Reformers. Lord Hartington and Goschen were also invited to become members of the Cabinet: Hartington as Postmaster-General and Goschen as President of the Poor Law Board.

This was an exceptionally able Cabinet and Goschen was thus privileged to participate in one of the great reforming administrations of the nineteenth century. In his election address he had ridiculed Disraeli's cry that Protestantism was in danger because Gladstone proposed to disestablish the Irish Church. It was rather a long overdue act of justice. Goschen pledged his support to cutting expenditure, reforming the universities, establishing a system of national education, and investigating and changing the system of local taxation. He was again returned for the City of London although the Liberal attempt to win all four seats under the provisions of the Reform Act of 1867 which gave each elector in the City only three votes resulted in failure. One Conservative was returned along with the Liberals.

Goschen had been much too optimistic about carrying all four seats as a letter to Gladstone on 15 November makes clear. It was estimated that there were 8500 Liberals and 5600 Conservatives in the City and Goschen confidently proclaimed: 'We *must* win, if there is no confusion.' But he knew that the attempt to distribute the Liberal votes might end in disaster and cause them to lose 'three out of the four'.[1] That very nearly happened since the Conservatives only put forward three candidates. Goschen topped the poll with 6520 votes.

Gladstone apparently hoped that Goschen's financial training would enable him to effect both economies and administrative reforms in the Poor Law Board. Poor relief in England and Wales had been placed in the hands of a Poor Law Commission by the 1834 Poor Law. In 1847 the Commission had been replaced by the Board over which Goschen was appointed president. The Poor Law of 1834 was designed to build a free labour market and

[1] GP, Goschen to Gladstone, 15 November 1868, Add. Mss 44161, ff. 224-5.

to end the system of allowances and outdoor relief on the part of the parishes. Larger units than the parish were desired and elected Boards of Guardians – supervised by Whitehall – were to administer these new areas. Workhouses were to be constructed in which conditions would be so miserable that the pauper would desire any other type of employment. It was a strange mixture of paternalism, *laissez-faire* and utilitarianism.

Several of Goschen's speeches and his 'Question Time' answers provide the background for the two comprehensive bills he introduced in 1871 to reform local government and taxation in the counties. Queried as to what he was doing to assist hungry paupers, Goschen replied that this was the responsibility of the Boards of Guardians concerned. More workhouses were needed in London but he contemplated no emergency relief in the London area. That would only draw 'pauperism to the metropolis'.[1] There was quite too much out-of-door relief instead of the strict application of the workhouse test.[2] For Goschen, the Poor Law provided both 'respect for the liberty of the subject' and the 'right which the law had conceded to every man to be supplied with the first necessaries of life at the public expense'. In England, 'every single life, however poor and miserable' was valued yet he specified that 'it would be impossible effectively to deal with the most pressing evils of vagrancy unless the public guarded themselves against the exercise of indiscriminate charity'.[3]

The terrible tragedy of children without parents also confronted Goschen. He sympathized with the orphans but was uncertain as to the best policy to pursue. Continued unemployment led to a proposal, supported by Florence Nightingale among others, that the government assist overseas emigration. Miss Nightingale was not impressed by the president of the Poor Law Board:

I don't think he will ever do much. He is a man of considerable mind, great power of getting up statistical information and Pol. Econ. but with no

---

[1] *Hansard*, CXCIX (15 February 1870), 327–8.
[2] *Hansard*, CXCIX (25 February 1870), 826–32.
[3] *Hansard*, CCI (13 May 1870), 655–5.

practical insight. It is an awkward mind – like a pudding in lumps. He is like a man who has been Senior Wrangler and never anything afterwards.[1]

When a plan for state-subsidized emigration was debated, Goschen admitted that 'there was much misery in some places' but he wondered if they should 'legislate for a particular district'. This was 'a semi-communistic plan' which would mean 'dangerous and novel legislation'. He preferred to place his 'faith . . . in the unfailing energy, the irrepressible elasticity, and the spontaneous efforts of an industrious, high-spirited and self-reliant people'.[2]

The fact that Goschen was a practising politician with a commercial background and not simply a *laissez-faire* doctrinaire may be seen by his support for a proposal to provide loans to the Metropolitan Board of Works to build parks in the London area. Not only did he advocate the construction of more parks but he also agreed

that where land for a park was taken in a populous district, the Board should have power to make what he should call 'a fringe' to the park itself – that was, should have power to build a decent class of houses around the park, instead of allowing the miserable tenements that might be in the neighbourhood to stand around it, or contractors to come in and run up a wretched description of houses. It was a most expensive proceeding to construct parks in the midst of populous districts, and the least that could be done was to reserve a small portion of the land for the purpose of recouping some of the expenses incurred.[3]

Goschen was also responsible for justifying the assessment of the local rates designed to provide sufficient funds for the various Boards of Guardians. Local rates were a major political issue since the landed gentry felt it was taxed exorbitantly. Its spokesmen condemned the high rates on land as compared with the lower rates on personal property. Sir Massey Lopes, a leader of the Conservative gentry, demanded a royal commission to investigate the incidence of local taxation. Goschen rejected this proposal and informed Gladstone that 'it is perfectly out of the

---

[1] Cecil Woodham-Smith, *Florence Nightingale* (London, 1950), p. 504.
[2] *Hansard*, CCII (17 June 1870), 407–48.
[3] *Hansard*, CXCVIII (2 August 1869), 1130–1.

question to allow an extra-parliamentary authority to deal with taxation'.[1]

In early 1870 Goschen became chairman of a select committee set up to investigate local taxation. Sir Massey Lopes was also on the committee and led the successful opposition to Goschen's draft report. Goschen conceded that rates had doubled in England and Wales in the previous thirty years but he argued that real property was not taxed excessively. He had convinced himself, contrary to the wishes of the gentry, that the rates must be shared between owner and occupier and not paid solely by the occupier as provided by the Reform Act of 1867.[2]

As Goschen continued his investigation of the confusion which existed in the administration of the Poor Law he became converted to the view that only total reform of both local government and local taxation could begin to meet the problem. In September 1870 Earl Spencer queried him about the working of the Poor Law near his home at Althorp. Goschen replied that 'these questions as to the redistribution of parishes and Unions are most knotty. The greatest anomalies exist – in every part of the country, so that if one once begins to recast the Unions, there is no saying where one can stop.'[3]

Not knowing exactly where to stop Goschen decided to reorganize the entire system. He introduced two comprehensive bills on 3 April 1871 and denounced the existing system. There was 'a chaos as regards authorities, a chaos as regards rates, and a worse chaos than all as regards areas'.[4] Goschen endeavoured to use the smallest unit, the parish, as the basis for his reconstruction of local government and local taxation. He suggested that only one consolidated rate be assessed. The rate-payers in each parish were to elect a chairman of the Parochial Board. These Parochial Boards would assume the executive functions of the vestry and all those duties which were now in the hands of the overseers,

[1] GP, Goschen to Gladstone, 15 January 1869, Add. Mss 44161, ff. 150-2.
[2] The development of Goschen's ideas on local taxation and local government may be followed in George J. Goschen, *Reports and Speeches on Local Taxation* (London, 1872).
[3] Spencer Papers, Misc. Papers, 1869.
[4] *Hansard*, ccv (3 April 1871), 1115-43.

highway surveyors and lighting and watching inspectors. Above the Parochial Boards would be a County Financial Board composed equally of Chairmen of the Parochial Boards and Justices of the Peace. These far-reaching proposals never had a second reading as the government decided to withdraw them in the face of opposition on both sides of the House.[1]

The landed gentry feared it would lose control of the counties and abhorred Goschen's proposal that rates be shared equally by occupiers and owners. It wanted relief for itself and not for its tenant farmers and agricultural labourers. The squires were so excited that they were even prepared to enlarge the authority of the central government if this was the only way relief could be obtained. Sir Massey Lopes' resolution in March 1871 to transfer such local charges as justice, police, paupers and lunacy to the consolidated fund was defeated when Goschen moved the previous question. There were a number of Liberal defectors and when Lopes moved his resolution again in the following year it was passed by a substantial majority. It was a pity that Goschen failed to conciliate the landlords, for the parishes desperately required reform and his proposals were a sensible move in a needed direction.

In the summer of 1870 the peace of Europe was shattered by the outbreak of hostilities between France and Prussia. While the idea of German unification was appealing, Goschen deplored the harsh tactics employed by Bismarck and referred to him once as an 'incarnate fiend'.[2] The Cabinet had to decide what role Britain should play in these revolutionary events which were fundamentally altering the European state structure. When it appeared that the defeated France was prepared to open negotiations, Granville, though pessimistic, wrote to Goschen on 19 September 1870 that peace would be 'a blessing'. He hoped that

---

[1] See the criticism in Bryan Keith Lucas (ed.), Joseph Redlich and Francis W. Hirst, *The History of Local Government in England* (London, 1958), pp. 210–14. See also Lady Victoria Hicks Beach, *Life of Sir Michael Hicks Beach, Earl St. Aldwyn* (London, 1932), vol. 1, pp. 25–6; Thomas F. Hedley, *Local Taxation: Observations on The Right Honourable G. J. Goschen's Bill on Parochial Assessments* (London, 1873); and R. Dudley Baxter, *Local Government and Taxation and Mr. Goschen's Report* (London, 1874).

[2] Granville Papers, Goschen to Granville, [?] September 1870, P.R.O. 30/29/54.

the war would end without any English involvement in the conditions of peace 'which will be considered by the Germans as insufficient, and by the French humiliating'.[1] Gladstone, however, tried unsuccessfully to convince Granville and the Cabinet that Britain should rally the neutral powers in an attempt to prevent Prussian seizure of Alsace-Lorraine without reference to the wishes of the inhabitants.[2]

In early October, Goschen switched from Granville's to Gladstone's side. He justified his reversal to Granville on 3 October:

What I have been opposed to, in common I believe with all the Cabinet, is the giving advice, the offering mediation, the useless attempt of bringing people together who won't be brought together. . . On the whole I have cordially sympathised with the German victories and quite think the downfall of the military prestige of France will be of incalculable benefit. But I confess I see great danger ahead in the unbounded success not only of the German arms, but of Bismarck's unscrupulous, cynical, and cruel policy. . . . But Mr Gladstone's draft despatch seemed to me to afford some standing ground. It was not advice, or meddling or mediation. It was practically a protest against a principle which is universally rejected by the Liberal Party throughout Europe.[3]

Granville responded that Britain should not resort to 'a principle at an inopportune moment'. It would only mean 'that, although we cannot prevent it, the Prussians are not to take any territory from the French'. The time might arrive when Gladstone's 'bit of buncombe' could be usefully employed 'and possibly help Bismarck by doing so'. There was no other ground 'upon which we can make a stand against France being utterly humiliated'. It was imperative, therefore, not to use their one bargaining device when it 'would only complete the anger of the Germans and encourage the French to hold out'.[4]

The resignation of Hugh C. E. Childers as First Lord of the Admiralty in March 1871 led to Goschen's being shifted from the

---

[1] Granville Papers, P.R.O. 30/29/54.
[2] Lord Edmond Fitzmaurice, *Life of the Second Earl Granville* (London, 1905), vol. 2, p. 62.
[3] Granville Papers, P.R.O. 30/29/54.
[4] Granville Papers, copy of letter, Granville to Goschen, 5 October 1870. Partly printed in Elliot, vol. 1, pp. 131–3.

Poor Law Board to the Admiralty. Childers was ill from over-work and as a result of the death of his son who perished along with 500 other men when the turret ship *Captain* was lost in the Bay of Biscay in September 1870. Ensor speculated that the opposition of the landed gentry to Goschen's local government plan caused Gladstone to move him to the Admiralty.[1] This is unlikely since Goschen introduced his bills on local government and local taxation after his elevation to the Admiralty. He was next in line for advancement to a higher post after Hartington became Chief Secretary for Ireland in December 1870. Nothing pleased Gladstone more than economies in the army and the navy. A man of Goschen's temperament and training would not be likely, Gladstone probably reasoned, to permit armament zealots to carry him along in great ship-building schemes.

There were few politicians in nineteenth-century Britain who managed to master the great departments of state which they administered. Their few years in control were inadequate for anything less than a superficial understanding of the depart-ment over which the Cabinet member was nominally the chief. More often than not he relied upon the permanent staff of civil servants and career officials for guidance and advice. At the War Office and the Admiralty it was also necessary to contend with generals and admirals. The admirals and civil servants in the Admiralty usually wanted to increase the size of naval estimates and were shocked at any suggestion of reduction. They justified their demands for a large navy, which somehow never seemed large enough, by an appeal to international tensions, decay of existing ships and the absolute necessity for Britain to maintain the strongest navy in the world.

Gladstone's expectation that a former financier would be able to reduce the navy's budget was disappointed. Ironically, when Goschen was at the Admiralty, his tendency was to agree with his naval advisers and to reject appeals from the Chancellor of the Exchequer or the Prime Minister for such economies. When he was Chancellor of the Exchequer from 1887 to 1892 he greatly

---

[1] R. C. K. Ensor, 'Some Political and Economic Interactions in Later Victorian England', *Transactions of the Royal Historical Society*, 4th series, XXXI (1949), 18.

modified his views about defence needs and requested the spending departments to reduce their expenditure. He was then working under a different set of assumptions and with a different type of civil servant. The civil servants and naval personnel at the Admiralty wanted a strong navy no matter what the cost. The Treasury officials were usually aghast at the demands made by the Admiralty and the War Office and emphasized economies and a balanced budget.

When Gladstone asked Goschen in September 1871 to reduce naval estimates for the following year Goschen responded that Childers had been so successful in eliminating wasteful practices that further savings would touch the policy of the government itself rather than simply the Admiralty. Gladstone had hoped that the cessation of hostilities in France would carry with it a reduction in British naval estimates.[1]

The Cabinet was also perturbed at the intransigence of the United States in reaching a final decision on the 'Alabama Claims', resulting from the depredations caused by Confederate ships constructed in Britain. Demands by the United States that indirect claims be considered by the Geneva arbitration tribunal were denounced in Great Britain. The British had made a number of concessions in the treaty which set up the arbitration tribunal and confidently expected the Americans to withdraw the indirect claims. When, however, the United States presented both sets of claims the Cabinet was forced to reconsider its earlier 'indulgence'. Goschen was not satisfied with Granville's handling of the affair and insisted that the indirect claims must be rejected. On 16 June 1872 Goschen notified the Prime Minister that he did 'not see how, holding the views I do, I could remain a member of the Cabinet'. Granville's persistent retort was that his questions were too hypothetical but Goschen protested that they had a 'practical bearing' to him.[2]

Gladstone maintained on the following day that the Cabinet should make no formal statement on the indirect claims since they did not come within the present arbitration agreement. His

[1] GP, Add. Mss 44161, ff. 177–82.
[2] GP, Add. Mss 44161, ff. 204–5; Elliot, vol. 1, pp. 134–5.

personal view was that 'they lay cast aside, a dishonoured carcass, which no amount of force, fraud, or folly can again galvanise into life'.[1] Goschen accepted the reassurances of Gladstone who as Prime Minister was 'decisive in his Cabinet'.[2] This exchange of letters took place just before the advisory opinion of the tribunal that 'indirect claims' did not constitute 'good foundation for an award of compensation or computation of damage between nations'. By September the arbitrators had decided that Britain must pay the United States £15,500,000.

Goschen was also involved in many departmental problems of peripheral historical importance but which required numerous hours of work. Public opinion had been aroused by the loss of the *Captain* in 1870 and in 1871 the troopship *Megara* ran aground while carrying soldiers to Australia. In the same year the *Agincourt* went onto the rocks near Gibraltar and the commander of the Channel squadron was removed from his post. This decision led Goschen into a minor conflict with Queen Victoria and her new private secretary, Colonel Ponsonby. The queen wondered why this change had taken place without her being first consulted. Goschen explained that flag officers were not appointed by the queen but by the Board of Admiralty. As a mark of courtesy and respect the queen was promptly informed as soon as the decision had been taken.[3]

Of more importance was Goschen's plan for overhauling the Board of Admiralty which he presented to the Cabinet on 6 March 1872.[4] He had feared the public was losing confidence in the Board of Admiralty.[5] In his Cabinet Paper, Goschen carefully evaluated the administrative changes which Childers had introduced three years ago. Childers' decision to divide the work of the Admiralty into three great divisions, 'personnel', 'material', and 'finance' had been sensible but there were several defects which had to be changed. In order to meet these failings

[1] Elliot, vol. 1, pp. 135–6.
[2] GP, Goschen to Gladstone, 17 June 1872, Add. Mss 44161, ff. 202–3.
[3] Ponsonby to Goschen, 27 August 1871, RA E52/73 and Goschen to Ponsonby, 30 August 1871, RA Add. A12/22.
[4] A nine-page Cabinet paper, GP, Add. Mss 44161, ff. 197–201 and Granville Papers, P.R.O. 30/29/54.
[5] GP, Goschen to Gladstone, 18 November 1871, Add. Mss 44161, ff. 191–2.

Goschen proposed to reconstruct the Board of Admiralty. The tasks of the various members of the new Board were then sketched in on broad lines as Goschen felt the definition of duties had in the past been too rigid. Board meetings would discuss all important questions but the First Lord of the Admiralty remained supreme and ultimately responsible for all the actions taken by his colleagues.[1]

Goschen was First Lord of the Admiralty during a period of rapid change in naval construction and tactics. Considering Britain's dependence upon power at sea for the defence of the empire, it is remarkable how conservative her naval chiefs remained. There was no desire to innovate and most changes were borrowed from other countries. The transition from wood to iron continued at a reasonably rapid pace and sails were eventually abandoned. In 1873 the *Devastation*, first of the truly modern warships, was completed. But the guns used by the navy were of poor quality. Until 1886 the navy depended upon the army for its guns and the ordnance branch of the army passionately insisted that the erratic muzzle-loaders must be kept.

Goschen soon discovered that the royal family could sometimes be more demanding than the most annoying honours seekers and more relentless in the defence of its 'rights' than the most pugnacious admiral. Goschen's crisis with Queen Victoria began delightfully enough with a naval display off Portland in August 1872. He then came face to face with two immovable objects – the 'rights' of royalty and the 'prerogatives' of admirals. On 11 August 1872, an irritated and annoyed Goschen wrote to Granville who was with the queen.

A disagreeable incident has happened with regard to the Prince of Wales, who has thought fit to think that he had supreme command over the fleet as 'the representative of her Majesty' because deputed to take part in a ceremonial for her. The incident was trivial but the Prince is rabid. At first the question was between Sir Sydney Dacres and Prince Leiningen, the Captain of the Royal Yacht, on a question of Regulations and Naval etiquette.

Prince Leiningen asked for a decision and got one adverse to himself. On which the Prince gave an order to the Captain which involved a breach of

[1] See the favourable comment in Michael Lewis, *The British Navy* (London, 1948), p. 380.

the orders given by the Admiralty. The point at issue was the firing of the evening and morning guns which are fired by a 'flag officer' senior to all others present.

I have heard privately that the Prince goes the whole length of considering himself supreme . . . because he flies his Standard, and represents the Queen. This is quite wrong and politically dangerous.[1]

No easy solution was found. On 26 September Ponsonby informed Goschen that the queen insisted upon her supremacy when afloat and wanted the regulation made clear on this point. After several more months of acrimonious correspondence, a compromise was finally hammered out. Goschen agreed that if the queen or the Prince of Wales as her deputy were on the royal yacht, it should fire the morning and evening salute, and the senior flag officer should then fire his gun. But Goschen insisted that the senior flag officer was still in command.[2]

While this Gilbert and Sullivan operetta was being performed, the Cabinet had many more serious problems to face. The numerous reforms which the government had passed aroused hostile sentiments. Some felt the reforms had gone too far while others contended they had barely scratched the surface. Speaking at Bristol late in 1872 Goschen praised the Liberal party for having passed an Education Act, a Ballot Act, an Irish Land Act and for having disestablished the Church of Ireland. He emphasized, at the same time, that the Liberals were not hostile to property or excessively sympathetic to any special groups or classes. He rebutted Nonconformist criticism of the government which had steadily increased since the passage of the Education Act with provisions to protect the schools administered by the Church of England. The government needed and wanted Nonconformist support but it was wise for them to remember that the Liberal party was not their possession.[3]

Disaster followed on the evening of 11 March 1873 when the government was defeated by three votes on its proposal to establish a new university in Dublin which both Protestants and Roman Catholics would be able to attend. Within a week the

[1] Granville Papers, P.R.O. 30/29/54.
[2] Goschen to Queen Victoria, RA Add. A12/76.
[3] Elliot, vol. 1, pp. 127–30.

Cabinet had resigned. Disraeli, however, refused to take office, believing that the Conservative cause would be vastly improved if a tottering Liberal ministry remained in power. Gladstone disagreed vehemently with Disraeli's constitutional arguments but agreed to resume the premiership. Neither leader wanted a dissolution at that time.

A new problem presented itself to a weary and quarrelling Cabinet in September of the same year. The Ashanti tribe in the African Gold Coast was threatening to destroy a number of coastal stations as well as the tribes which had co-operated with the British. The Cabinet finally decided that action must be taken, though there was little enthusiasm for the project. Sir Garnet Wolseley was sent out with a military expedition which successfully punished the Ashanti in early 1874. Goschen was in close contact with Kimberley at the Colonial Office and Cardwell at the War Office as plans ripened for an assault on the Ashanti. His main tasks were to supply transportation to move the British troops to the Gold Coast and to provide a hospital ship for the care and removal of the sick and wounded. Goschen informed Gladstone on 8 September 1873 that he had insufficient funds for a hospital ship and doubted the wisdom of the entire campaign. The Ashanti were now in retreat but Kimberley still seemed eager to go on with plans for an invasion of the interior. 'I feel so uncomfortable about the expedition and *now* so doubtful as to its necessity that I feel bound to unburden myself of my views on the subject before we go further in preparing ships.'[1] Two days later Goschen wrote to Cardwell: 'The more I study the news from the Gold Coast the more qualms I have as to the proposed expedition.'[2]

Goschen eventually convinced himself that war had been '*forced*' on the British.[3] The Cabinet agreed to provide Wolseley with the material and troops he required for an assault upon the Ashantis in their home territory. There were numerous administrative problems which had to be surmounted and the governmental machinery was not too well oiled. Goschen and Cardwell

[1] GP, Add. Mss 44161, ff. 240–1.
[2] Cardwell Papers, Goschen to Cardwell, 10 September 1873, P.R.O. 30/48/5/27.
[3] GP, Goschen to Gladstone, 22 September 1873, Add Mss 44161, ff. 247–8.

fought to maintain the prerogatives of their individual departments and sharp words sometimes passed between them.[1] But the combined operation was a success, for the Ashanti capital fell in February 1874.

Scandals in the Post Office department prompted a Cabinet reshuffle in the summer of 1873. Robert Lowe was moved from the Exchequer to the Home Office and Gladstone contemplated moving Goschen or Childers to the Exchequer. He finally took the post himself in order to revive a spiritless ministry. There was a constitutional question whether Gladstone must submit himself to his constituency for re-election.

The annual problem of the service estimates now reared its head and Cardwell and Goschen resisted the reductions demanded by Gladstone.[2] The constitutional question, the service estimates, and the Cabinet resignation of the previous year convinced Gladstone that it was time to recommend a dissolution of Parliament. He proposed an electoral appeal on the issue of abolishing the income tax. If the electorate supported a tax cut it would signify agreement with Gladstone's aim to decrease military and naval expenditure. The Cabinet concurred when Gladstone divulged his plans and agreed that its lack of harmony over the service estimates should not be made public. Cardwell acquiesced as did Goschen who affirmed that 'it is best not to state differences where the statement of them is not indispensable'.[3]

Neither Gladstone nor Goschen thought the business depression of the previous year would affect the chances of the Liberal party. On 2 November 1873, Goschen reported to Gladstone that his two brothers – one a director of the Bank of England and the other a director of the London Joint Stock Bank – were convinced 'that *mercantile* affairs are on the whole on a sound footing'.[4] Gladstone's decision to base his electoral campaign on the abolition of the income tax ended in disaster, for the Conserva-

---

[1] See the letters which passed between Goschen and Cardwell in mid-November 1873, Cardwell Papers, P.R.O. 30/48/5/27.
[2] GP, Goschen to Gladstone, 11 January 1874, Add. Mss 44161, f. 253; Cardwell Papers, Goschen to Cardwell, 16 January 1874, P.R.O. 30/48/5/27.
[3] GP, Goschen to Gladstone, 22 January 1874, Add. Mss 44161, f. 256.
[4] GP, Add. Mss 44161, f. 253.

tives scored a resounding victory – their first since the Peelite split of 1846. They won about 350 seats while the Liberals were reduced to just under 250 and the Irish Home Rule party obtained almost 60.

Gladstone tried to blame the defeat on his Licensing Bills which, he believed, had mobilized the wine trade, brewers and publicans behind the Conservatives. The victory was, however, due much more to the normal swing against the party in power, to an effective Conservative organization in the boroughs, and the resolute activity of the landed magnates in the counties. The most significant development of the election was the continued trend to Conservatism in all middle-class areas, especially in the growing suburbs. The swing which had been noticeable in 1868 when W. H. Smith and Lord George Hamilton were elected gained additional momentum.[1]

The City of London illustrates the shift. After Rothschild's victory at a by-election in 1869, the Liberals held all four seats for the City. In 1874 their monopoly was permanently shattered as the City marched decisively into the Conservative camp. It will be recalled that Goschen had topped the poll in 1868 followed by two Liberals and one Conservative and the Liberals had been so sure of their strength that they had hoped to win all four seats by a careful distribution of their votes. In 1874 Goschen finished fourth behind three Conservatives.[2]

The Liberal party seemed to have alienated a section of all the groups which traditionally supported it. The Whigs muttered indignantly at the growth of Radical influence in the party while the Radicals thundered their objections to so many Whigs in high office. The working class was dissatisfied with the Trade Union Act of 1871 which had been coupled with a Criminal Law Amendment Act that made picketing illegal. Employers, on the other hand, thought Gladstone had conceded too much to the trade unions and organized The National Federation of Associated

[1] H. J. Hanham, *Elections and Party Management* (London, 1959), pp. 225–6.
[2] *Dod's Parliamentary Companion for 1875*, p. 133. The biographical sketch of Goschen (pp. 221–2) is shorter than in previous years and mentions only that he was in favour of the repeal of the rate-paying clauses of the Reform Act of 1867. His other proposals of 1863, 1865 and 1868 had already passed into law.

Employers of Labour in Manchester in 1873 to counter the Trades Union Congress which had been formed in 1868.

A few days after the election Goschen's wife confided to her mother-in-law that 'George was in *lower* spirits about the *chaos* in the Party than about himself.' They had dined with Gladstone a few days before and found him 'very down' although 'quiet and resigned'. It was rumoured that Gathorne-Hardy would be sent to the Admiralty and this gratified Goschen for he was 'a sensible man and a true gentleman'.[1]

The Cabinet assembled for the last time on 17 February 1874 and Gladstone's surprise announcement that he wished to resign as party leader created bewilderment and alarm. His colleagues finally convinced him that no one else could hold the squabbling Liberal groups together and he consented to retain the leadership through the first session of the new Parliament. Gladstone had intended to give up the leadership but to remain in the Commons. Such a course would create difficulties for a new Liberal leader since Gladstone's commanding presence was not easily overshadowed.

As George Goschen prepared to leave office he seemed to be marked out for a long and active career as a leader of the Liberal party. His ideas and general political position placed him near the centre of the party as it then existed; his views were not far from Gladstone's although he was willing to follow a stronger line in foreign policy. But the next few years would find Goschen traversing a path which made it impossible for him ever again to accept office in a Liberal ministry.

[1] Elliot, vol. 1, p. 143. Disraeli decided, however, to send G. Ward Hunt to the Admiralty.

CHAPTER 4

EGYPT AND ELECTORAL REFORM

Gladstone's absolute refusal to continue as Liberal leader beyond early 1875 forced Whigs, Moderates and Radicals to consider naming a successor. The choice was important as, potentially, it meant the creation of a new Prime Minister even though Granville remained leader of the Liberals in the House of Lords and was, at least in Gladstone's eyes, titular head of the entire party. Speculation centred on Hartington or Forster as Gladstone's successor while Goschen was considered a possible compromise candidate. Superficial observers expected Hartington to be supported by the Whigs and Forster by the Radicals. Forster's gruff manners and lack of social polish antagonized the Whigs but he had alienated many of his Nonconformist friends during the debates on his Education Act in 1870. The older radicalism of John Bright and Forster appeared pale and timid to the new Radical leaders, Sir Charles Dilke and Joseph Chamberlain.

Hartington was not enthusiastic about the leadership but Forster coveted the honour and grew bitter as it slipped from his reach. He believed that all factions within the party were using him as the scapegoat for the controversial aspects of his Education Act which had angered the Nonconformists. Goschen had already protested to Gladstone about Forster's independent conduct and complained that he seized 'every occasion to follow his own line in speaking'.[1] Gladstone replied that he, too, was exasperated at Forster's tactics.[2]

Goschen still hoped that Gladstone would keep the leadership and rebutted Sir William Harcourt's accusation that the Liberal party had become too radical and too subservient to Gladstone.[3]

[1] GP, Goschen to Gladstone, 15 June 1874, Add. Mss 44161, ff. 237–8.
[2] Elliot, vol. i, p. 155.
[3] Alfred G. Gardiner, *Life of Sir William Harcourt* (London, 1923), vol. i, pp. 287–8.

While Goschen defended Liberal policies before Harcourt's on-slaught, he responded in a different way to Granville.

> The absence of the chief must necessarily lead a dispirited party to murmur against the innocent lieutenants and I say frankly that Gladstone is placing us (in the House of Commons) in a humiliating and *intolerable* position, if he persists in the same course which he followed last year. . . The party and the country come before us, of course, and both require his [Gladstone's] services, but I think the consideration due to those with whom he has worked is entitled to some weight too. To continue on the same footing as last session would be to some of us, clearly political ruin. . . It would be rather ridiculous if the members of the late Cabinet were to dot themselves about the back benches as independent members; yet after the first laugh, I doubt if they would present a more ridiculous appearance than we should do if we were to repeat the experience of last session.[1]

Attempts to alter Gladstone's decision were unsuccessful. His expectation that Hartington would succeed to the leadership without complications was shattered when almost half the party voiced a preference for Forster. If Forster had not been respon-sible for the Education Act of 1870 it seems likely that the prize would have been his. But the party leaders finally convinced Forster that he must withdraw in the interest of party unity.[2] The Whigs had been written off as a significant political force after Gladstone's rise to the leadership of the Liberal party but they were still very much alive as their leader stepped into Gladstone's shoes. Unfortunately, the old slogans of Whiggery no longer satisfied the Radicals who were demanding extensive social legislation. Reforming programmes and mass agitation were not smiled upon by the Marquess of Hartington.

It was just before the election of 1874 that Goschen had the satisfaction of putting the final touches on the new home he had been planning for the last five years. This amount of time was required to transform the house and property which he had pur-chased at Seacox Heath near the tiny town of Flimwell in Sussex. The nearest large town is Hawkhurst in Kent – from this place Goschen later took his peerage designation. It was here that

[1] Fitzmaurice, *Life of Granville*, vol. 2, pp. 138–9, Goschen to Granville, 5 January 1875.
[2] Sir T. Wemyss Reid, *Memoirs and Correspondence of Lyon Playfair, First Lord Playfair of St. Andrew, 1818–1898* (London, 1899), p. 282.

Goschen passed many of his happiest hours.[1] Lyon Playfair described it in 1878 as

the most lovely place in Sussex. . . The scenery is the perfection of English landscape with undulating hills and the wide plains richly wooded. The house is quite palatial in the size of the rooms, and the central hall is square, with two galleries, one above the other, running right around. I am in a bedroom on the upper gallery, and have an English landscape from my window from which I have always fresh enjoyment.[2]

George and Lucy Goschen still kept their house at 69 Portland Place in London but it was at Seacox Heath that they felt most at home. In 1875 their sixth and final child was born. Lucy Maude had been born in 1858, George the younger in 1866, Alice in 1868, William Henry in 1870, Beatrice in 1872, and Fanny Evelyn in 1875.

Fanny Evelyn must have provided some consolation for a rather dreary Parliamentary year as the Liberals sought to re-group behind their new leader and to win back their lost followers in the country. Later in the year, after the adjournment of Parliament, the government announced that it intended to purchase the khedive's shares in the Suez Canal Company. This would give the British government 44 per cent of the shares in a privately managed company. The Liberals were in a quandary. Some favoured what seemed both an excellent business proposition and an increase in the strength of the British Empire. A few saw this initial step as leading inevitably to the occupation of Egypt. Others were disturbed over Disraeli's acting without reassembling Parliament and over the high commission which the House of Rothschild was to receive.

Hartington informed Granville on 25 November 1875 that the news was 'well received in the country' and 'was likely to turn out a most successful coup'.[3] Reginald Brett wrote in his journal on 2 December that Goschen regarded the purchase as 'wise and advantageous and . . . would like to have an opportunity of saying at once that he approves of the step as a sound commercial and

---

[1] George and Lucy Goschen along with most of their children are buried in the graveyard adjoining the parish church of St Augustine in Flimwell.
[2] Reid, *Lyon Playfair*, p. 282.
[3] Fitzmaurice, *Life of Granville*, vol. 2, pp. 157–8.

political transaction'.[1] But Goschen expressed a slightly different
view when he differed with Granville on 7 December: 'Commercially little could be said for the step taken . . . But politically
I confess I approve. Doubtless there is very great force in your
arguments, but you do not deal with the risk of the shares being
bought by others.'[2] When Parliament met in early 1876 and the
purchase of the Suez Canal shares was debated, the Liberals,
unable to agree on a policy, failed to press for a division.

The vast Egyptian loans floated by Fruhling and Goschen on
the London money market meant that the purchase of the Suez
Canal shares had not been Goschen's first opportunity to observe
the turbulent world of the Egyptian economy. He had also helped
the Egyptians to purchase guns and other weapons in Britain.[3]
What exactly was the relationship between British foreign policy
and overseas investment? No easy answer is possible. Still, when
all the necessary qualifications have been made, a connection
between capitalism and imperialism is discernible. Leland Jenks
has effectively demonstrated that a common social group con-
trolled both British foreign policy and British investments
abroad. Many of the great banking and commercial houses had
partners, or former partners such as Goschen, in Parliament.
There was nothing necessarily scandalous about this but it
meant that the government of the day would be automatically
alive to the interests of the financial community.[4]

British investors may have shed a small tear for the plight of
the Egyptian peasant; they could console themselves with the
thought that the khedive might employ some of the loans for
social reform. But the standard of living about which British
investors were primarily concerned was their own and this meant
that they wanted the 6, 7 or 8 per cent interest pledged by the
Egyptian government. But it was a country – still technically

[1] M. V. Brett (ed.), *Journals and Letters of Reginald, Viscount Esher* (London, 1934–8), vol. 1, p. 35.
[2] Fitzmaurice, *Life of Granville*, vol. 2, pp. 158–9.
[3] F. E. Hamer (ed.), *The Personal Papers of Lord Rendel* (London, 1931), pp. 278–9.
[4] Jenks, *Migration of British Capital*, pp. 284–5. See Appendix I for the financial interests of the Goschen family.

under the control of the Ottoman Empire – which was utterly unprepared to service such large loans.

In order to protect their investments abroad, the Council of Foreign Bondholders, later to become the Corporation of Foreign Bondholders, was organized in London in 1868. Its primary mission was to compel all foreign governments to satisfy the interest and redemption payments upon bonds held by British subjects. At the same time the council acknowledged an obligation to the people in those lands where money had been sent and it hoped to act as a conscience to all overseas investors. If foreign governments were to default on their payments should the British government aid the bondholders? The problem was posed in 1868 by an M.P., H. B. Sheridan, who exhorted the British government to aid its foreign bondholders. Goschen, presiding over this particular meeting, disagreed.

I think it is dangerous to have the idea go forth that when an Englishman lends his money to a foreign government he is creating a national obligation, guaranteed by the full weight of the English government. The Englishman lends his money to a foreign government, and gets high interest, because he incurs a risk. I believe the duties of the Council will be most important . . . by exercising a moral power over the foreign governments contracting loans; and also by exercising a moral power over our own government by inducing them to interfere, if by their good offices they can do anything.[1]

Despite the sale of his Suez Canal shares, the khedive of Egypt failed to improve his financial predicament. Bankruptcy and a cancellation of interest payments on foreign bonds seemed imminent. In April of 1876 the khedive suspended all payments of Egyptian Treasury Bills and in May – to pacify his creditors – he established a Commission of the Public Debt which was to contain delegates from Britain, France, Austria and Italy. But the British government refused to participate. The khedive then announced that the entire Egyptian debt was to be unified. This alarmed the British bondholders, as it was more beneficial to the French and Italian holders of Egypt's floating debt. The Council of Foreign Bondholders asked Goschen to negotiate with the

[1] *Ibid.*, pp. 288–91.

khedive as its representative.[1] Goschen replied that he would undertake the project only so long as it was agreed 'no money should be made by anybody out of the protection of the interests of English bondholders'; nor would he permit this assignment to interfere with his political freedom; and he declared that he 'could not urge any steps on the English Government which though useful to the Bondholders, I might deem politically inexpedient'. He and Joubert, the representative of the French bondholders, reluctantly decided that a trip to Egypt was essential. Shortly after his arrival in Cairo, though not in any way accredited by the British government, Goschen reported to Sir Stafford Northcote, Chancellor of the Exchequer in Disraeli's ministry:

> For my own part, I think it would be very dangerous except in the case of extremity to consent to a single reduction of interest as a reward for extravagance and lying. And I shrink from the danger of the precedent being followed again a few years hence. The Viceroy has not said a single word in favour of the tax-payers. . . It will be very necessary to be exceeding firm with him. His attitude is hostile. . . We are surrounded by every kind of intrigue, and the Viceroy [khedive] telegraphs in all directions for Counsellors, but I still hope he may be induced to accept our plan.[2]

The harassed khedive finally accepted most of Goschen's plan and the khedival decree of 18 November 1876, designed to provide European supervision of Egyptian finances, was often referred to as the Goschen decree. When Goschen returned to London, he delivered an optimistic report to the bondholders. The agreement which had been reached was favourable, he alleged, to both the people of Egypt and the bondholders. The interest would be reduced from 7 per cent to 6 per cent for the next nine years and then return to the higher rate.

Part of the Goschen decree permitted the British government to select a number of officials to serve in specified financial and administrative positions in Egypt. The British Conservative

---

[1] The relevant material may be found in the publications of the Council of Foreign Bondholders. The most useful document, *Mission of the Right Hon. G. J. Goschen*, was published by the Council in December 1876. See also Elliot, vol. 1, pp. 166–75.
[2] Iddesleigh (Northcote) Papers, British Museum, Goschen to Northcote, 21 October 1876, Add. Mss 50021, ff. 245–7.

government decided not to avail themselves of this prerogative. This led a confused khedive to ask Goschen to suggest several candidates. Goschen still hoped to obtain government support for his Egyptian arrangements and on 19 December 1876 asked Northcote to assist him in choosing a Commissioner of the Public Debt. Goschen fancied someone of 'position and character' in order 'to have a nucleus of first class men in Cairo with the feelings and traditions of the best style of official life'. He was also worried that the government's refusal to designate would lead the khedive to think it was indifferent to Egyptian affairs. 'I state this to you *privately* but I repeat, I shall take care not to raise such a point in public as I wish to keep out any political question from what I have done.'[1] Goschen requested Northcote on the following day to ask Lord Derby, the Foreign Secretary, to indicate 'by a word or two . . . that the objection is not to my plan but to appointing under any circumstances'. He wanted it known that in May the British government had opposed the khedive's scheme while now it did not oppose Goschen's plan but simply did not wish to participate in its operation.[2]

Goschen discussed the appointment of a Commissioner of the Public Debt with Sir Louis Mallet, Under-Secretary at the India Office, and the returning Viceroy of India, Lord Northbrook. Both recommended Captain Evelyn Baring, Northbrook's cousin, who had recently served as his secretary in India. Baring, Lord Cromer after 1892, accepted Goschen's offer and thus began the career which was to identify his name permanently with Egypt. Goschen decided that Baring would be an 'excellent choice'.[3]

As one of the four Commissioners of the Public Debt (from Great Britain, France, Austria and Italy), Baring's major responsibility was to see that the bondholders received their interest on time. The two Controller-Generals (one British and one French), on the other hand, were supposed to concentrate on the reform of the Egyptian financial system so that it might be made more

[1] Iddesleigh Papers, Add. Mss 50021, ff. 254–5.
[2] *Ibid.*, Add. Mss 50021, ff. 254–5.
[3] Cranbrook (Gathorne-Hardy) Papers, Ipswich and East Suffolk Record Office, 11 January 1877, T 501/24.

efficient and better suited to benefit both the autocratic khedive and his suffering subjects. Baring – like Goschen – was related to a famous family of merchant bankers. Originally from Groningen in West Friesland, the Barings arrived in England in the early eighteenth century and later established the firm of Baring Brothers. While Baring never worked for the family concern, he maintained a weekly correspondence with his brother, Thomas, a partner in the company.[1]

While Goschen was only eight years older than Baring, he looked upon the younger man as something of a protégé since he had been responsible for his appointment and an extensive correspondence between the two men soon developed. Baring later wrote: 'During the years 1877–79 which were very critical years in Egyptian history I was practically serving under Goschen's orders.'[2] He quickly became convinced that the Goschen–Joubert agreement had been based upon faulty information supplied by the khedive's government. Several months after his arrival in Cairo, Baring visited both Paris and London accompanied by the French Controller-General, Baron de Malaret. Goschen and Joubert agreed that the terms of their settlement might be modified and that a full and detailed inquiry into Egypt's financial problems was required.[3]

While the Europeans in Egypt were apt to call the Khedive Ismail an incorrigible liar and an oriental intriguer, he must himself have been awed by the intricate philosophical webs which they could spin. On 11 January 1878 Baring informed Goschen:

The fact is that throughout I have been hampered by the anomalous position of wanting the enquiry, and at the same time being obliged to hold to the principle – in which I quite agree – that the Khedive must in the first instance say he wants it. If the Khedive says to me 'You want the Enquiry?' I am obliged to say, 'No, I don't; *you* want it.' And if he replies: 'I don't want it', I am forced to shake my head and give him to understand that he ought to want it. All of which is a very pretty instance of reasoning in a circle, but

[1] Marquess of Zetland, *Lord Cromer* (London, 1932), p. 22.
[2] Elliot Papers, Philpstoun House, Linlithgow, West Lothian, Scotland, Cromer to Arthur Elliot, 2 May 1911. For further extracts from this letter see Appendix 2.
[3] Zetland, *Cromer*, pp. 60–1.

inevitable in dealing with a potentate whose ways are so circular and tortuous as our Khedive.[1]

In an effort to deflect the demands of Baring and the other commissioners for a full enquiry in which they would participate, the khedive suddenly turned to General Gordon, at this time in his service in the Sudan. Gordon was asked to become president of a commission which would investigate the sources of revenue but would be excluded from analysing the khedive's expenditure. Baring was thoroughly opposed to this proposal but de Lesseps had indicated he would work with Gordon. It seemed clear to Baring that 'sooner or later, the English Government will be driven out of its policy of non-intervention in Egyptian affairs. . . You may depend upon it that they will be obliged to step in at last whether they like it or not.'[2]

Though Goschen was concentrating upon the strained relations which existed between British and Russia as a result of the Russo-Turkish War, he kept a keen eye on Baring's voluminous reports. On 14 February 1878 Goschen wrote in his diary that he was 'working to get the Viceroy deposed if he won't give way'.[3] By early March, Baring was more insistent than ever that all four Commissioners of the Public Debt must be on the Commission of Enquiry. He remarked that he had just seen General Gordon and had

begged him not to get into his head that we were blind to the interests of the fellah. . . He has written a long rigmarole to Vivian, winding up with calling on God to witness that he cares for the opinion of no one in this world, and that all he prays for is 'a speedy death'. Altogether, he impresses me so far as an excellent, simple, good-hearted, and impracticable man, about as much fit for the work he has in hand as I am to be Pope.[4]

But a few days later Baring was able to intimate success. The khedive accepted the four Commissioners of the Public Debt and Sir Charles Rivers Wilson of the British Treasury as members of

---

[1] CrP, Public Record Office, F.O. 633/2.
[2] *Ibid.*, Baring to Goschen, 1 March 1878, F.O. 633/2.
[3] Elliot, vol. 1, p. 188.
[4] CrP, Baring to Goschen, 8 March 1878, F.O. 633/2.

the Commission of Enquiry. At Ismail's insistence de Lesseps was to be chairman though this turned out to be purely nominal and Rivers Wilson was the effective presiding officer. Gordon had been cast aside even more quickly than he had been unveiled. Several days later a delighted Baring reported that they had obtained 'absolutely all for which we have been contending'.[1]

Before leaving for Egypt, Rivers Wilson had several interviews with Goschen. After a few months of searching investigation the Commission of Enquiry produced a report in August which chastised the khedive's regime and insisted that the government of Egypt must be reformed before the bondholders could be asked to make any further concessions and a new loan negotiated. Feeling trapped, the wily khedive decided upon almost complete capitulation to give himself time to prepare a counterattack.

In April 1879 Ismail struck and tried to free himself from Anglo-French control. The pro-European ministry was removed and replaced by an entirely native administration which was to be responsible to an elected Chamber of Notables. Baring was disgusted and promptly resigned and returned to England. The British might have gone along with the change if it had not been for Bismarck's sudden interest in the region. Salisbury had expressed his distress in April at appearing to be in any form of partnership with the bondholders but he was equally determined not 'to part company with France' nor to allow the French to acquire a 'special ascendancy' in Egypt. He concluded that 'subject to these two considerations I should be glad to be free of the companionship of the bondholders'.[2] But German intervention and a growing disenchantment with Ismail convinced Salisbury that he must join with the French in demanding the khedive's abdication. The sultan – after some reluctance – deposed his vassal in late June 1879 and Ismail was replaced by his son, Tewfik.

At the time of Goschen's return to London from Egypt in late

[1] *Ibid.*, Baring to Goschen, 16 March 1878, 18 March 1878, F.O. 633/2.
[2] Lady Gwendolen Cecil, *Life of Robert, Marquess of Salisbury* (London, 1921–32), vol. 2, to Lyons, 10 April 1879.

autumn 1876, Gladstone's short-lived partial retirement was over and he was thundering against Turkish brutalities in Bulgaria. Gladstone looked to Russia as the saviour of the Christian Bulgarians while Disraeli feared that Russia might seize the entire patrimony of the 'sick man of Europe' and thereby imperil British power in the Mediterranean. Gladstone's denunciation of the Bulgarian horrors had been published on 6 September, a few weeks before Goschen left for Egypt. It would appear that Goschen was already in disagreement with his former chief. On 13 September 1876 Queen Victoria informed Disraeli (now the Earl of Beaconsfield) that Goschen had dined with her and had spoken

with great good sense and moderation, greatly deprecating the wild, sense-less agitation of the country, and the dangerous and absurd extent to which the philanthropy is carried. . . He said that he thought it most unnecessary and ill-judged that 'we should perform the part of sister of charity to the rest of Europe' which is an excellent mode of putting it.[1]

Gladstone tore himself away from this great debate on 29 November 1876 to compliment Goschen on the success of his Egyptian mission and to denounce 'the whole Turkish case'.[2] Goschen agreed that the financial system of the Ottoman Empire looked 'almost hopeless'. But he argued that the Turks seemed more willing than usual to pay their debts. The Chief Liberal Whip had visited Goschen the day before and seemed 'rather cheerful as to liberal prospects. I cannot say that I am very hopeful myself.'[3]

The usually imperturbable Hartington was ruffled over Glad-stone's tactics. Hartington was more anti-Russian than the former Prime Minister and Gladstone's vigorous re-entry into active politics weakened Hartington's control of the divided party.[4] On 7 May 1877 Gladstone introduced five resolutions on the recently declared war between Russia and Turkey. Turkey was censured, self-government was advocated for the Balkans and Great Power

[1] W. F. Monypenny and George E. Buckle, *Life of Benjamin Disraeli* (London, 1910–20), vol. 5, p. 64.
[2] Elliot, vol. 1, p. 174.
[3] GP, Goschen to Gladstone, 7 December 1876, Add. Mss 44161, ff. 266–7.
[4] Spencer Papers, Hartington to Spencer, 12 November 1876, Misc. papers, 1876.

intervention was recommended if necessary. The Conservatives rallied behind Disraeli while Gladstone was threatened by Hartington and the moderate Liberals with a mass defection unless he withdrew the last three of his five resolutions. He conceded defeat and the Liberals voted fairly unanimously for the two mild resolutions which merely censured Turkey for violating treaty obligations and warned that Turkey no longer had any claim to British support. The resolutions were lost in the Commons by a vote of 354 to 253. Goschen spoke in support of the two resolutions and also rebuked the 'silent and cynical' government of Germany which had failed to take action. 'He trusted this country was great enough and strong enough not to feel jealous of any Russian victories which might be in favour of the Christian population in Turkey.'[1]

Russia's rapid victories opened the door to Constantinople and propelled a number of moderate Liberals such as Goschen into Disraeli's arms. They disliked his excessive jingoism but were basically in agreement with the broad outlines of his anti-Russian policy. Goschen wrote in his diary on 29 January 1878:

Meeting at Granville's at 12 to decide on course about vote of credit. Everybody except Hartington and me quite enthusiastic about fighting the Government. Hartington hung back and almost resigned leadership. I back him. Row with Harcourt. He holds me personally responsible for separating Hartington from Liberal party. . . My fear of being left in the lurch, etc.[2]

Childers was also reluctant to deny Disraeli's request for £6 million to meet the emergency. After a confused debate the Conservatives scored a decisive triumph by a vote of 328 to 124. About twenty Liberals voted with Disraeli while Hartington, Goschen and most of the other Liberal leaders abstained. Gladstone, however, voted with the minority.

Goschen's feeling of alienation from his party over foreign policy grew greater and he wondered what the future held for the 'moderate men'. 'I am coming to the conclusion that a schism must come. We cannot be dragged any further by Gladstone and

[1] *Hansard*, ccxxxiv (11 May 1877), 807–18.
[2] Elliot, vol. i, p. 183.

Bright. We are compromised by them every moment. This is my ruling idea. We have no opportunity of showing our anti-Russian feeling.'[1] British public opinion was inflamed by the terms of the Treaty of San Stefano which augmented Russian influence in the Balkans. Disraeli demanded a European Congress. It seemed for a moment as if Britain were poised on the brink of war. Lord Derby, the Foreign Secretary, disagreed with Disraeli and resigned his post at the end of March. The reserves were called up and Indian troops were sent from India via the Suez Canal to Malta for possible action against Russia. The great majority of Whigs and moderate Liberals were aghast at the Prime Minister's bellicose actions but sympathized with his policy. Only Gladstone and a handful of Radicals consistently opposed the government.

An annoyed Goschen was no longer satisfied with mere abstention when the Radicals introduced a variety of censure motions in the House of Commons. He advised Hartington in May that he could be present at the next meeting of Liberal leaders but warned that he might be 'more trouble than use'. 'I know you will think we can't walk out a third time and so I see no help for it but that some of us who think a censure on the Government inopportune or unpatriotic at this critical moment must vote *against* any such motion.'[2] At the close of a debate on the constitutional question raised by sending Indian troops to Malta without parliamentary approval, Goschen wrote in his diary: 'Shall we vote with the Government or stay away? Harcourt and I fought over Hartington's body. He yields to former. I am very cross, but it turns out for the best. Hartington makes a good speech in favour of not opposing Government further. On this occasion *nearly all* the Liberals followed him and walked out.'[3]

Even before these last debates on the eastern question, Goschen had exacerbated his breach with the Liberal party. His views on Russia and Turkey were, in fact, similar to Hartington's and the

[1] *Ibid.*, vol. i, p. 187.
[2] DP, Chatsworth, Goschen to Hartington, May 1878, 340.764.
[3] Elliot, vol. i, p. 192.

majority of the Liberal party. But in June 1877 he had publicly rejected the party's decision to support the extension of household suffrage to the counties. Goschen was then forty-six years of age and could have expected a major office in the next Liberal government. By opposing an important measure which a future Liberal majority expected to bring into law, he was saying that he could not serve in such a government.

Two years before, Sir Charles Dilke and G. O. Trevelyan had introduced a bill to extend household franchise to the counties. Hartington, speaking as the leader of the Liberal party, abstained. He refused to oppose the bill on principle and merely argued that the agricultural workers were not yet ready for the vote. Franchise reform, he thought, should be accompanied by a redistribution of seats. The extension of household suffrage to the counties would mean an increase of the electorate from about 3,000,000 to 5,000,000.

At this time Goschen supported Dilke's proposal to investigate the implications of another measure of electoral reform. Wisdom dictated that they must ascertain what the voteless would request from Parliament and how Parliament would respond to their wishes.[1] The Liberal party's decision in 1877 to accept the extension of household suffrage to the counties made further equivocation and abstention impossible. Robert Lowe dusted off his old anti-democratic speeches but advised Goschen to be silent.[2] Nor did the Conservatives wish to identify themselves with Goschen and Lowe. Disraeli had been the architect of the Reform Act of 1867 and everyone realized, including Goschen, that eventually universal manhood suffrage would be granted. For a party to place itself on principle against it could be disastrous since both Conservatives and Liberals hoped to win votes from the agricultural labourers – the largest group to be affected. The Conservatives opposed another Reform Bill at that time for tactical reasons and not on principle.

Goschen delivered his momentous speech in the House of

---

[1] *Hansard*, ccxxv (15 July 1875), 1550–74.
[2] A. Patchett Martin, *Life and Letters of Robert Lowe, (Viscount Sherbrooke)* (London, 1893), vol. 2, pp. 439–40.

Commons on 29 June 1877. He accused both parties of bargaining for votes and felt obliged to speak out now that the Liberal leadership had capitulated. 'He was told that the change was inevitable, and that, therefore he ought not hesitate to vote for it.' It was not that easy for him to veil his misgivings. The urban population which would be added to the electoral rolls did not worry him excessively but the rural population had no training in self-government and was much too dependent in old age upon the Poor Law. Not for a moment did he think they would be disloyal to the throne. Republicanism was dead and the House of Lords strong and popular. The last ten years, however, had been prosperous and the newly enfranchised of 1867 had not yet been called upon to make any sacrifices. Would they be willing to make the necessary sacrifices when they were demanded? It was disturbing to chronicle the growing demand for remedial legislation during the last ten prosperous years. Would these demands reach a crescendo with an economic downturn? Political economy was being dethroned by philanthropy. The New Radicals

were in favour of the view that Government should lay its hands upon every trade and remedy its abuses – adjusting the relations between capital and labour – and that Parliament should do what the old school of political economists and Radicals thought that men should do for themselves. It was the teaching of history that the reign of numbers endangered not the throne, not the Constitution, not property – those were all bugbears – but political economy and the teaching which made Englishmen self-reliant.

He asserted that he had no fear of the new voters as individuals but 'he wanted to know what safeguards there would be that the class proposed to be enfranchised would not vote in such numbers as would overwhelm the expression of opinion of the other classes.'[1] The motion to extend household suffrage to the counties was defeated by a vote of 276 to 220 with Goschen voting with the Conservatives.

The *Spectator* praised Goschen's courage for breaking 'with his party on a proposal which may at any minute become the turning point of an election, and on which the ultimate victory of his opinions, as he is well aware, is morally impossible'. It concluded,

[1] *Hansard*, CCXXXV (29 June 1877), 557–68.

however, that Goschen had vindicated the case of Trevelyan and Dilke:

It used to be said that though not electors, they were constituents, and were indirectly represented because they agreed with their representatives; but Mr Goschen specifically denies that, declares that they and the enfranchised classes differ radically, and that their opinions are so separate as to be dangerous to legislation. Surely this assertion, if it is true – and it is partially true – establishes Mr Trevelyan's case beyond argument.[1]

The usually calm Goschen prepared himself to serve as a parliamentary watchdog against the concentration of political power in the hands of a meddling Parliament. It was to reverse this trend that he sought to reform local government and to encourage local authorities to undertake their own programmes of self-help without looking to Westminster for assistance. He rang the tocsin when Disraeli introduced a Prison Bill in 1876 and angrily rejected the argument that the national government should undertake everything which it could do more 'cheaply and efficiently' than various intermediate authorities. This pernicious doctrine could 'lead to changes of a most dangerous character' such as 'the transfer of the police to the State'. The squires on the Conservative side, however, shouted their approval since it would mean reduced local rates.[2]

In the following year he argued that he and Joseph Chamberlain were in basic accord over the value of 'local life and institutions'. Localities must be encouraged to 'draw into the service of the State as many men belonging to as many classes' as possible so that these individuals could acquire 'fresh responsibilities' and thereby 'increase the dignity of their local life'. The House of Commons was already overworked and dangerous nostrums such as Home Rule for Ireland were being advocated. It would be much better to strengthen local bodies rather than delegating more authority to Parliament.[3]

Foreign disturbances and domestic affairs did not complete Goschen's interests. The former merchant banker was carefully

[1] *The Spectator*, 'Mr. Goschen on County Suffrage', vol. 50 (7 July 1877), 846–7.
[2] *Hansard*, CCXXX (3 July 1876), 914–15.
[3] *Hansard*, CCXXXII (5 February 1877), 442–7.

watching the rapidly declining value of silver as compared with gold. The value of silver had been decreasing since 1873 as a result of the discovery of new mines in the United States, the number of Western European countries which had left a silver standard for the gold standard and the restrictions which several countries had placed upon silver coinage. The silver interest demanded bimetallism and Britain was especially concerned because of her extensive financial commitments and because India remained on a silver standard until 1899. Goschen's first reaction was to call for further study of the problem.[1] In 1878, at Northcote's request, he agreed to attend an International Monetary Conference in Paris where bimetallism was to be discussed. Northcote had some doubts about Goschen's opposition to bimetallism at this time for he wrote to the Secretary of State for India and asked him to recommend someone 'who can be trusted? Goschen seems inclined to accept; but he does not hold the Catholic faith so fully as to make it safe to yoke a heretic with him.'[2]

The International Monetary Conference accomplished little. Goschen hoped that his 'main object' of 'stemming the tide' against the panic of 'substituting gold for silver, where silver is still current, has on the whole been promoted by the Conference'.[3] His flexible position was confirmed when he spoke in Parliament. The monometallists were mistaken in their attempt 'to convert all nations to the use of gold only'. He hastened, however, to show that he was not a bimetallist:

I am in favour of gold and silver being left to continue to perform the aggregate work of currency together; but it is a perfectly different thing to say, as the bimetallists say, that those countries which have a gold currency now ought to supply themselves with a silver currency as well.[4]

By 1878 Goschen was wondering whether he should look for a

[1] Goschen, *Essays and Addresses*, 'The Depreciation of Silver', pp. 131–84. This essay was first published in the *Edinburgh Review* of October 1876.
[2] Cranbrook Papers, Ipswich and East Suffolk Record Office, Northcote to Cranbrook, 2 July 1878, T 501/271.
[3] Iddesleigh Papers, Goschen to Northcote, 29 December 1878, Add. Mss 50021, ff. 259–80. See the Report of the Commissioners appointed to represent Her Majesty's Government at the Monetary Conference held in Paris in August 1878, C-2196.   [4] *Hansard*, CCXLVI (12 June 1879), 1770–84.

new constituency. He sensed that the City of London would probably return only one Liberal again and it might be more favourably disposed to someone in closer accord with the official leadership. On 10 May 1878 he spoke to the Liberal Club of the City of London and found that everyone 'buttered each other' much too much. A few days later he recorded that he was 'beginning to think seriously of retiring from the City representation'. He was 'annoyed at the state of the party in the House and at the prospect of standing with Lawrence and Rothschild, at the vulgarity of the City people, at their false estimates of everything, at the separation of Liberals from National sentiment, at the absence of any friends "on the bench" etc.'.[1]

Lord Ripon, a former colleague in Gladstone's cabinet, had the constituency of Ripon virtually in his pocket. He advised Goschen that his views on the county franchise would cause no harm in this region. 'As you probably know I have followed Hartington on the subject; but I am pretty nearly the greatest radical in Ripon.'[2] The incumbent, a relative of Ripon, had been elected without opposition in 1874. In 1880 Ripon had only 1081 registered electors. Goschen replied with thanks but was reluctant 'to disturb the existing arrangements'. Since he sought

another constituency, in consequence of a difference with the leaders of my party on an important question, it would be out of the question I think that they should exercise any influence to induce a liberal who will vote for them to make way for a liberal who would not vote with them on some questions, especially as I have no connection with Ripon.

If the Liberal organization in Ripon expressed an interest in him he would certainly give such an offer every consideration. 'I am not at all anxious with regard to finding a Constituency, nor in any hurry whatever. I only wrote because Ripon seemed particularly attractive.'[3] In the following year he was adopted by the

[1] Elliot, vol. I, p. 189. In the elections of 1880, the three Conservatives who were successful received slightly more than 10,000 votes while the three Liberals, only one of whom was elected, received slightly more than 5,800 votes.

[2] Elliot, vol. I, p. 193, Ripon to Goschen, 25 November 1878. For the history of this constituency see Norman Gash, *Politics in the Age of Peel* (London, 1953), pp. 219–42 and Hanham, *Elections and Party Management*, p. 410.

[3] Ripon Papers, British Museum, Goschen to Ripon, 27 November 1878, Add. Mss 43592, ff. 193–4.

constituency Liberal organization of Ripon as their candidate and informed Gladstone on 24 August 1879 that he was told 'Ripon is a safe seat for me, but who can know?'[1]

When Goschen first appeared before the electors of Ripon he explained that his principal reason for leaving London was to enable him to contest a single-member constituency in a straight party fight with a Conservative. He reaffirmed his belief in religious equality though he was opposed to disestablishment. The Conservatives had interfered too much with private enterprise and their foreign policy was characterized by excessive 'swagger' and 'bombast'. He still found it impossible to support household suffrage in the counties.[2]

Disraeli and his Cabinet decided to dissolve Parliament early in 1880 and agreed to make opposition to Irish Home Rule the principal issue in their appeal to the electorate. The moderate Home Rule policy which Isaac Butt had championed was no longer acceptable to many of the Irish Nationalist Members of Parliament nor to their supporters in Ireland. Charles Stewart Parnell, first elected to the Commons in 1875, was rapidly emerging as a new and more radical leader of the Irish in their demand for a Parliament in Dublin. At this time, however, Disraeli's remarks about Liberal willingness to concede Home Rule to Ireland seemed to many a blatant piece of demagoguery. The *Ripon Gazette and Times* failed to be impressed by Disraeli's 'lamentable twaddle about the "disintegration" of the United Kingdom and "decomposition of the Colonies"'.[3]

The Ripon Conservatives selected a native son, Francis Darwin, as their candidate. He challenged the Liberals for bringing in an outsider and noted his own approval of Goschen's stand against extending the suffrage. It would be better, he argued, to return a genuine Conservative rather than a disaffected Liberal.[4] Goschen's election address rejected all arguments for a Parliament in Dublin and stressed his support for 'the greatness and integrity of the Empire'. In foreign policy, however, he was

---

[1] GP, Add. Mss 44161, f. 268.
[2] Elliot, vol. 1, pp. 193–4.
[3] *Ripon Gazette and Times* (11 March 1880), 4.
[4] *Ibid.* (18 March 1880), 6.

especially harsh on Disraeli's policies. The Prime Minister and his Foreign Secretary, Lord Salisbury, had acted in 'un-English ways'. They had failed to uphold 'the honour of the country without a recourse to diplomatic devices and surprises'. Britain's support had been placed 'on the side of militarism instead of constitutionalism' and the seizure of Cyprus 'impaired the reputation of England as the most clean-handed member of the European family'. While pleased that Constantinople was not in Russian hands, he regretted that 'the rising nationalities of the East were not taught to look to England as one of their staunchest friends, and that the claims of Greece are still unsatisfied'. A policy of isolation, however, was not possible since Europe and all her many problems were of concern to Britain. He denounced the Conservatives for a lack of confidence in the people and for being 'afraid to ask the people to pay'. The problem of temperance could best be handled, he felt, on the basis of local option rather than national legislation.[1]

The elections of late March and early April 1880 were further confused by uncertainty as to which Liberal leaders would form a ministry if they won the election. Would it be Hartington, Granville or the rejuvenated Gladstone whose Midlothian campaigns were in the nature of a religious revival. Goschen won his seat by a vote of 591 to 362 and to the horror of the queen and the dismay of Disraeli, the Liberals were triumphant. The final results gave almost 350 seats to the Liberals, 240 to the Conservatives and more than 60 to the Irish Nationalists.

[1] *Ibid.* (20 March 1880), 5, and Elliot, vol. 1, pp. 194–5.

CHAPTER 5

DIPLOMACY AND HAREM LADIES
1880—1881

Once the elections of 1880 were over, Granville and Hartington prepared to step aside for Gladstone. To the mass of Liberal electors Gladstone was once again the leader of the party and they expected him to become Prime Minister. Gladstone had procrastinated about resuming the leadership and never seemed to realize the difficulties which he placed in Hartington's path. There had been much speculation about Goschen's role if the Liberals won the general election. Lord Acton, friend of both Gladstone and Goschen, found Goschen 'on the road that leads away from the Liberal party, through Brookes's', and into a coalition of moderates from both parties.[1]

The queen, encouraged by Disraeli, asked Hartington to form a ministry immediately after Disraeli's resignation. She indicated her lack of confidence in Gladstone but Hartington insisted that a government without Gladstone would be unworkable. Since the former Prime Minister would not serve in a subordinate capacity, he must be sent for at once.

The process of Cabinet-making now began. The *Spectator* thought Goschen would make a perfect Viceroy of India.[2] Gladstone agreed and offered this post to Goschen since his opposition to the extension of the franchise made him impossible for the Cabinet. This usually meant a peerage and a four-year tour of duty. He declined this position of great prestige because both he and Mrs Goschen did not wish to be away from their children and because he was not certain 'he would see eye to eye with the Prime Minister and his colleagues either on matters of high imperial policy or of native administration'. Goschen's refusal apparently left Gladstone 'stunned and out of breath'.[3] The post

[1] Herbert Paul (ed.), *Letters of Lord Acton to Mary, Daughter of the Rt. Hon. W. E. Gladstone* (London, 1904), pp. 3–4.
[2] *The Spectator*, vol. 53 (10 April 1880), 453–4.
[3] Elliot, vol. 1, p. 196 and Morley, *Life of Gladstone*, vol. 2, p. 629.

was finally accepted by Goschen's friend and sponsor in the Ripon constituency, the Marquess of Ripon.

The Conservatives also eyed Goschen carefully. Sir Stafford Northcote, their leader in the Commons, wrote in his diary on 26 April 1880:

> I think it is likely enough that a Conservative cave may be formed on the Liberal side, with perhaps Goschen as its centre, and that if we manage our opposition discreetly, we may often join hands with them, and perhaps ultimately bring some of them to take part in a Conservative Cabinet. At the present moment one thinks of such things only in the spirit in which the Roman purchaser bid for the fields occupied by the Carthaginian army. Still, it is necessary to lay our foundation properly.[1]

The ever-watchful queen, eager to aid a moderate, voiced her distress at Goschen's exclusion from the Cabinet.[2] She should instead have sighed with relief when the Cabinet was complete. After much discussion and negotiation only Joseph Chamberlain was selected from among the Radicals to serve in the Cabinet. Sir Charles Dilke and Henry Fawcett did accept important posts in the ministry and Dilke was destined to enter the Cabinet two years later. Forster and Bright were in the Cabinet but were not regarded as representatives of the new Radicalism. The Cabinet then was dominated by moderate Liberals and Whigs. Gladstone foolishly decided to become Chancellor of the Exchequer as well as Prime Minister and Leader of the House of Commons. This was far too great a burden for a man of seventy and he never succeeded in gaining adequate control over his Cabinet.

Goschen was next offered the embassy at Constantinople in succession to Sir Austen Henry Layard, the archaeologist and former Liberal Member of Parliament. In 1868 Layard had accepted the embassy at Madrid and in 1877, as the Russians and Turks moved towards war, Disraeli had switched him to Constantinople. Known as a Turcophile, Layard had vigorously supported Disraeli's anti-Russian policies. After some hesitation

---

[1] Andrew Lang, *Life, Letters and Diaries of Sir Stafford Northcote (Earl of Iddesleigh)* (Edinburgh, 1890), vol. 2, pp. 149–50.
[2] Buckle (ed.), *Letters of Queen Victoria*, 2nd series, vol. 3, pp. 87–90.

Gladstone and Granville decided that he would have to be replaced. Goschen's first reaction was to decline but Gladstone found the refusal 'very weak' and urged Granville to try again.[1] Success resulted. Goschen agreed to become a Special Ambassador without pay for the sole purpose of quickly working out the territorial arrangements prescribed by the Congress of Berlin in 1878. This enabled him to retain his seat in the House of Commons.[2]

Goschen now set out to master the intricacies of that swamp called the eastern question. The diagnosticians at the Congress of Berlin had been able to read the symptoms but were unable to agree on a remedy. Portions of the Ottoman Empire could be partitioned among the Great Powers, the present *status quo* could be maintained and the empire called upon to reform itself or the demands of the subjugated nationalities in the Balkans could be fulfilled by the grant of autonomy or independence. Unable to accept any of these proposals in full the Great Powers attempted to orchestrate several variations of these three major themes but eventually found that no one was really satisfied with their discordant finale.

In 1878 Disraeli and Salisbury had scored a minor success at the Congress of Berlin when Russia was forced to give up a number of the gains she had wrested from Turkey in the Treaty of San Stefano which had concluded the Russo-Turkish War. Since 1878, Abdul Hamid II, the Ottoman sultan, had procrastinated in order to evade the decisions of the Congress of Berlin. Britain had been granted the right to occupy and to administer the Ottoman island of Cyprus so as to have a base in the Eastern Mediterranean but in return Disraeli had pledged himself to protect the Asiatic part of the Ottoman Empire. Recognizing that the British public would not be very enthusiastic about protecting a government known for its oppression of the

---

[1] GP, copy of letter, Gladstone to Granville, 2 May 1880, Add. Mss 44172, ff. 47–8 and Granville to Gladstone, 4 May 1880, Add. Mss 44172, ff. 49–50.

[2] See Elliot, vol. 1, pp. 196–240. Much of the material which follows is based upon the two excellent studies by W. H. Medlicott, *The Congress of Berlin and After* (2nd edn. London, 1963) and *Bismarck, Gladstone, and the Concert of Europe* (London, 1956).

Armenian minority, Salisbury had insisted that there must be reforms which could be observed by military consuls from Great Britain.

Goschen had been against the seizure of Cyprus as it seemed to put England in the same class as the other Great Powers – prepared to dirty its hands by grabbing what it could from the defeated Turks. And he seems to have realized that Salisbury had obtained French acceptance of the Cyprus deal by intimating that Britain would not object to France's occupation of Tunis. By 1880 the Porte was still delaying execution of the clauses which pertained to Turkey's frontiers with Greece and Montenegro, and the Greeks, despite their military inferiority, were growing ever more obstreperous.

The Liberal electoral victory of early April was a source of delight to the Russians who regarded Gladstone as a friend; the Turks were horrified. Both Russian and Turk failed to appreciate the strong anti-Russian feeling which existed in the Liberal as well as in the Conservative party. Indeed Gladstone set out not to overturn the agreements reached at Berlin but to see that they were finally implemented. Gladstone hoped to base his policy on the creation of a genuine Concert of Europe which would attempt to thrash out differences in a conciliatory fashion. This brought Gladstone face to face with Bismarck who regarded Gladstone's talk of a 'Concert' as a cover for British designs.

The Cabinet was still undecided about the amount of pressure to be exerted on the sultan. They eventually decided to say that while the British government 'invited the concert of the other Treaty Powers in order to exercise united pressure upon the Porte' it wanted Goschen to

clearly convey to the Sultan and to the Porte that the representations which you are instructed to make to them are essentially of a friendly character, that it is in the interests of Turkey itelf that the pending questions with Greece and Montenegro should be settled, and that the only hope for the maintenance of the Turkish Empire lies in a thorough and searching reform of its administration both at the capital and in the provinces.[1]

[1] Granville Papers, Granville to Goschen, 18 May 1880, Corrected 7 June 1880, P.R.O. 30/29/210.

Layard reported that the news of his replacement by Goschen had been received with alarm by the Turks. Britain had not even asked whether Goschen was satisfactory. This had been an unintentional snub but it increased the sultan's qualms: he remembered that Goschen had gone to Egypt in 1876 and recommended certain financial reforms. Three years later the khedive had been deposed. Given Abdul Hamid's suspicious nature it is easy to imagine the apprehension he felt.[1]

Considering the need to obtain Bismarck's support for any coercive measures it is surprising that Goschen failed to visit Berlin on his way to Constantinople. Instead, it was decided that he should go by way of Paris and Vienna and thence by sea from Trieste. Stopping in Paris, Goschen and Lord Lyons, the British Ambassador to France, were granted an interview with the French Premier, Freycinet, on 19 May. Freycinet gave Goschen 'the impression that he had not mastered the Eastern Question at all and had no policy except to draw a new frontier line in Greece and to be very cordial to the English'. He regretted very much that he had not seen Gambetta 'who has been in the country where he has an Egeria, and is not visible'.[2] The French seemed fearful that Goschen's 'financial knowledge and reputation . . . might gain a financial ascendancy for England in Turkey'. It was obvious to Goschen that France was prepared to co-operate with Britain though being 'very careful' about employing force against the Turks. This was equally true of the attitude of the Austrian Foreign Minister, Haymerle, whom Goschen met in Vienna several days later. Goschen hoped that he might 'say openly that England thinks that if Turkey does not accept this award she must be forced to do so, of course keeping the Concert of Europe in view'.[3] Goschen did not shrink from forceful action against the Turks if it was required but he had found little support from either France or Austria. A similar view was maintained by Prince Reuss, the German Ambassador to Vienna, with

---

[1] *Ibid.*, Layard to Granville, 9 May 1880, P.R.O. 30/29/371.
[2] *Ibid.*, Goschen to Granville, 19 May 1880, P.R.O. 30/29/188.
[3] Dilke Papers, British Museum, Goschen to Dilke, 23 May 1880, Add. Mss 43911, ff. 55–6. Dilke was Under Secretary for Foreign Affairs.

whom Goschen also had a private interview. Reuss doubted that British public opinion would support the use of force.[1]

On 28 May Goschen was in Constantinople and he quickly endeavoured to bring the entire Turkish area under his personal control. It was understandable that he expected to be fully briefed about the actions of all his subordinates but he exhibited one of his most conspicuous administrative failings – an excessive interest in detail, a desire to check on too many unimportant problems and the impossible ambition to know everything that was happening. Goschen insisted that all consular reports must go through the embassy so that he would be fully informed. It was intolerable that the consuls should be acting as 'independent agents' and communicating directly with the Foreign Office.[2]

A few days later Goschen had his first official audience with the sultan and this was followed by a private interview of some thirty minutes. The sultan had been much distressed at the British government's argument that since he was 'all-powerful' he was responsible for a large share of Turkey's misfortunes. This had frightened Abdul Hamid, but Goschen concluded after listening to several other opinions that the 'general impression seems to be that the Sultan and the Porte will meet us with practical resistance even if they use fair language'.[3] The sultan's ministers told Goschen of their master's anguish. Goschen retorted that the sultan should 'summon a Parliament' and replace his 'utterly discredited' advisers with a 'respectable and responsible Ministry'.[4]

After a few weeks in Constantinople Goschen began to evaluate his fellow ambassadors and to offer suggestions of his own. He was happy to report that the new French Ambassador, Tissot, had 'the strongest instructions to act with me on everything'. Not content with the hurdles to be surmounted on the Montenegrin and Greek frontiers, Goschen thought that the time might be right to grant autonomy to the fierce Albanians.[5] During the

[1] Granville Papers, Goschen to Granville, 23 May 1880, P.R.O. 30/29/188.
[2] *Ibid.*, Goschen to Granville, 1 June 1880, P.R.O. 30/29/188.
[3] *Ibid.*, telegrams, Goschen to Granville, 3 and 4 June 1880, P.R.O. 30/29/371.
[4] *Ibid.*, telegram, Goschen to Granville, 5 June 1880, P.R.O. 30/29/371.
[5] Dilke Papers, Goschen to Dilke, 8 June 1880, Add. Mss 43911, ff. 64–5.

last weeks of June Goschen concentrated on the Montenegrin frontier and the Armenian oppression since the new Greek frontier was being drawn – or so it was hoped – by the ambassadors of the Great Powers in Berlin. This Berlin Conference of June 1880 (not to be confused with the Congress of Berlin in 1878) eventually drew a line which gave the Greeks far more in Epirus and Thessaly than the Turks were willing to concede.[1]

Goschen's relations with the sultan were not good, but this did not make the new ambassador unhappy. He believed that Layard had been too friendly with Abdul Hamid when a certain amount of rigidity had been required. 'I think the fact is he is afraid of me, though as you told the Queen I never fail to be perfectly courteous. . . My manner leaves the impression on him that I thoroughly mean business, and that is what he doesn't like.'[2] His letters to Granville throughout the summer reflected his grave apprehensions that war might break out in the Balkans and ultimately involve the Great Powers. The Turks refused to make the required concessions to Montenegro and Greece and the poorly prepared Greeks were muttering about going to war. While Goschen was strongly pro-Greek in sentiment he wondered if it was wise to give the Greeks all they were demanding.

It was at this time that Goschen reported a 'disagreeable incident'. A former member of Sultan Murad's harem had taken refuge in the embassy. Afraid of being 'forced to marry against her will' and worried that she had 'compromised herself by flight to the Embassy', she feared that 'death might be the consequence'. Goschen hoped for an amicable settlement but was 'inexorable as to yielding anything without lady's full and free consent'. On the following day he was able to report that the 'Turkish lady' had left the embassy and 'returned to Constantinople of her own accord'. Assurances had been given 'that she is in no way to be molested in consequence of her flight, and she left perfectly cheerful'.[3] With the departure of this lady and the arrival of his wife and family Goschen was a happier man. But he missed the

[1] Medlicott, *Concert of Europe*, pp. 97-112.
[2] Granville Papers, Goschen to Granville, 2 July 1880, P.R.O. 30/29/188.
[3] *Ibid.*, telegrams, Goschen to Granville, 9, 10, and 11 July 1880, P.R.O. 30/29/188.

House of Commons and was eager for information about Irish troubles and the Bradlaugh case.

Never happy with the Cyprus Convention, Goschen made it clear to the Turks that the British guarantee for Asiatic Turkey was dependent upon reforms in Armenia.[1] Mid-August found Goschen irritated with the vacillation of his fellow-ambassadors. 'Things look bad.' The other Powers seemed to be looking for an escape from the proposed naval demonstration which was designed to coerce Turkey into co-operation. 'It is going too far to say that I am probably the only Ambassador who holds quite unflinching language, but there is certainly a change of tone about many of my colleagues.'[2] It was 'disheartening' to see so much 'shuffling going on'.

Goschen was disgusted with the lack of concern evinced by the other ambassadors for Muslim minorities in Roumelia and Bulgaria. 'We are the only humane people and we alone have care for protecting right and justice. The others only look to see how it affects their political position.' This feeling of outrage at the other Powers soon shifted to Granville. Goschen wondered why his advice was never followed.

You are not inclined to compromise. The decision of Europe must be carried out, but in the mode of carrying out the decision you seem sanguine of being successful by means in which I have not equal confidence and which do not equally recommend themselves to me. *I* might be less high-handed as to the amount of what I would ask, but having asked it I should be quite as high-handed, probably more high-handed in carrying it through. To use the word 'recommend' in a note, which if not obeyed is to lead to coercion seems to be inconsistent. I should have thought it would have been far better to tell the Turks straight out – the peace of Europe, the general interest, even your own interest, require that you should accept such a line and you must bow to the will of Europe, than to invite and recommend something to them as within the Berlin treaty which they will never allow to be there.

Goschen acknowledged that his 'comments and criticisms' on Granville's policy were

[1] *Ibid.*, telegrams, Goschen to Granville, and Granville to Goschen, 22 and 23 July 1880, P.R.O. 30/29/371.
[2] *Ibid.*, Goschen to Granville, 10 August 1880, P.R.O. 30/29/188.

the consequence of appointing as Special Ambassador, one who has been your intimate colleague and who therefore takes the liberties of a colleague rather than those of a simple agent. At the same time I will remind you of what I said before I left, that you need never scruple to replace me the moment it seems desirable. There will be no blow to my amour propre in any way.[1]

While favouring a strong stand against Turkish intransigence, Goschen was not blind to the merits of the Turkish case. He agreed with Granville that the European Powers should issue a 'self-denying Protocol' stating that they would not take advantage of Turkey and would work to prevent further concessions being demanded by minor Balkan states.[2] Queen Victoria, however, believed that Goschen was too anti-Turk and was *'pushing to hostilities'*.[3]

As summer passed into autumn, the unresolved Greek frontier question was gradually overshadowed by the decision of the Powers to settle the Montenegrin frontier. An attempted naval demonstration designed to wrest Dulcigno from the Turks collapsed in the last days of September when the Montenegrins, fearful of Turkish power, refused to move their army forward. The Concert seemed to have fallen apart but Goschen and Granville continued to press for united action. When Goschen heard of the fiasco in Montenegro he concluded that it might be necessary to bring the fleet immediately to the Dardanelles if the other Powers agreed. It was essential 'to go ahead'. Granville objected to the Dardanelles at that stage of the conflict but the Cabinet agreed to propose the occupation of Smyrna to the Powers if Turkey remained obstinate.[4]

When the Turkish note of 4 October proved to be as stubborn as ever, Gladstone decided to act with as many other Powers as cared to follow. Goschen concluded that his mission would soon be over. 'We may either go forward so much that the Ambassadors must withdraw or we must go back and then my position

---

[1] *Ibid.*, Goschen to Granville, 19 August 1880, P.R.O. 30/29/188.
[2] *Ibid.*, Goschen to Granville, 24 August 1880, P.R.O. 30/29/341.
[3] Buckle (ed.), *Letters of Queen Victoria*, 2nd series, vol. 3, pp. 141–2.
[4] Granville Papers, copy, Goschen to Granville, 28 September 1880 and telegram, Goschen to Granville, 5 October 1880, P.R.O. 30/29/188.

would clearly be untenable.'[1] Gladstone and Granville could only obtain the support of Italy and Russia for the occupation of Smyrna. But France and Germany warned the sultan that Dulcigno must be given up at once. Their action coupled with the news that the British, Italians and Russians were prepared to seize Smyrna convinced the Turks that further procrastination on the Montenegrin frontier was no longer possible.

On 9 October the Turks agreed to cede Dulcigno immediately. Goschen was elated: 'Smyrna has done it, that is clear.'[2] Granville congratulated his Special Ambassador on the completion of step one 'of a tiresome journey'. Now they would have to decide on the next move and Granville liked Goschen's suggestion that Turkish finance be tackled. This might not be too divisive an issue between the Powers.[3]

Goschen was deeply disturbed over reports in *The Times* which called for a pause in the pressure on the Turks. Goschen was, of course, absolutely opposed and wondered if someone in the Cabinet had planted the stories. This was the belief of his fellow ambassadors. If the stories were based upon official British policy he wanted to be relieved at once.[4] Granville immediately replied that *The Times* articles were 'not inspired'.[5] A few days later Granville remarked that it was 'pleasant to find out that even one's best friends have some defects – and I was rather relieved than otherwise when I was incidentally told the other day, that in the City it was thought that your only fault in business was being somewhat suspicious'. Granville conceded that Goschen had demonstrated this trait to him in only 'one or two instances'.[6]

Goschen did not think anything could be accomplished unless the financial question was brought up as part of 'strong and

[1] *Ibid.*, Goschen to Granville, 5 October 1880, P.R.O. 30/29/188.
[2] *Ibid.*, Goschen to Granville, 12 October 1880, P.R.O. 30/29/188.
[3] *Ibid.*, copy, Granville to Goschen, 14 October 1880, P.R.O. 30/29/210.
[4] *Ibid.*, Goschen to Granville, 24 and 25 October 1880, P.R.O. 30/29/188.
[5] *Ibid.*, copy of telegram, Granville to Goschen, 25 October 1880, P.R.O. 30/29/210.
[6] Gladstone Papers, copy, Granville to Goschen, 28 October 1880, Add. Mss 44172, ff. 270–1. See also Agatha Ramm (ed.), *The Political Correspondence of Mr. Gladstone and Lord Granville 1876–1886* (Oxford, 1962) vol. 1, pp. 204, 209–11.

energetic measures'. The Turks could never be 'cajoled into any-thing like a financial enquiry'. He was sure that the Berlin Conference of June 1880 had granted too much territory to Greece and he advocated a compromise. While the Turks were angry and disappointed with England at that time, Goschen still believed 'that the affection for England and the belief in her is so deeply rooted that *when we like* we can have their friendship back'. Goschen denied Granville's charge of being excessively suspicious.

You were wrong though to say I was suspicious, or that my chief defect when I was in business was want of faith in my neighbours. On the contrary I always was and am 'naif'. Indeed I told one or two of my colleagues the other day that this was one of my chief characteristics. Indeed I only suspected one man when I was in the City and have spotted him as the man who is likely to have made the remark to you.[1]

Believing that he had fulfilled his mission, Goschen wanted to return home. Granville and Gladstone appealed to him to remain at his post for a little time longer. Goschen was not enthusiastic but finally agreed provided that he might visit England for a rest and for talks with the Cabinet.[2] His six-week leave in England was both an enjoyable interlude and a time of intense diplomatic activity. The Turks continued to delay while the Greeks bellowed loudly that they would wage war if the award of the Berlin Conference was not granted to them. Gladstone knew that the Turks could be coerced, since the projected occupation of Smyrna had convinced the sultan that he must be conciliatory on the Montenegrin frontier. But in order to employ this pressure Gladstone had deviated from his first principle, that of trying to insure an harmonious concert. Gladstone and Granville now sought to reconstruct the Concert but they did not know that Bismarck cared little for European co-operation. At this particular moment he was absorbed in his plan to recreate the Three Emperors' League.

Granville and Gladstone wanted Germany to play a more direct

---

[1] Granville Papers, Goschen to Granville, 2 and 9 November 1880, P.R.O. 30/29/188.
[2] *Ibid.*, telegram, Goschen to Granville, 25 November 1880, P.R.O. 30/29/188.

role in achieving a solution. The co-operation of Britain and Germany, they thought, would bring the other Great Powers into line, re-establish the Concert and compel the Turks and the Greeks to do what they were told. It was finally agreed that the ambassadors at Constantinople should open negotiations with the Porte about the Greek frontier and should attempt to propose a line which would give the Greeks more than the Turks had offered in their unacceptable note of 3 October 1880 and less than that proposed by the Berlin Conference in June 1880. Lord Odo Russell, the British Ambassador in Berlin, informed his government that Bismarck would welcome a visit from Goschen on his way back to Constantinople. Gladstone, Granville and Goschen were delighted, for it meant that the Prussian might be willing to take the lead in arranging a satisfactory settlement and thus remove everyone's chestnuts from the fire. But Bismarck was not likely to further anyone's interests but his own.

Goschen met Bismarck during the first week of February and later recorded that it had been 'a great privilege to discuss high matters of state with a man whose insight was so clear and quick, whose grasp of detail as well as of principles was so perfect and immediate, and who knew his own mind so absolutely'.[1] In a long letter to Granville on 7 February, Goschen summarized the results of his talks.

Bismarck has now taken the initiative and thrown himself into the question heartily. He seems to have Russia and Austria in his pocket. . . If his proposals are sufficiently acceptable to *you*, they will in all probability be unanimously agreed to, so far as they go *at present* but when the more energetic steps become necessary, which Bismarck contemplated as a contingency, France may refuse to go forward. Bismarck spoke however of 'some of the Powers', as if he were prepared to go forward without having all the six together. This struck Lord Odo and me as very important.

The Chancellor seemed 'more Greek' than Goschen had anticipated. Much of their first interview had dealt with the need to localize any armed conflict between Greece and Turkey. They evaluated the ways in which Greece might be assisted if the Turks attacked.

[1] Elliot, vol. I, p. 211.

It was on the second day of talks that Bismarck 'dropped the localization plan for the present' and proposed instead that 'the Powers must agree on a new line. They must tell Greece what they consider reasonable; for this they must first agree among themselves.' Bismarck had been as much impressed by the fierce Albanians as Goschen.

I gather this is to be the ostensible motive for the change from the decision of the Berlin Conference. The Albanian Mussulmans have shown by their action since the Conference what dangerous customers they are. Greece 'could not digest them': but let her have Crete instead. He asked me whether you would object to Crete. I told him that you had not liked the idea of Crete, as it brought into prominence that territory belonging to the Turks was simply handed over to the Greeks irrespective of the frontier considerations which had determined the action of the Powers at the Berlin Congress and Conference, but that I thought you would accept the idea in view of the immense advantage of giving the King of Greece and his Ministers the opportunity of declaring that they had got as good a bargain as that of the Conference.[1]

It seemed to Goschen that a great success had been achieved. The ambassadors of the Great Powers under German and British leadership would agree on a frontier for Greece and Turkey which would compensate Greece for deviations from the line drawn by the Berlin Conference. The consent of Greece would be obtained and only then would the package be presented to the Turks with the full weight of the Great Powers placed squarely behind it. Turkey would be unable to resist. But Goschen was to discover, once again, that the words spoken by diplomats were often altered beyond recognition when it came to moving from talk to action.

Within a week of Goschen's arrival in Constantinople, the Bismarck–Goschen scheme had been scuttled because of the German Ambassador's failure to press it. By 21 February the ambassadors were again negotiating with the Porte in the hope of finding just how much territory the Turks would cede to the Greeks. Goschen was thoroughly disgusted. He reminded the

---

[1] Granville Papers, Goschen to Granville, 7 February 1881. P.R.O. 30/29/189.
See also Elliot, vol. 1, pp. 208–16 and Medlicott, *Concert of Europe*, pp. 215–18.

German Ambassador, Hatzfeldt, of Bismarck's comment that 'immoral support' might be required to dragoon the Turks into line. Hatzfeldt accepted Goschen's recollections but did nothing to mend his ways.[1]

It was in the midst of interminable discussions about the territory which Turkey should cede to Greece that Goschen 'conceived' what he called 'a daring idea' when he later wrote a full account of his mission to Constantinople. Why not restore Cyprus fully to the Ottoman Empire?[2] Goschen had never been happy with the Cyprus Convention and he no doubt remembered that Gladstone had called the agreement 'insane' and talked of 'filching the island'. But Gladstone had also made it clear that his government would not repudiate binding agreements made by the Conservatives.[3]

While it is undeniable that Goschen wanted to get rid of Cyprus, there is some confusion as to whether he wished to give it back to Turkey or to grant it to Greece. It is obvious in the record of his mission mentioned above, written some years after the event, that he wanted to return Cyprus to Turkey as partial compensation for the territory Turkey was to cede to Greece. Michel Lhéritier is, as Professor Medlicott wrote, 'clearly in error in stating that Goschen proposed that Cyprus should be given to Greece'.[4] Lhéritier's only reference is to Elliot's book, where Goschen concluded that Cyprus should be restored to Turkey.[5] But it appears that Goschen considered both alternatives: returning Cyprus to Turkey in order to compensate her for the cession of Crete and territory in Thessaly and Epirus or ceding Cyprus to Greece in order to pacify the Greeks for Turkish unwillingness to give up both Crete and territory on the mainland. He seems to have felt that the Greeks would be content with parts of Thessaly and Epirus plus Cyprus. This would have

[1] Granville Papers, Goschen to Granville, 21 February 1881, secret, P.R.O. 30/29/189.
[2] Elliot, vol. I, p. 221.
[3] W. N. Medlicott, 'The Gladstone Government and the Cyprus Convention, 1880–1885', Journal of Modern History, XII (June 1950), 186–208.
[4] Medlicott, Concert of Europe, p. 223, note 102.
[5] Michel Lhéritier, Histoire Diplomatique de la Grèce de 1821 à Nos Jours (Paris, 1926), vol. 4, p. 121, note 3.

given the Greeks much less than they had expected on the mainland but granted Cyprus by way of compensation.

It was in a secret letter to Granville on 25 February 1881 that Goschen – irritated with the lack of progress since his return to Constantinople – asked a 'startling question. Is it out of the question to do something with *Cyprus*?'

> Suppose at the last moment Turkey and Greece cannot be brought to agree, or if the Turks will not give enough even to satisfy the Powers, if there is deadlock, would it not be a fine coup de théâtre, much finer than Dizzy's in seizing it, if we were to throw in Cyprus to avoid a European War. . . In the first place we should place Europe under a great obligation and give this most striking proof of our disinterestedness. Still more, we should undo in the minds of the Turks the immense harm that was done by the acquisition. . . . Again we should, not in a shabby way, but in a brilliant way, get rid of a most embarrassing Convention, the embarrassments of which have only begun. What are we to do in Armenia? What an immense advantage if we could get off from our separate line more or less imposed by the Convention and only share responsibility with the other Powers.[1]

Granville replied that Goschen's idea was 'very well argued, but it does not smile to me at present'.[2]

Goschen continued to grumble that war between Greece and Turkey seemed imminent. Throughout the first three weeks of March negotiations continued between the ambassadors and the Turks with little success. Goschen continued to fight for the interests of the Greeks, sometimes receiving lukewarm support from Hatzfeldt, while the other ambassadors insisted that the Turks must be conciliated if war was to be prevented. They were convinced that the Greeks were bluffing and secretly wanted to be presented with a *fait accompli* acceptable to the Turks and the ambassadors. Goschen warned the Greeks that they must be prepared to accept less territory than the Berlin Conference had proposed. Greece would be delighted with Crete but was far more interested in Epirus and Thessaly. The Turks insisted that if they gave up Crete they would surrender virtually nothing on the mainland and this the ambassadors rejected Goschen

[1] Granville Papers, Goschen to Granville, 25 February 1881, P.R.O. 30/29/189.
[2] *Ibid.*, copy Granville to Goschen, 3 March 1881, P.R.O. 30/29/210.

informed Granville on 22 March that 'war is very possible. Hatzfeldt thinks it inevitable'.[1]

The crisis suddenly came when on the following day the Turks made a fairly generous proposal. It was a strictly mainland solution which excluded Crete. The Greeks would obtain a sizeable chunk of Thessaly but the city of Prevesa in Epirus would be retained by the Turks. This was a bitter pill for the Greeks. They wanted Prevesa desperately, as the first step towards eventually obtaining the whole of Epirus. Goschen knew how badly the Greeks wanted Prevesa but he favoured the Turkish offer as did the other ambassadors. They doubted that the Greeks would ever get a better deal.

A solution was in sight if only the Greeks could be reconciled. Goschen had an inspiration. He promptly cabled Granville on 25 March and reminded him of his Cyprus proposal of 25 February. It is absolutely certain from the context of this telegram that Goschen wanted to give Cyprus to Greece as compensation for Prevesa.

Let me simply add that if Cyprus were thrown in with present Turkish proposal the programme of compensation for Epirus would be carried out; the present difficulties would vanish; England would acquire an immensely strong position for pressing Greece; the total offered would be more valuable than the Berlin award. Peace ought to be certain. Europe grateful; Turkey convinced of indisputable disinterestedness and England relieved in a most honourable way of a Convention which Mr. Gladstone called an act of madness. My taint of Jingoism is a guarantee to you that this suggestion does not come from one who is usually addicted to giving up.[2]

Granville and Gladstone, however, rejected Goschen's idea. They were convinced that the recent Turkish proposal would turn out to be acceptable.[3] Though there were still some trying moments to be faced during the month of April as the Greeks were badgered into accepting the arrangement, Goschen thought that he could now escape from the world of diplomacy. It had been decided that the career diplomat, Lord Dufferin, then ambas-

---

[1] *Ibid.*, see Goschen's long and interesting letters to Granville of 10, 11, 17 and 22 March 1881, P.R.O. 30/29/189.
[2] *Ibid.*, telegram, Goschen to Granville, 25 March 1881, P.R.O. 30/29/189.
[3] *Ibid.*, copy of telegram, Granville to Goschen, 26 March 1881, P.R.O. 30/29/210.

sador to Russia, should succeed Goschen as soon as the Greco-Turkish frontier question had been resolved. By the first days of May both Greece and Turkey had accepted the settlement and Goschen began the final preparations for his departure. Goschen wanted Dufferin to come to Constantinople while he was still there but Dufferin objected to the presence of two ambassadors at the same time and to 'learning his lesson' from his predecessor.[1] Goschen had already written to Dufferin on 28 March about the servants, cooks, carriages and horses at the British embassy in Constantinople. He also observed: 'Quite between ourselves, I don't think the Government are as anxious to see me in my place in Parliament as I am to see myself there.'[2]

Goschen was intensely annoyed by the French move into Tunis at this very time. It meant that another plum had been plucked from the areas under the nominal control of the sultan.[3] Nor was Granville very happy but he could not envisage any British action to prevent it. He informed Goschen that the Cabinet had decided nothing could be done since 'Cyprus, and the language of Salisbury leave little ground under our feet to take a strong attitude.'[4] By the end of May, Goschen was on his way back to London.

While the embassy failed to welcome any harem ladies in 1881, Goschen did have to contend with representatives of British nonconformity. In mid-March his office had been invaded by a delegation from the Bible Society, one of whose missionaries had been expelled from Crete. With heavy sarcasm Goschen informed Granville that they were willing to 'wait a few weeks before the whole force of the Empire will be expected to fight the cause of religious liberty on this occasion'. He implored Granville not to leave this matter to his 'discretion' as he did not know the 'precedents' and had 'no sympathy with and no confidence whatever in the operation connected with forcing the Bible on Mussulmans or Greeks'. The 'behaviour of the Cretans' seemed 'very natural' to Goschen and while he tried to be 'reserved and neutral' when

[1] Ramm (ed.), *Correspondence of Gladstone and Granville*, vol. 1, pp. 265–6.
[2] Dufferin Papers, Public Record Office of Northern Ireland, D1071 H/K1/1/178.
[3] Granville Papers, Goschen to Granville, 11 April 1881, P.R.O. 30/29/189.
[4] *Ibid.*, copy, Granville to Goschen, 13 May 1881, P.R.O. 30/29/210.

the deputation was in his office, 'a fiery Scotchman' had 'threatened' that he would take the issue to the Liberal party 'if the case were not actively pursued'.[1]

When Goschen reported to his constituents at Ripon on 20 July, he proved that he had thoroughly mastered one of the most important aspects of diplomatic life. He discussed his ambassadorial colleagues thus: 'We were social. We were fast friends. Some of us played lawn tennis together. Others rode, and we all dined together; and the more critical the moment the more assiduously we dined.'[2]

[1] *Ibid.*, Goschen to Granville, 17 March 1881, P.R.O. 30/29/189.
[2] Elliot, vol. 1, p. 240.

CHAPTER 6

THE 'MODERATE' LIBERALS
1881—1885

The formation of Gladstone's Cabinet in 1880 had been a pleasure for the moderate Liberals and a disaster for the Radicals since it was overwhelmingly Whiggish in composition. How much longer would Gladstone be able to strike a balance between Whig and Radical – between Hartington and Chamberlain? A split appeared certain though no one could be sure if it would come over Ireland, social welfare legislation or foreign policy. The chief political representatives of the Liberals of the Right were Goschen and Hartington, once Lowe had given up active politics. Hartington, the hereditary Whig, knew that Gladstone was moving in directions which were distasteful to the class he led but it was Goschen who provided the intellectual arguments to justify resistance to the emerging democracy. The Home Rule Bill of 1886 was the last item on a lengthening list and served as the final impetus for many Whigs and moderate Liberals who thought Gladstone had joined the attack on the 'rights of property'.[1]

When Goschen returned to London from Constantinople in December 1880, there had been speculation about his attitude towards the policies of the government. After meeting with Goschen, Granville sent a report to Gladstone and remarked that Goschen had not asked 'a single question about the position of home politics and when I made some allusion to them, was perfectly reticent'.[2] Goschen agreed with Queen Victoria that Gladstone's speeches had done 'much harm'. 'No one, he remarked, seemed nowadays to have courage. Everyone seemed to dread unpopularity and bid for popularity.'[3] Lord Acton, however, was

[1] See John Roach, 'Liberalism and the Victorian Intelligentsia', *Cambridge Historical Journal*, XIII (1957), 58–81.
[2] Ramm (ed.), *Correspondence of Gladstone and Granville*, vol. 1, pp. 234–5, Granville to Gladstone, 21 December 1881.
[3] Buckle (ed.), *Letters of Queen Victoria*, 2nd series, vol. 3, p. 178.

'impatient' with Goschen for not 'making overtures as to joining the Cabinet'.[1] On 2 February 1881 Lord Acton informed Gladstone's daughter that he had advised Goschen of 'the error of his ways' but he warned:

Goschen is above sordid motives. He dreads the Radicals . . . and, if left to himself and the nearest influences, he will drift away. His lips have never been touched with the sacred fire of Liberty. His international soul has never glowed with the zeal of the good old cause. He is moved by the fears to which City men are prone, and there are people more calculating than he is, who work those fears, partly to check the Government, partly to provide a new chief for the Opposition. Nobody can keep him straight but Mr Gladstone.[2]

What Goschen really feared was equality or any attempt to build a new meaning for liberty in terms of equality.

But Gladstone recognized the insuperable barrier of franchise reform and even Acton predicted that Goschen would not enter the Cabinet when he completed his task at Constantinople.[3] Gladstone and Granville hoped, however, to woo him with the offer of a G.C.B., kept vacant especially for him. It was to be a reward for his fine work as a Special Ambassador. Goschen's refusal upset Granville's equanimity but Gladstone urged tolerance.[4]

Within six weeks Gladstone had lost his benevolent attitude. He grumbled to Granville on 27 July 1881 that he was 'sorely vexed about Goschen'.

He voted against us last night. He did not vote on the life and death business of the Transvaal motion. He says the weak-kneed Liberals are the strong-kneed Liberals, and represents Liberalism as a torrent which they bravely stand against. (I thought such work had been the business of the Tories.) This gives me an indigestion.[5]

Goschen had voted in favour of a Whig amendment to Gladstone's Irish Land Bill of 1881 which would have exempted tenancies of £100 rental. The government only had its way by

[1] Elliot, vol. 1, p. 205.
[2] Paul (ed.), *Letters of Lord Acton*, pp. 64–6.
[3] *Ibid.*, p. 88.
[4] Ramm (ed.), *Correspondence of Gladstone and Granville*, vol. 1, pp. 276–9.
[5] *Ibid.*, vol. 1, pp. 286–7.

the comparatively narrow majority of thirty-six. Three weeks later Goschen informed Lord Dufferin that the Irish Land Bill had passed into law. 'The belief in Gladstone became so strong towards the end that any expression of qualified feelings towards the Bill were considered a sin against the Holy Ghost.' It seemed to Goschen that the House of Commons was being 'demoralized by having to swallow so much'. In the future, 'Nothing will seem too strong for it. . . The attitude of the party seems to me rather alarming.'[1]

Goschen's unwillingness to accept the G.C.B. was a part of his desire to be free of obligations so that he might be as independent as possible. The House of Commons which Goschen returned to in June 1881 was, after only one year, a wild sea of controversy.[2] The Bradlaugh incident, the failure of Gladstone's Irish Land Bill of 1880 in the House of Lords, the Boer victory at Majuba Hill, the death of Disraeli in April 1881, and the resignation of the Duke of Argyll from the Cabinet in May over the new Irish Land Bill served to intensify the rivalry between Liberals and Conservatives. The Irish Nationalists under Parnell were in the process of destroying the friendly atmosphere which had usually pervaded the House of Commons in the past. A record sitting of forty-one hours in early February 1881 provoked by the Parnellites led to the passing of severe closure resolutions. The House of Commons was determined to carry out its constitutional functions but the 'tone of the House' which mattered so much to many members seemed to have changed irreparably.

Both major parties were themselves badly divided. The divisions within the Liberal party grew worse as the Radicals pressed for concessions in Ireland while the Whigs demanded coercion and strong government. Fortunately for the Liberals, cleavages also existed within the Conservative party. The death of Disraeli heightened party divisions which had erupted immediately upon the opening of the new Parliament. The Bradlaugh

[1] Dufferin Papers, Goschen to Dufferin, 17 August 1881, D 1071 H/K1/2/249.
[2] The best contemporary account of this Parliament is Henry W. Lucy, *A Diary of Two Parliaments: The Gladstone Parliament 1880–1885* (London, 1886).

affair led to the formation of the 'Fourth Party', a 'ginger' group within the Conservative party. Guiding the four-man 'Fourth Party' was the sparkling and dynamic Lord Randolph Churchill who rejected the mild opposition tactics of Sir Stafford Northcote.

Goschen's return to England from Constantinople and the independent stand which he took on the Irish Land proposals marked him as a potential leader of the discontented moderate Liberals. The Duke of Argyll confided to Goschen on 31 July 1881 that 'the effect on the Cabinet would be great if a good body of independent Liberals were *to set up their backs a little.* You are the only man in a position to give such a party some coherence just now.'[1] Wishing to prove he was still a Liberal and not a Conservative, Goschen delivered a series of speeches. He advocated firmness in Ireland, ridiculed the Fair Traders, supported Gladstone's proposals against parliamentary obstruction, discussed the advantages of local government as opposed to the concentration of power in London, and upheld Gladstone's 'genius' and 'character', which made his continuance in office 'a matter of imperative national necessity'.[2] Early in January 1882 Acton considered Goschen to be 'travelling towards the Ministry, and no longer away from them'.[3]

When Parliament reassembled in early 1882 it seemed as though Acton might be correct. Goschen defended the government's agricultural policy and rejected the arguments of protectionists whose plans would raise the price of the people's food; he supported Gladstone's closure proposals; and he spoke in favour of permitting Bradlaugh to affirm and to enter the House of Commons.[4] On 10 March 1882 Goschen informed Lord Ripon, Viceroy of India, that the political situation at home was not good. The government had been having 'bad luck' while the Conservatives were 'behaving very badly and are horribly led . . . We

[1] Elliot, vol. 1, p. 253.
[2] *Ibid.*, vol. 1, pp. 255–8.
[3] Paul (ed.), *Letters of Lord Acton*, pp. 118–19, Acton to Mary Gladstone, 7 January 1882.
[4] *Hansard*, CCLXVI (17 February 1882), 1030–3; (20 February 1882), 1181–6; and CCLXVII (6 March 1882), 205–6.

should do much better with a stronger and more intelligent opposition.'[1]

Any movement on Goschen's part towards the Cabinet was retarded by disturbances in Ireland. Gladstone, under pressure from Chamberlain and because he saw the futility of coercion, came to an agreement with Parnell in April 1882. Known as the Kilmainham Treaty, it was supposed to improve relations between Great Britain and Ireland. A part of the arrangement called for an end to coercion and a return to ordinary legal procedures in Ireland. Forster, Chief Secretary for Ireland, resigned in protest. Goschen doubted the wisdom of Gladstone's tactics. He disclaimed a policy which seemed to pander to violence. The Liberal party would disintegrate 'if the idea is to be fostered that we are not powerful enough and not strong enough for the suppression of disorder, and for grappling with these disturbances, and that it is only by retreating, and by concession after concession, that we can govern'.[2] The terrible assassination of Lord Frederick Cavendish, the new Chief Secretary for Ireland, and T. H. Burke in Phoenix Park a few days later led to the reintroduction of coercive legislation for Ireland which Goschen was very happy to support against the protests of Irish M.P.s who were 'steeped in treason'. He was called to order by the Speaker and withdrew this expression. [3]

Goschen reported these exciting events to Lord Ripon on 9 May 1882:

Forster's retirement began a week of more painful and concentrated interest than I can remember before in politics. . . As regards the political effects, the principal one may perhaps be the blow dealt to the Parnellites. On Thursday they were considered masters of the situation, now they are nowhere, probably crushed between two forces, and it is said that they would scarcely dare show themselves in Ireland. . . I myself sympathize more with Forster than with his colleagues.[4]

Nor was Goschen sorry to inform Dufferin that the 'stringent'

---

[1] Ripon Papers, Add. Mss 43532, ff. 201-2.
[2] *Hansard*, CCLXVIII (2 May 1882), 1989-92.
[3] *Hansard*, CCLXIX (11 May 1882), 514-17.
[4] Ripon Papers, Add Mss 43532, ff. 203-5.

new Crimes Bill for Ireland meant that the 'Gladstone–Parnell alliance' was 'shattered'.[1]

Gladstone wanted to strengthen his Cabinet after this disastrous mishap and also to lessen his own burden by giving up the Exchequer. Hartington was encouraged to take the Exchequer in order to acquire additional governmental experience. Granville advised Gladstone that Hartington was willing to give up the India Office to Goschen but would prefer to remain where he was and let Goschen replace Childers at the War Office with Childers taking the Exchequer.[2] One of Goschen's votes seemed to imply that he was now willing to accept county suffrage extension and Gladstone wrote on 1 June 1882 to offer the post of Secretary of State for War. Gladstone stated that 'next year' would be devoted to the reform of local government.[3]

It seems strange that Gladstone should once again have passed over Goschen for the Exchequer. According to Edward Hamilton, Gladstone was 'prejudiced against Goschen for this place, believing that no man connected with the City can make a good Chancellor of the Exchequer'. Hamilton doubted that Goschen would accept the War Office.[4] Gladstone's mention of local government must have served as tempting bait but the fish refused to bite. Goschen replied on the following day that he could not accept, as his opinion on county suffrage had not altered.[5] Many years later he observed that 'his opinions on many matters were so different from Gladstone's that he could not with any ease have accepted that post'.[6] John Bright remarked that Goschen was 'going backward rather than forward in his political opinions'.[7] Joseph Chamberlain, however, was not unhappy. He informed Dilke a few days later: 'I hear G. has refused to join the Government. *Tant mieux*.'[8]

---

[1] Dufferin Papers, Goschen to Dufferin, [May 1882], D 1071 H/K1/3/29.
[2] Ramm (ed.), *Correspondence of Gladstone and Granville*, vol. 1, p. 372, Granville to Gladstone, 18 May 1882.
[3] GP, copy of letter, Gladstone to Goschen, Add. Mss 44161, ff. 282–3. Partially printed in Elliot, vol. 1, pp. 258–9.
[4] HP, British Museum, diary entry for 1 June 1882, Add. Mss 48632.
[5] GP, Add. Mss 44161, ff. 284–5. Partially printed in Elliot, vol. 1, p. 259.
[6] Elliot, vol. 1, pp. 259–60.
[7] Walling (ed.), *Diaries of John Bright*, p. 480.
[8] ChP, University of Birmingham Library, 11 June 1882.

Goschen energetically supported the new Coercion Bill for Ireland which was introduced and passed by the government but he recoiled from a bill designed to decrease evictions in Ireland. Gladstone and the Radicals were unwilling to employ a simple policy of ruthless enforcement of the existing law in Ireland. They insisted upon a constructive programme too and it was this aspect of the Cabinet's Irish policy which many moderate Liberals and Whigs refused to accept since it meant further tampering with the rights of property and contract. Each Irish land measure which Gladstone introduced seemed but the prelude to another one of an even more advanced and radical nature. Goschen summarized his own views in Parliament on 6 July 1882:

I believe the wish of all in this house is that we should be able to make progress in settling this question – that we may know that the last demand has been made for legislation on the Irish Land Question; that the rights of the landlord and tenants have been defined; that capital may once more go to Ireland in the confident expectation that no further legislation is likely to weaken that security which is at the foundation of all national prosperity.[1]

It was perhaps fortunate for both Goschen and the Cabinet that he had not accepted office. Riots in Alexandria on 12 June 1882 led to the death of some Europeans. The bloodshed was part of a struggle for power in Egypt between the khedive and a nationalist movement led by Colonel Ahmed Arabi which opposed British and French economic control over their country. Events moved quickly. The British, acting alone when France refused to co-operate and Turkey procrastinated, were determined to protect both their nationals and the Suez Canal. They bombarded Alexandria on 11 July and British troops were landed. By the middle of September Arabi had been defeated and Gladstone had carried out his own prediction about the probable outcome of the purchase of the Suez Canal shares. Much British money was invested in Egypt and Goschen was identified in the public mind as a representative of the Egyptian bondholders.

To the Radicals and the Parnellites, Goschen was among those chiefly responsible for exploiting the Egyptian peasants so that the khedive might pay off greedy British investors. Goschen

[1] *Hansard*, CCLXXI (6 July 1882), 1694–701.

answered this criticism as he had in the past and as he would again when he was Chancellor of the Exchequer. He had severed all connections with the firm of Fruhling and Goschen and had gone to Egypt for the bondholders in 1876 only after having publicly stipulated that he would do nothing for the bondholders contrary to the British national interest. If Goschen had been in the Cabinet when the events at Alexandria and Tel-el-Kebir took place, the government's actions would have been much more open to suspicion and attack. After Tel-el-Kebir Goschen wrote to Granville to congratulate him on the 'immense success achieved in Egypt' and 'on the éclat which will be reflected in our Foreign relations generally by the brilliancy of the late victories'. He admitted:

Of course, I rejoice (as a bit of a Jingo) on the 'prestige' we have gained. I rejoice, as an Ex-Ambassador at the increased power which we shall acquire in the East, and in foreign questions generally. I rejoice as a Liberal in the success of an Army Reformer, such as Sir Garnet Wolseley, and in this striking proof that the reorganization plans have not damaged the fighting qualities of the soldiers and I am sincerely glad that the Government after all their troubles and misfortunes, should have this great satisfaction and have achieved a principle which will be most telling in every way.[1]

Granville consulted Goschen as to what course the British government should follow now that Arabi had been vanquished. Gladstone had hoped to smash Arabi and to withdraw as soon as a stable government under the khedive had been re-established in Egypt. Goschen's diagnosis of 19 September was not optimistic because of the need to conciliate British public opinion, France and Turkey. He returned the papers which Granville had sent him with the conclusion that he could 'scarcely give an opinion on a single point without knowing how far you will feel compelled or be anxious to humour France'. He did insist that the Treasury of the Public Debt, concerned with the bondholders, should be kept separate from the controllers, whose orientation was towards the Egyptian economy 'as a whole'. Baring was praised for having alleviated the suffering of the poorer classes of Egypt and Goschen warned that the controllers must never be

[1] Granville Papers, Goschen to Granville, 15 September 1882, P.R.O. 30/29/150.

considered to be 'Bondholders' men'.[1] It is apparent that Goschen was genuinely concerned about the misery and poverty which existed in Egypt but he did not want the bondholders to be denied their legitimate profit.

Gladstone and Granville were now scouting for someone to send to Egypt and had not yet decided to bring Baring back from India. Granville wrote to the Prime Minister on 21 September 1882: 'When you suggested sending a strong man to Cairo, the idea smiled to me much. Goschen would probably do the work best, but he has unjustly a flavour of bondholder about him, and there are other objections.' Gladstone agreed that Goschen was 'clearly impossible'.[2] The Cabinet eventually decided to send Sir Evelyn Baring back to Egypt as Consul General after a three-year absence as Financial Member of the government of India. Baring arrived in Egypt in mid-September of 1883 and on 25 October, Goschen sent a letter of congratulation.

We are all agog now to know what is going to take place about evacuation. The Foreign Office people proper seem to be violently opposed to it, and to fear it may lead to ultimate difficulties with France, who would move if we gave them a chance and afterwards give us trouble if we wished to keep them out again, but all this seems based on the idea that evacuation would mean abandonment, which it certainly would not. . . After a little time it will be *you* who will direct *them* [the British government], rather than they who will direct you, and an agent who *has* a policy decently in accord with the general feeling of the Government has an immense advantage, seeing that the tendency to drift is not one from which our friends are entirely free.[3]

Whigs, moderate Liberals and Radicals were eager to criticize various aspects of Gladstone's policies but all could agree that when he retired the party would face a 'time of troubles'. Goschen feared 'chaos' when Gladstone departed while Chamberlain and Dilke shuddered at the prospect of Hartington in Gladstone's place.[4] The platform of the Radicals was set forth in a series of unsigned articles in *The Fortnightly Review* and endorsed by

[1] *Ibid.*, Goschen to Granville, 19 September 1882, P.R.O. 30/29/150.
[2] Ramm (ed.), *Correspondence of Gladstone and Granville*, vol. 1, pp. 427–8, 438.
[3] CrP, F.O. 633/7.
[4] H. D. Acland (ed.), *Memoirs and Letters of Sir Thomas Dyke Acland* (London, 1902), pp. 345–6.

Chamberlain. These proposals, which included free education and land reform, provided the foundation of his 'Unauthorized Programme' in 1885. The Radical leader was also hurling thunderbolts at the House of Lords because that heavily Conservative body was determined to scuttle a Reform Bill unless it was coupled with a redistribution of seats.

Chamberlain's personal friend and political associate, Jesse Collings, spoke against coercion in Ireland on 21 February 1883 and Goschen wrote in his diary that Collings had ignored 'all the terrible crimes. I was exceedingly glad to hear him as a specimen, and wondered whether he really represents the democracy of which he spoke.'[1] Some Whigs and moderate Liberals pleaded with Goschen and Hartington to step forward as leaders of a formal moderate Liberal organization which would serve as a counter-weight to the National Liberal Federation. They refused, as it might split the party.[2]

The great debate about the organization and purpose of the two great political parties continued in the journals of opinion. The Whigs were urged again and again to join forces with Conservatism against destructive Radicalism. The spectre of *laissez-faire* being destroyed and state socialism constructed before their very eyes plagued the Whigs and moderate Liberals. In 1883 Goschen delivered an address entitled 'Laissez-Faire and Government Interference' to the members of the Philosophical Society in Edinburgh. He declared that *laissez-faire* was losing support 'chiefly owing to moral considerations, to the assertion of the claims of other than material interests, and to a growing feeling that it is right deliberately to risk commercial and industrial advantages for the sake of reforming social abuses, and securing social benefits'. Goschen maintained that the Irish Land Act of 1881 was 'probably the most gigantic invasion of the principle of "Laissez-faire" in recent times'. The new democracy regarded the state as its 'servant' and sought to 'control the individual' in a 'distinctly Socialistic' way. But a demand for public housing was

[1] Elliot, vol. 1, pp. 267–8.
[2] Moisei Ostrogorski, *Democracy and the Organization of Political Parties* (London, 1902), vol. 1, pp. 246–8.

not the solution to the slum problem. How much better it would be to punish 'house-owners who let out rooms unfit for human occupation, as tradesmen who offer putrid food for sale'. The greatest danger of all was the transference of duties to the state which might weaken 'the belief of the community in the value of natural liberty'. A partial response to the dangers he foresaw would be the revival of local authorities so that responsibilities could be delegated to them rather than to the central government.[1]

When he perused this lecture some twenty years later he thought that his analysis of the decline of *laissez-faire* was substantially correct but he conceded that government interference had been less rapid than he expected. He was especially irritated by municipal authorities which had failed to act as a bulwark against government interference and socialism. 'Vast undertakings, carried out without much regard for financial considerations, frequent charges of jobbery, risky experiments, an increasing army of dependents upon municipal generosity – such are the concomitants of the extension of the over-energetic efforts of civic authorities.' The London County Council had done good work 'but the spirit of State Socialism is active within their ranks'. All of the things which he had 'feared for the Executive Government have dogged the footsteps of municipal administration. In no direction have blows more serious been struck at the very foundation of private enterprise.' He had also to admit that his fears about the redistribution of property had not been fully justified. 'On the whole I am inclined to think that work undertaken by the State has been better done, and with less friction than I anticipated; while on the other hand I fear that the spirit of self-reliance has suffered in the process, and the sense of individual responsibility, as was foreseen, been sensibly injured.'[2]

Goschen reported periodically on political events to the Marquess of Ripon and mentioned on 1 July 1883 that several constituents had criticized him for his anti-Liberal votes and for not visiting his constituency often enough. The Irish and the Radicals

[1] Goschen, *Essays and Addresses*, pp. 294–325.
[2] Goschen, *Essays and Addresses*, pp. 282–93.

made the most trouble at home and affected both domestic and foreign policy. The Irish were doing their best to show that the English were brutal in their dealings with all subject peoples and not only with Ireland. Goschen commented that

> our extreme Radicals are very much that way themselves. We will soon see how a democracy will succeed in keeping subject races in order. Gladstone keeps the democrats in order now: and we see only the beginnings of what may take large dimensions hereafter. But the democratic radicals are longing in many ways to make war on the Executive, and to limit its actions in some directions, tho' quite prepared to compel its extension in others.[1]

Joseph Chamberlain was not sorry when he wrote to Mrs Leonard Courtney on 31 October 1883 and expressed doubts that Goschen would 'ever come to the front again'.[2] A month later, however, Goschen was on the main stage when Gladstone offered him the office of Speaker of the House of Commons in succession to Henry Brand. The Solicitor-General, Herschell, had been the first choice but he had declined the offer. Henry Lucy suspected that the Prime Minister was trying to remove 'a dangerous combatant' from the political arena.[3] After some hesitation and to his own surprise, Goschen decided to accept the post if his weak eyes proved strong enough. Dr Bowman, the famous oculist, was consulted and expressed reservations to both Gladstone and Goschen. Goschen would be fine during quiet periods of debate but he would be at a grave disadvantage during moments of excitement in the House of Commons. This convinced Goschen that he must decline the office.[4]

Goschen's refusal left him free to continue his independent role. In 1884 the Liberals were determined to redeem their election pledge and extend household suffrage to the counties. There were numerous hurdles to be surmounted, for the Conservatives, while unwilling to follow Goschen by opposing the measures on principle, insisted that a redistribution of seats be coupled with the extension of the vote. The realization that the Irish electorate

[1] Ripon Papers, Add. Mss 43532, ff. 206–9.
[2] George P. Gooch, *Life of Lord Courtney* (London, 1920), p. 194.
[3] Henry W. Lucy, *Sixty Years in the Wilderness* (London, 1909), pp. 239–41.
[4] GP, Add. Mss 44161, ff. 268–94.

would be greatly enlarged while Ireland retained her one hundred M.P.s was a disturbing one to moderates in both parties. They correctly foresaw that this would put all of Ireland – with the exception of a part of Ulster – in Parnell's pocket and double the size of the contingent under his command. The Franchise Bill went through the House of Commons early in 1884 with only Goschen, among the Liberals, voting against it. The House of Lords threw the measure out and insisted that it be joined to a Redistribution Bill. Gladstone was indignant at this attempt by the Lords to impose their will and decided to re-introduce the Franchise Bill in the autumn. Chamberlain and Morley denounced the Lords while the queen pleaded for restraint and compromise. Finally, direct talks between the party chiefs led to an agreed settlement. The Reform Bill was to be passed as a separate measure and a Redistribution Bill was to be introduced immediately. The electorate was increased from about 3,000,000 to 5,000,000 and most of the United Kingdom was divided into single-member constituencies.

When Goschen spoke in March during the first reading of the Franchise Bill he acknowledged that his fears about the urban working class had not been realized. But they had been trained through participation in the activities of local authorities while the agricultural labourers lacked any preparation for the proper exercise of the vote. He demanded that the government reveal in detail its plans for Ireland and its plans for a redistribution of seats. On the second reading of the bill, Goschen defended the rights of minorities and pleaded that all classes must be represented in Parliament. He envisaged the masses outvoting the business, social and intellectual elite in every single-member constituency. It was essential that the present Parliament pass a Redistribution Bill for if it did not, a democratically elected Commons might grant permanent superiority to the masses at the expense of the classes. The House of Commons was already losing its independence. He concluded: 'My Party seems to breathe an atmosphere of Utopia, and to feel a confidence I cannot share.'

The suggestion that women be enfranchised caused Goschen

to shudder and protest since 'it assumes an equality between men and women which never has existed, and which I believe never can exist'. In 1873 and again in 1875 he had voted to retain the Contagious Diseases Acts. When the Franchise Bill was read for the third time Goschen chided the Conservatives for failing to join him in a general assault on the principle of the bill. Rumour had it that the Conservatives did not wish to alienate the new voters by opposing it on principle in the House of Commons and would simply permit their overwhelming majority in the Lords to carry out the task for them. Constitutionally, this did not seem wise to Goschen and it proved that party tactics and slick manoeuvres had replaced principles and statesmanship.[1]

Albert Grey (later the fourth Earl Grey) considered resigning his seat in protest in late 1883 when he realized that a Franchise Bill was to be introduced without a Redistribution Bill attached to it. Goschen urged the younger man to wait before taking such a drastic step since all moderate Liberals were badly needed in the Commons. It would be 'awkward' for Goschen to press this particular point about the separation of the bills as much as he wanted to since he had been a member of the Russell Cabinet in 1866. At that time the two issues had been separated and Goschen had made 'speeches defending that course'.[2] A few days after the House of Lords had rejected the Reform Bill because it was not coupled with a Redistribution Bill, Goschen complained to Albert Grey: 'I cannot for the life of me understand why the House of Lords should not be allowed the power of forcing an appeal to the people. It seems a peculiarly good function for them to exercise, especially in a serious change of the constitution.' Nothing much could be done until Parliament reassembled in the autumn and then, if the Liberal leaders had been 'truculent' during the recess 'or if there should be anything like violence, I should like to beat the Government in the Commons so as to force a dissolution, and *avowedly* to *force* a dissolution, as the best means to conclude the controversy with its attendant risks'.[3]

---

[1] *Hansard*, CCLXXXV (3 March 1884), 416–30; CCLXXXVI (7 April 1884), 1867–80; CCLXXXIX (12 and 26 June 1884), 182–90, 1444–5.
[2] Grey Papers, University of Durham, Goschen to Grey, 19 December [1883].
[3] *Ibid.*, Goschen to Grey, 20 July 1884.

After a summer of harsh political speeches a compromise was finally hammered out by the Liberal and Conservative leaders. The general outlines of the agreement followed a memorandum which Goschen submitted to the Prince of Wales and Queen Victoria on 31 October 1884. This is not to say that Goschen was the driving force behind the agreement but rather that his common-sense approach probably appealed to both sides as they grappled for a solution. Goschen attempted to remove all 'partisan' considerations from his mind. This led him to conclude that the Conservatives genuinely feared that 'a dissolution based on the existing electoral areas, but with the addition of 2,000,000 new voters, would strike a heavy almost irretrievable blow not only to themselves as a party but at the landed and agricultural interest generally'. It was true that the government had promised to pass a Redistribution Bill before the present Parliament was dissolved but the Conservatives were afraid that 'time' or 'circumstances' might make it impossible.

The Liberals, on the other hand, argued that 'if the two bills are tied together, they widen the opportunities for the Lords to throw out the Franchise Bill'. The Reform Bill might then 'be wrecked, if the Government did not give way to the Conservatives in any changes they might propose in the Redistribution Bill'. Since a compromise seemed impossible it was necessary 'to endeavour as far as possible (for it cannot be done completely) to obtain the same results as the union of the two bills would secure, from some other course of proceeding'. The solution was not too difficult. 'As the Bills cannot be tied together, let them at all events follow on each other's heels so closely as to minimize the risks of one being passed without the other.' The government should 'be urged to introduce and carry forward their Redistribution Bill, as soon as the Commons have disposed of the Franchise Bill, and without waiting for the latter to be finally passed by the Lords'.[1]

When the Franchise Bill was read for a second time in early November, Goschen stated that he would no longer oppose it as

[1] Goschen to the Prince of Wales, 31 October 1884, RA L15/41.

'the country and the House have decided that the suffrage is to be extended'. But he did criticize the decision to establish single-member constituencies. This could mean that the members of the Commons would only represent the class interests of their constituents. He then went on to talk vaguely about his belief that communities of every description needed representation.[1]

If the extension of the franchise had been the only point on which Goschen disagreed with his party, it might have been possible for him to co-operate with the Liberal leaders now that this was no longer an issue. But other areas of conflict remained. Ireland, foreign policy, and the growth of bureaucratic power in London kept him at a distance. The whole tone of British politics seemed to have changed as he looked back over his twenty years in the House of Commons. When he spoke on Gordon's mission into the Sudan he extolled the 'prestige and moral effect of the British soldier' but he wondered why these 'most delicate and difficult questions' could not be discussed 'without their being obscured by the smoke of Party spirit'. It seemed as though there was no longer a 'continuity of national will'.[2] On 2 June 1884 he reported to Lord Ripon in India: 'I have been in a peculiar and not very pleasant position during the whole of this Parliament. But even apart from this, politics have lost almost all their charm since the whole tone of the House of Commons was changed by the Irish Nationalists.'[3]

The accumulated tension and anxiety of the previous four years led Goschen to take a momentous step for a nineteenth-century politician. He resigned from the two most important Liberal clubs to which he belonged, the Reform and the Devonshire. But he remained a member of the Liberal party and began to search for a new constituency since Ripon was to disappear under the terms of the Redistribution Bill. Trying to explain these resignations he wrote:

---

[1] *Hansard*, CCXCIII (7 and 11 December 1884), 1297–305, 1463–8; and CCXCIV (4 December 1884), 711–22.

[2] *Hansard*, CCLXXXVIII (13 May 1884), 260–72.

[3] Ripon Papers, Add. Mss 43532, ff. 210–13.

The immediate motive was economy. I belong to too many Clubs; but if I analyse my motives, I fancy there is a feeling too of not caring to be *tied* to the party or at least to wear its livery. I am in a devil-may-care humour as to what people may say or think as regards my political future.[1]

[1] Elliot, vol. I, p. 290.

CHAPTER 7

THE IRISH NATIONALISTS AND THE ELECTION OF 1885

It was in 1884 that Alfred Milner, thirty years of age and still writing part-time for the *Pall Mall Gazette*, came to work for Goschen as a private secretary. Their friendship had started a few years before and quickly ripened, so that Goschen, impressed with Milner's great ability, did everything possible to advance his career. Perhaps Milner's German heritage helped to bring the two men together.

Milner agreed with Goschen that Gladstone's vacillating foreign policy was a national disgrace and recommended that the members of the 'Foreign and Colonial Offices' be swept 'right out into the street'. These offices were 'entirely manned *with Whigs*' and he wondered if Goschen could name a group of Radicals who could 'possibly make a greater mess of things'. A fatal error was made by those who failed to distinguish between the Whig and the moderate Liberal. 'For a real Moderate Liberal is a man whose moderation is based on principle, as strong, maybe stronger, and better digested than that of the more advanced men. But the moderation of the Whig is the result not of moderate principles but of the accident of birth and of having no principles at all.'[1] Queen Victoria, disgusted with Gladstone, Chamberlain, Randolph Churchill and Parnell, was also shopping about for Moderates but she wanted them from both major parties. On 7 October 1884 she wrote to the Duke of Argyll that she longed 'for the moderates of both sides to form a third party'. Goschen seemed 'very eager' to support such a tactic.[2]

Goschen was outraged at Chamberlain's speech in Birmingham on 5 January 1885, which he found, 'Quite detestable. . . Setting class against class; all against property, which he implies

---

[1] MP, Milner to Goschen, 21 August 1884, Box 182.
[2] Buckle (ed.), *Letters of Queen Victoria*, 2nd series, vol. 3, p. 547.

but does not actually say is landed property'.[1] Chamberlain later wrote that it was in this speech that he used the expression 'What ransom will property pay?' which he admitted 'was not perhaps a very happy one, but curiously enough it was borrowed from Mr. Goschen, who had used it in a private conversation we had had a few days before on the subject of these social reforms'.[2]

Milner assisted Goschen in the preparation of several speeches which Goschen was to deliver in Edinburgh in late January and early February as the Liberal leaders of the Edinburgh East constituency had displayed an interest in securing him as their candidate. While Goschen prepared for his journey to the Scottish Lowlands Milner continued his reports and comments on the latest political incidents. On 20 January 1885 he wrote that 'a good many Liberals, and Advanced Liberals too, will be very glad if you give Chamberlain some hard knocks'. A few days later Milner informed Goschen that the majority of provincial newspapers still regarded Goschen as a Liberal and they were 'anxious that your influence should increase rather than decrease'. What they feared was that Goschen might be 'too conclusively critical and too little constructive. They want to swear by you but they must have a programme to swear by and not merely an ethos.' There were many Liberals who were 'seriously alarmed and disgusted with Chamberlain, but unless they have an alternative policy offered them they will "swim with the stream" or else give up the game and sink into apathy or desert to Conservatism'.[3]

The great care which Goschen devoted to his two Edinburgh speeches and the importance he attached to them are made abundantly clear from his correspondence with Milner and Albert Grey. He found himself in the uncomfortable position of wanting to be adopted by the Edinburgh East constituency as a Liberal although he had not been in harmony with his party for some years. In order to be selected and to win the election, working-class support would be necessary but it was already confidently

[1] Elliot, vol. 1, p. 290.
[2] Joseph Chamberlain, *A Political Memoir 1880–1892* (ed. C. H. D. Howard) (London, 1953).
[3] MP, Milner to Goschen, 20 and 25 January 1885, Box. 182.

asserted that the Radicals of Edinburgh East would not tolerate Goschen and had their own nominee.

Goschen, however, was determined to state his opinions clearly and resolutely even if they brought political disaster. In his speech in the Music Hall at Edinburgh on 31 January 1885 he returned to his theme that the 'new democracy' had been achieved at a time of 'momentous crisis in the History of this country'. He defended his independent position and affirmed his 'allegiance to the principles, the Liberal principles, in which I have been brought up'. The old principles of the Liberal party could still be applied to this new situation. 'The object of all politics must be to secure the greatest happiness for the greatest number – to endeavour to spread the prosperity of this country over an ever-widening area of the population.' No one wanted Britain to be simply 'the paradise of the rich'. It was the Liberal party which had 'struck off the fetters from industry' and 'promoted the union of classes'.

Goschen hoped that the new electors would not endorse 'the dethronement of Gladstonian finance'. Surely they would not demand a 'ransom for abstaining from plunder'. The new democracy had every right to further its class interests just as other classes had done. He was convinced that the new problems could be faced 'in the old spirit' and without reliance on 'crude panaceas', and visionary utopian proposals which were not grounded on solid fact. By 'crude panaceas' he meant such things as the nationalization of land and the establishment of a land court to fix rents. Goschen proposed that they 'try freedom first, before we try the interference of the State'. All hereditary restrictions should be removed from the ownership of land so that owners might be able to sell more easily to their tenants. Goschen warmly approved the Liberal party's desire to see a larger number of independent landholders. This goal could be achieved by setting up a 'Land Register in every great local centre' so that 'transfers of land might take place with not very much greater difficulty than transfers of Consols take place in the Bank of England'.

He went on to reiterate proposals and reforms with which his name had long been associated – reform of local government in the counties; an increase in the activities assigned to local government in order to curtail the London bureaucracy; a demand that slum landlords be punished rather than allow public authorities to undertake the construction of public housing for the poor; public houses to be licensed by local authorities; a word of caution about tax legislation which might 'drive capital out of the country'; and contempt for those who wanted a return to protective tariffs. Goschen had no doubt that 'the new democracy will do its duty, if those who aspire to lead it will only tell the truth'.

Earlier in the speech in a particularly revealing passage, he had analysed Gladstone's Irish Land Act and its principles of fair rent, free sale and fixity of tenure. Goschen argued that free sale would destroy fair rent and in seeking to show that slogans might often be contradictory he decided to look at the famous expression – liberty, equality, fraternity.

> Liberty and Equality almost destroy each other. (Oh.) Liberty is the power to possess as much as you please or as little as you please, to work, to get forward, to rise in the scale of life, if you can. Equality is against all that, and says every man must be exactly the same as his neighbour. (Cries of No, no; laughter, cheers, and some hissing.) I should like to argue that out, because I have a very strong opinion about it. Equality in France killed liberty. (Hear, hear; hisses and cheers.) I am astonished that that is not accepted. (A voice, 'That's right.') I am not speaking against equality in the slightest degree. I am only showing that these catch-phrases of three words often involve fallacies.[1]

Goschen reported that an 'attentive and intelligent audience' had received him 'very well'. There had been many Radicals in the audience but they had 'behaved perfectly'. It seemed to Goschen that he had succeeded in establishing the contrast which Milner had suggested. Goschen's policy was based upon 'union, freedom, justice and common sense' while Chamberlain stood for 'class conflict and wild schemes'.[2] Twenty years later Goschen remarked to Milner that this speech had been 'a kind of landmark

---

[1] George J. Goschen, *Addresses* (Edinburgh, 1885), pp. 3–22. This small booklet contains Goschen's Edinburgh speeches of 31 January and 3 February 1885 and his Liverpool speech of 11 February 1885.

[2] MP, Goschen to Milner, Sunday [1 February 1885], Box 184.

in my life'. Goschen regarded it as 'distinctly constructive'.[1]

Three days later he spoke again in Edinburgh; this time on foreign policy. He emphasized the importance of the empire and the colonies to the working men at home. But they must be willing to make sacrifices in the interest of the empire since other European states were now competing with Britain for colonies and trade. He urged them to think of the importance of colonial trade to Britain: 'I should like to know whether this country would do the same business with India if India were under a Russian protectorate – which Heaven forbid. . . . You will remember that goods follow the flag to an extraordinary degree; and, what is more, men follow the flag.' Trade with the colonies even where protective tariffs had been imposed, 'stood the depression which has existed with far greater strength than our trade with foreign countries not under our own flag'. He hoped that Britain and her colonies might be drawn closer to one another. The great strength of Germany and the 'colonising mania' sweeping the continental states were disturbing but there was no reason to be an 'alarmist'. It was essential, however, to avoid 'drift' and to 'make up our minds what we consider essential and what we do not, and then stand by what we consider to be the rights and duty of this country'.[2]

Two days after this speech the news of Gordon's death at Khartoum reached London. Goschen wondered: 'What will happen to the Government? Will the country be furious at last? I don't feel much confidence.'[3] When he spoke on foreign policy in Liverpool a week later he insisted that Britain must have a free hand in Egypt and not allow any other nation to meddle. Britain must remove 'any impression of weakness or "squeezability"'. He conceded to his Radical critics that he was 'a moderate man' but he was also 'a fighting man, always willing to take up a challenge which has been thrown down'.[4]

In the parliamentary debate on the Gordon tragedy, Goschen voted along with Forster and a few other Liberals for Sir Stafford

---

[1] *Ibid.*, 1 January 1906, Box 45.
[2] Goschen, *Addresses*, pp. 23–8.
[3] Elliot, vol. 1, pp. 291–2.
[4] Goschen, *Addresses*, pp. 38–51.

Northcote's censure motion. The government prevailed by only 302 to 288 and disaster seemed imminent. Goschen had his own plan for the reconquest of the Sudan and it went far beyond the doctrine of concentration. Argument revolved about a proposal to construct a railway into the Sudan along the Nile River valley and one to build a railway from Suakin, on the Red Sea and in the Sudan, almost directly west to Berber. Goschen expounded his preference for the Suakin–Berber route in a letter to Sir Stafford Northcote on 5 March 1885. It would mean that Britain could then 'act independently of internationalizing Egypt. It is another door, of which the Great Powers will not have the key.'[1] Northcote wondered if Goschen wanted a 'key' to central Africa. 'That is a large room, and one which will absorb a goodly proportion of our strength.'[2]

The closest but most discontented part of the empire was again disrupting the Cabinet. Gladstone had been convinced since late 1884 that Ireland would get some kind of legislative body but he failed to carry a majority of the Cabinet with him when the Chamberlain–Dilke proposal for a central board – but no separate Parliament – came to a vote on 9 May 1885. Once Chamberlain's scheme had been dropped the Cabinet was left to decide whether or not to extend the Coercion Act for Ireland and if so, for how many years. Goschen vehemently opposed its extension for only one year as this would mean that a new Parliament, shortly after the expected general election in late 1885 or early 1886, would have to decide whether to maintain it, permit it to lapse or rewrite it. Goschen implored Hartington on 25 May 1885:

Are we to start with a furious fight over the Crimes Bill in the new Parliament? Is that to be the 'pièce de résistance' of the first session? It would be risking the character of the new Parliament before it has settled down and demoralising it from the beginning. It would be most unfair to England and Scotland, but it might be worse than unfair: it might be disastrous to our parliamentary institutions.

Gladstone might well have retired and the political parties could be 'in a state of chaos'. It would be much better to make it

---

[1] Iddesleigh Papers, Add. Mss 50021, f. 265.
[2] *Ibid.*, Add. Mss 50021, ff. 263–4.

necessary for a new Parliament to change an existing statute. 'If a majority wants to repeal it – OKAY – but if a majority has to pass a new bill it may be impossible with determined minority efforts.' He recognized Hartington's difficult position but regarded the first session of the new Parliament as 'the most critical session; the session most likely to determine the course of English politics for a long period to come'.[1]

Goschen's desire to be a member of that new Parliament was partially fulfilled when the Liberals of the Edinburgh East constituency adopted him as their candidate. But after his selection new doubts entered his mind as to whether he would be able to run as a Liberal. A long, 'fighting' talk with Albert Grey in late May made Goschen consider

retiring from Edinburgh and endeavouring to bring a party together before the election, so that people might stand knowing where they were; programme: Honesty: Secondary Education: Local Government: Representation and Taxation: Distribution of burdens between the whole Community: Sympathy with Colonies: Administrative Reform: Sympathy with fighting Services: Concentration but Firmness. . . If the Irish Crimes Bill is renewed only for a year, I shall oppose that provision *coûte que coûte*. But the Conservatives may prove most unreliable. They have been behaving abominably about the budget.

At about the same time he sighed that he was 'more disheartened and disgusted than ever before: to such an extent that I have thought of going off to the Colonies – Australia for instance, for six months, till the Election is past'.[2]

There seemed to be no haven in sight as Goschen's distrust of the Conservative party had not abated. The actions of Lord Randolph Churchill alarmed him, for the shrewd young opportunist was courting the Irish in order to turn out Gladstone. The Conservatives intimated that they would allow the Coercion Act to lapse. On 8 June 1885 a coalition of Conservatives and Parnellites defeated the Liberals on a budget clause by a vote of 264 to 252. Perhaps with a gasp of relief, Gladstone and his Cabinet resigned on the following day. Goschen had voted with

[1] DP, 340.1784. Hartington sent this letter to Gladstone.
[2] Elliot, vol. 1, pp. 293–5.

Gladstone this time and was surprised that this relatively minor issue had toppled the government. The queen sent for Lord Salisbury since Churchill had done such an effective job in elbowing aside Sir Stafford Northcote. Salisbury obtained guarantees of support from the Liberals since a general election could not take place until the end of the year.

During the summer of 1885 Goschen asked Gladstone to define his reaction to Chamberlain's plan for 'several *central* national councils for the different parts of the United Kingdom'. This would reach 'deep down to the foundations of the Constitution'. While opposing Chamberlain's national councils, Goschen underscored his support for 'decentralization and the devolution of important functions to provincial or other bodies'.[1] Gladstone was determined to hold his umbrella over the entire Liberal party and refused to commit himself. Throughout the month of August and into September a fierce internecine struggle raged between Radicals and Whigs while Gladstone picked his way skilfully between the opposing factions and sought to rally behind him all who were willing to campaign as Liberals.

Goschen was exultant over Hartington's first major electoral speech and prepared to harmonize his declarations with those of Hartington, the natural leader of the Whigs and moderate Liberals.[2] The Whig leader replied two days later that Chamberlain realized his own weakness and did not wish to split the party. Speeches by Goschen in support of Hartington's programme would be 'most useful' but he cautioned Goschen 'not to advance the position and attack Chamberlain more than can be avoided'.[3] Goschen had advised Lord Richard Grosvenor, the Chief Liberal Whip, that he would speak wherever he might help the Liberal cause. 'I concluded from his silence that he thinks me compromising; but I don't see that I need be considered so.' Having been rebuffed by the Chief Liberal Whip, Goschen now offered to speak wherever Hartington thought he might be useful. 'Of course not in such radical places as would be vexed at my intru-

---

[1] GP, Goschen to Gladstone, 10 July 1885, Add. Mss 44161, ff. 313–17.
[2] DP, 6 and 11 September 1885, 340.1803 and 340.1807.
[3] Elliot, vol. 1, pp. 308–10, 13 September 1885.

sion: and I am not well suited to an agricultural audience.' Hartington's comments about Gladstone's thoughts on Ireland were 'indeed ominous' and made him feel 'uneasy'.[1]

Albert Grey had already asked Goschen about Hartington's reliability in a struggle with Gladstone and the Radicals. Goschen replied that he thought Hartington was 'slowly coming round to see that he must face the possibility of a break'. On 20 September, Goschen remarked to Grey that Gladstone's election address had not been entirely satisfactory on the Established Church. Disestablishment was something which Goschen was prepared to resist 'à outrance' but it would be difficult for him to take a leading role on this topic since he was not unsympathetic to demands for disestablishment in Scotland. Goschen suspected that few questions would 'be dealt with in the next Parliament, because the next Parliament must be extremely short'.

The Parnellites will break it up, and if not, Gladstone's retirement will break it up. I hate this Umbrella policy but I admit that the attitude of the Conservatives toward the Irish question has much modified the situation. I will tell you what I think the best plan to pursue. I have told no one yet except my wife. It is to prepare myself, if the occasion comes, to join a Cabinet formed by Gladstone (of course *if* I am asked, which may be very doubtful), thus to keep Hartington up to the mark in resisting the Radicals in the Cabinet, to keep them strictly to the accepted programme put forward by Gladstone, and then when the latter retires, either to assist toward making Hartington the first power, or to split off: – to keep up the idea throughout that the Moderates will be as outspoken against Radical schemes as the Radicals are in their favour, and to see to it that the Cabinet does not drift. If all this could be done, the split, which must come, might find the Moderates in a stronger position than now: at any rate personally I should be able to act and come forward in defence of Moderate Liberalism, as one of the joint heirs of Gladstone and of his 'sound economic school' instead of as a malcontent and outsider. Gross Conservative profligacy almost drives one to this course and Gladstone's comparative moderation makes it possible. I shall take no one into confidence about this but tell me how it strikes you.[2]

Gladstone's election address of 18 September 1885 accomplished its purpose. Hartington found it 'a weak production' but

[1] DP, Goschen to Hartington, 14 September 1885, 340.1811.
[2] Grey Papers, 1 and 20 September 1885.

leaning 'to the side of moderation'[1] while Chamberlain thought that 'by a somewhat strained interpretation' it was possible 'to extract comfort from between the lines of his lengthy lucubration'.[2] Chamberlain and Dilke emphasized their 'determination not to be lay figures in a Cabinet of Goschens'.[3] Attacking Hartington would not be easy if party unity was to be maintained; the solution was to reach Hartington's Whiggish programme by letting 'Goschen have it hot'.[4] And to Dilke, Chamberlain wrote: 'If you can include a few hits at Goschen do so. We must make him our Whipping boy – and reply to Hartington etc. through him. Above all we must try to make him impossible for next Cabinet.'[5] As yet no Conservative opponent had appeared in Edinburgh. Instead a Radical, B. F. C. Costelloe, had entered the hustings against him.

Goschen recognized his dilemma when he informed Albert Grey that he would prefer 'to speak somewhere in reply to the Conservatives instead of having so often to face the Radicals'. He insisted that, 'The forecast of my own position which I sent you certainly does not imply any abating one jot from my independence.' While wanting Hartington to take a forceful stand against Chamberlain, Goschen was distressed when the Whig leader spoke 'of *leaving* the party. It is far better to give the idea of the Radicals dividing it.' Goschen was determined to 'remain good humoured while Chamberlain fumes'. 'I intend pinning our Moderate leaders to their programme when I speak next Wednesday and to show that it would be a gross breach of faith if a majority secured by Gladstone's manifesto were to be turned to other and wider purposes.'[6] It was Goschen who baptized Chamberlain's platform the 'Unauthorized Programme', in a speech of 14 October 1885, in order to differentiate it from Gladstone's more orthodox proposals. The main points of Chamberlain's

[1] Bernard Holland, *Life of the Eighth Duke of Devonshire* (London, 1911), vol. 2, p. 73.
[2] ChP, typed copy of letter, Chamberlain to Dilke, 20 September 1885.
[3] *Ibid.*, typed copy of letter, Chamberlain to Dilke, 28 September 1885.
[4] *Ibid.*, Chamberlain to Jesse Collings, 12 October 1885, 5/16, f. 109.
[5] *Ibid.*, typed copy of letter, Chamberlain to Dilke, 13 October 1885.
[6] Grey Papers, Goschen to Albert Grey, 26 September 1885 [Autumn 1885], and 18 October 1885.

programme centred on reform of local government, land for the agricultural labourer, free education, and a reduction of taxation for the lower classes. Chamberlain often over-emphasized the differences between Gladstone, the Whigs and himself in order to put his programme in its most shining and distinctive light. In fact Hartington wrote to Queen Victoria's secretary that the Radical proposals were inexpedient but not 'revolutionary'. He regretted many of the Radical speeches because they raised 'hopes and expectations which the measures actually indicated would fail to satisfy'.[1] But real differences did exist over free education and over Chamberlain's desire to permit local authorities to purchase land compulsorily and to use it for the creation of small-holdings ('three acres and a cow').

A month before the election Goschen informed Sir Rowland Blennerhassett that Gladstone's head was full of ideas about large concessions to the Irish. But Goschen thought he could be 'kept straight'. 'I suppose it is certain that the Liberals will win and prettily heavily. Some policy as regards Ireland will have to be decided on. If it is a firm policy, the Irish will be quite unmanageable. If it is a policy going beyond the limits of safe concession, it must break *us* up.'[2] Goschen now turned to his own constituency. His Radical opponent hammered away relentlessly at the refrain that Goschen was no longer a Liberal. So long as there was no Conservative candidate in the East Edinburgh constituency, which contained more than 7,000 electors, Goschen would be able to count on a sizeable number of Conservative votes. But Lord Salisbury and Richard Middleton, chief party agent for the Conservatives, were hoping that their supporters in Edinburgh would find an opponent for Goschen.[3] A Conservative nominee failed to appear and after Goschen's victory Salisbury lamented that a real opportunity for an upset win had been lost by default.[4]

[1] Hartington to Ponsonby, 6 October 1885, RA B36/96.
[2] Blennerhassett Papers, Goschen to Blennerhassett, 8 November 1885, Add. 7486/53.
[3] Viscount Chilston, *Chief Whip: The Political Life and Times of Aretas Akers-Douglas, 1st Viscount Chilston* (London, 1961), p. 54.
[4] Chilston Papers, K.A.O., Salisbury to Akers-Douglas, 26 November 1885, U564 C18/3.

Goschen campaigned strenuously in his constituency and was heartily supported by the principal Edinburgh newspaper, *The Scotsman*. His meetings in the various wards of Edinburgh East were rowdy and boisterous affairs with the Scots clamouring that all questions be answered. He refused to modify his opposition to compulsory insurance or to the nationalization of mineral properties. Nor would he acquiesce in giving land courts the power to purchase land compulsorily. Each meeting was followed by a vote of thanks and an expression of support but the Radicals were always present with an amendment rejecting Goschen because of his 'persistent opposition to the Franchise Bill, his Egyptian arrangements, and his desertion of the Liberal cause on critical occasions during Mr Gladstone's Ministry'. Costelloe made most of his speeches outside factory gates and in the streets. He demanded that Chamberlain's Radical policy be enacted:

Men like Mr Goschen maintained that the best thing they could do was to give every man fair play and leave him alone. He (Mr Costelloe) thought that they had too much of the let alone policy. It was a shame that the great industrial masses in the crowded quarters of our large towns should live as they did in dens where health was impossible, and where vice was almost a necessity in the training of youth.

Goschen admitted his inability to accept the principle of either universal manhood suffrage or women's suffrage. Talk of an eight-hour day caused him to mention the higher prices which would result and the effect on British exports. Unless conditions changed drastically, he would not be willing to give the Irish control over their own police. At one meeting a 'tipsy man' got up to speak while at another Goschen was asked to state his religious preference. He replied, 'Church of England' and the aroused questioner jumped down from the chair he had mounted and exclaimed 'that was as bad as a Catholic'. To shouts that he was 'a Tory in disguise' and a 'bondholders' man' he said: 'I have left business and devoted myself exclusively to the public service, and I am not a bondholder.'[1]

When the votes were counted Goschen had 4337 to Costelloe's 1929. Gladstone congratulated Goschen and blamed

[1] *The Scotsman* (17 November 1885), 5–6; *ibid.* (18 November 1885), 6; *ibid.* (21 November 1885), 6–8.

Liberal failures in the English boroughs on 'the two Bogies of the Church and Fair Trade, and chiefly the last which is the worst and in every way despicable.'[1] As the elections returns poured in, it was soon obvious that the Liberals were winning but that Gladstone would not obtain a commanding majority. In the cleanest and most democratic election in British history until that date, the Liberals elected 335 members, the Conservatives 249 and the Irish Nationalists 86. After the final count Goschen agreed with Hartington that 'the mess is the most inextricable into which a country ever got itself'. He did not anticipate a coalition at this point though Hartington had indicated that 'overtures' might be made. It might be necessary for them 'to promise the Government independent support, if they reject the Parnell alliance, and if, as I expect, Gladstone will be ready to grant what you and I would never agree to'.[2]

Goschen was not completely distraught at the election results for they also seemed to show that the 'advance of democracy' had 'not been so great' as he had 'anticipated it would be'.[3] He was no doubt thinking of the poor showing of the Liberals in the boroughs. And to Albert Grey he chortled: 'What a crushing defeat Radicalism has sustained. I agree with you that the elections are a complete justification of Moderate liberalism.'[4] But Goschen was not pleased with the fate of the anti-Parnell Liberals in Ireland for they had failed to save a single seat. Ireland now had eighty-five Nationalists and eighteen Conservatives from Ulster. Goschen complained to Blennerhassett, one of the Liberal loyalists in Ireland, that the Irish Loyal and Patriotic Union had not been very effective. 'It is fearful to think that not a man on our side will be able to speak in the name of any Irish constituency.'[5]

Queen Victoria was determined to retain Salisbury and to prevent Gladstone's return to power. She turned to Goschen as

[1] GP, copy of letter, Gladstone to Goschen, 26 November 1885, Add. Mss 44161, ff. 318–19.
[2] DP, Goschen to Hartington, 7 December 1885, 340.1846. For Hartington's reply see Holland, *Life of Devonshire*, vol. 2, pp. 96–7.
[3] Blennerhassett Papers, Goschen to Lady Blennerhassett, [? December 1885], Add. 7486/52.
[4] Grey Papers, Goschen to Albert Grey, 1 and 12 December 1885.
[5] Blennerhassett Papers, [14 December 1885], Add. 7486/53.

the person most likely to keep Hartington from falling back under Gladstone's spell. Her private secretary, Sir Henry Ponsonby, had already reported to her (9 December) that Goschen believed

Gladstone contemplates granting a Grand Council to Ireland, and if he does so the Liberal party will be split into two. If Lord Hartington is firm, he will lead a very strong Moderate Section, and if the liberal Conservatives will unite a powerful party could be organised. But the junction must grow from themselves and any external pressure would do harm.[1]

Herbert Gladstone's disclosure in mid-December of his father's willingness to approve a legislative body for Ireland outraged the queen. Ponsonby had warned her that Goschen had few followers of his own. All would depend on Hartington's decision.[2] Afraid that Ponsonby had not written to Goschen 'as strongly' as she might have wished, the queen decided to communicate directly with him.

I appeal to *you* and to all moderate, loyal, and really patriotic men, who have the safety and well-being of the Empire and the Throne at heart, and who wish to save them from destruction, with which, if the Government again fell into the reckless hands of Mr. Gladstone, they would be threatened, to rise above Party and to be true Patriots!

Goschen was prodded to keep Lord Hartington from succumbing to Gladstone's baleful influence. The queen suggested that the moderate Liberals call themselves 'Constitutionalists'. She was sure Salisbury 'would highly approve my telling you what I have done. *No* one knows of this letter, which I send, through Lady Ely, to Mrs Goschen for you.' Taking advantage of her sex she added a postscript: 'I do not speak of *myself*, but I may say I think a Queen and one well on in years, and who has gone through terrible anxieties and sorrows, ought not to appeal in vain to British gentlemen, who have known and served her long!'[3]

Hartington's usual calm was shaken by Herbert Gladstone's interview for he was convinced that 'if Home Rule is once

---

[1] Ponsonby to Queen Victoria, RA B36/112.
[2] Buckle (ed.), *Letters of Queen Victoria*, 2nd series, vol. 3, p. 712.
[3] Queen Victoria to Goschen, 20 December 1885, RA B66/2.

granted I doubt we shall stop short of separation'.[1] He had pressed Gladstone unsuccessfully for the details of his thoughts on Ireland but now Gladstone hastened to write that Ireland had spoken in the recent elections and 'an effort ought to be made *by the Government* without delay to meet her demands for the management by an Irish legislative body of Irish as distinct from Imperial affairs'. No doubt existed that 'a Tory Government can do it more easily and safely than any other'.[2] Hartington was not convinced and advised Gladstone he was going to London on the following day 'to see Goschen who is as much alarmed as I am at the position which has been created'. He doubted they would 'take any action'.[3] But action was decided upon as Hartington sent a letter to his election committee stating that he had in no way altered his opposition to a separate Parliament in Dublin. Goschen hoped he 'would not repent [his] step. It was, I still feel convinced, absolutely necessary: though it may have fallen like a shell in Hawarden. But hundreds of Liberals will be grateful to you.'[4]

Granville – the great conciliator – implored Hartington not to send this letter which would be made public.[5] But this time Hartington did not waver. Goschen confided to Albert Grey that Hartington had not been 'combative at all'.

> But I hope that a letter will appear in Monday's papers stating that he adheres to all his electoral declarations. I have not wished to act before him or without him, if it could possibly be avoided. I want him to act as the leader of the Moderates, so long as there is any hope that he will.
>
> What a crisis! What a mess![6]

The Radical programme was being rapidly forgotten as Ireland came to overshadow every other issue. Hartington and Goschen made the surprising discovery that their main antagonist in the recent election, Chamberlain, agreed with them in opposing

[1] Blennerhassett Papers, Hartington to Blennerhassett, 13 December 1885, Add. 7486/53.
[2] GP, copy of letter Gladstone to Hartington, 17 December 1885, Add. Mss 44148, ff. 167–8.
[3] *Ibid.*, Hartington to Gladstone, 18 December 1885, Add. Mss 44148, ff. 177–81.
[4] DP, Goschen to Hartington, 21 December 1885, 340.1864.
[5] Fitzmaurice, *Life of Granville*, vol. 2, pp. 468–9.
[6] Grey Papers, Sunday [20 December 1885].

Home Rule. Spencer and Harcourt, on the other hand, were moving towards support for Home Rule. Political speculation was intense and abundant as the year drew to a close. The fact that more was involved than Irish affairs was registered by the Duke of Argyll. He wrote to *The Times* on 26 December 1885 and argued that Home Rule challenged 'the fundamental principles of all civilized societies' such as 'the freedom of industry' and 'the security of property'. Goschen recorded his approval:

The point is to awaken the country to what the Irish demands really mean, and to analyse what it means to allow the Irish to 'manage their own affairs'. I saw some merchants, etc., from Dublin yesterday, who came over to see me, and expose the danger of Home Rule from their point of view. I told them nothing was more important than to convince the English public that the question is not one of landowning merely, but that there are menaces, not only to unpopular landlords, but to property of every kind.[1]

[1] Duchess of Argyll (ed.), *Autobiography and Memoirs of the Eighth Duke of Argyll* (London, 1906), vol. 2, pp. 411–17.

CHAPTER 8

HER MAJESTY AIDS THE OPPOSITION

Westminster was the centre of attention as Parliament assembled on 12 January 1886. Goschen had confided to the queen that most of Gladstone's key colleagues did not wish 'to force on any motion or to take any step which might compel the Government to resign' and 'they will use their utmost efforts to prevent his embarking on such a course'. Most Liberals, however, had just finished heated electoral campaigns in which they had denounced the Conservatives. This meant that they could not 'vote confidence' in Salisbury's government 'under any circumstances' though they were 'quite prepared and even anxious to abstain from any actual attack'. Since the queen too did not want a change of government 'every influence should be used to prevent the Conservative leaders from directly or indirectly *challenging* the Liberal Party in such a way as might be interpreted to mean a vote of confidence'.[1]

The tactics of their leaders irritated a large portion of the Liberal party, especially its Radical section, which wished to reap the benefits of an electoral victory. But Chamberlain, the major Radical leader now that Sir Charles Dilke was involved in a divorce action, opposed Home Rule and vacillated as to whether Salisbury should be kept in office or turned out. Chamberlain's cry for agricultural allotments had swept the counties for the Liberals and the agricultural labourers wanted their 'three acres and a cow'. Chamberlain, Harcourt, Dilke and Jesse Collings finally formulated an amendment to the Conservative address from the throne which criticized the government for failing to assist the agricultural labourers. What convinced Gladstone that he must turn out the Salisbury government was the Conservative announcement on 26 January 1886 that a new Coercion Bill for Ireland was imminent. Salisbury and Churchill had decided to end their brief flirtation with Parnell.

[1] Goschen to Queen Victoria, 3 January 1886, RA B37/3.

While the discussion that evening was technically on 'three acres and a cow', all realized that the main issue if the Conservatives were defeated would be the formation of a Gladstone ministry with Home Rule for Ireland as its avowed aim. After a sharp debate, the Conservatives were defeated by 331 to 252. The majority was composed of 257 Liberals and 74 Irish nationalists. The ministry had 234 Conservative and 18 Liberal supporters among whom were Goschen, Lord Hartington, Sir Henry James, Leonard Courtney and Arthur Elliot. There were more than seventy abstentions on the Liberal side, including the formidable John Bright.

The vote was a 'thunderbolt' for Queen Victoria as it meant Salisbury would resign and she must, distasteful though it might be, send for Gladstone. She was not too 'startled', however, to falter for an instant in her 'fishing' expedition for a coalition of moderates.[1] As she was then at Osborne on the Isle of Wight reporters were able to lie in wait and speculate upon the political implications of each arrival.

On the following day Goschen was warned by the queen: 'If Lord Hartington gets persuaded that Mr. Gladstone will drop Home Rule or a leaning towards it – and joins him – he will never regain his position.' All 'moderate, loyal and patriotic men' must join with Hartington and Goschen in the formation of 'a strong Whig party which the Conservatives would support and which might lead ultimately to an amalgamation or rather juncture of Conservatives and Whigs'.[2] With Salisbury's approval she wrote to Goschen again on 28 January 1886 and requested his presence at Osborne for consultations on the political crisis. Goschen, however, declined the request as gracefully as he could. Such a visit might be misinterpreted by many and 'further compromise' the 'critical situation'.[3] Salisbury formally resigned on the morning of 29 January 1886 but the queen could still not accept the inevitable. She had Salisbury contact Goschen but he was unable

---

[1] See the exchange of letters between Queen Victoria and Goschen on 27 January 1886, RA B66/7, and RA C37/162.
[2] Queen Victoria to Goschen, 28 January 1886, RA B66/8.
[3] Goschen to Queen Victoria, 29 January 1886, cypher telegram, RA C37/178.

to 'persuade' Goschen to go to Osborne.[1] Goschen informed Hartington that the queen had sent Ponsonby with a summons for Gladstone to form a government 'but he was to see Salisbury and myself first. I can't say for any particular reason.' He had immediately urged Ponsonby to contact Gladstone. 'The Queen was rather put out in receiving my message, but Ponsonby had told her beforehand, he was sure I would not come, and he had opposed her sending for me.'[2]

Goschen then explained to the queen why a moderate coalition was still not possible and why she had no choice but to send for the former Prime Minister. They must know the details of Gladstone's plan before it could be opposed. A premature attempt at an 'amalgamation of parties' might be disastrous and provide Gladstone with sufficient momentum to carry out his proposals.[3] The queen admitted 'the difficulty of a Coalition *at present*' but she regretted Goschen's failure to appear at Osborne.[4]

When Hartington and Goschen were asked to join the new Cabinet, they refused. The way in which Chamberlain was finally given the Local Government Board showed Gladstone at his worst in handling an ally who was absolutely essential if his plan was to succeed. A few days after the formation of Gladstone's new Cabinet, Lord Salisbury informed his Chief Whip, Akers Douglas, that Goschen had called to see him. They had talked about 'the possibility of some treaty between us to secure his friends from being opposed by us at an election if they joined in opposing the Government'.[5] The belief that Gladstone would retire if defeated on Home Rule conditioned the actions of many political figures. Hartington recognized the insuperable problem of Whig and Radical co-operating in a Liberal government again and he winced at the recollection of Gladstone's last Cabinet. But

---

[1] Salisbury to Queen Victoria, 29 January 1886, cypher telegram, RA C37/179.
[2] Devonshire Papers, Goschen to Hartington, [30] January 1886, 340.1883a. See also Arthur Ponsonby, *Henry Ponsonby: Queen Victoria's Private Secretary* (London, 1942).
[3] Goschen to Queen Victoria, two letters of 29 January 1886, RA C37/191 and RA C37/192.
[4] Queen Victoria to Goschen, 31 January 1886, RA B66/10.
[5] Chilston Papers, Salisbury to Akers-Douglas, 9 February 1886, K.A.O. U564 C18/6.

sentimental Whigs abhorred the idea of entering the Conservative party and hoped until the last that Gladstone would introduce a Home Rule proposal they could support.

Goschen was now confident that if 'a separate Parliament should be proposed', Lord Hartington would 'take a decided and *active* part in opposing it'. While 'the present state of uncertainty' was 'very deplorable', the numerous inquiries which Goschen had made demonstrated that the 'moderate men who would be likely to follow Lord Hartington' were 'not prepared to break with the bulk of their Party, *till* they see whether or not Mr. Gladstone proposes Home Rule. At present many still profess incredulity.' The queen remained disturbed at Hartington's 'want of *decidedness*'.[1] The momentary lull which had descended on the activities of Parliament as men awaited Gladstone's plans was broken by the resignation of Chamberlain and Trevelyan on 27 March 1886. They rejected Gladstone's outline of his Home Rule and Land Purchase proposals for Ireland. When Queen Victoria was notified of Chamberlain's resignation on 26 March, she informed Goschen that it would be 'a great thing' if some Radicals joined Hartington to beat Home Rule. But she wanted no permanent tie between Chamberlain and Hartington as this might frustrate her major aim: 'the object to be *obtained* for the safety of the Country *is* a *union* with the *Conservatives* to put a *check* on *revolutionary* changes'.[2] Her dream was a union of Whigs and moderate Liberals with the Conservatives. They could then call themselves Loyalists or Constitutionalists. So far there seemed to be no place for Chamberlain in her orthodox approach to the situation.

The Conservatives rejoiced as the Liberal party burst apart. They had counted upon Goschen and Hartington to lead the fight against Home Rule and now they had Chamberlain and some of his Radical supporters as well. This would introduce complications, however, since little love was lost between Chamberlain and the Conservative party, though he was admired by

---

[1] Goschen to Queen Victoria, 10 March [1886], RA D44/2 and Queen Victoria to Goschen, 18 March 1886, RA B66/12.
[2] Queen Victoria to Goschen, 26 March 1886, RA B66/13.

younger members such as Lord Randolph Churchill and Arthur Balfour. The Conservatives were pushing Hartington to take the lead by moving the rejection of the Home Rule Bill when it reached its second reading. On 8 April 1886 with a packed House of Commons waiting expectantly, Gladstone introduced his bill. The Prime Minister conceded that certain problems and technical difficulties needed to be ironed out but he argued that good will on all sides would provide an acceptable solution. The essence of Gladstone's plan was really his belief that Parnell could be trusted and the Irish reconciled and made loyal members of the empire if large concessions were made and sufficient trust exhibited on both sides. His opponents, however, regarded Home Rule as the first step on the road to an independent Ireland and the betrayal of the Ulster Protestants.

Goschen reported to the queen that Gladstone's Home Rule scheme 'was quite as far reaching as was expected, indeed on the whole more so'. He reassured her that Lord Hartington would not hesitate to denounce it immediately.[1] Two days later the dignified part of the constitution returned to the attack. It was essential 'to *sink* all *minor differences* and *unite as one man*' in order to prevent the destruction of the empire. Only in this manner would it be possible to establish a 'firm and *stable* government'. There was no alternative to a Hartington–Salisbury coalition. 'The Country calls loudly for it and I *earnestly* urge it . . . it is the *only chance* the Country has of a *strong government* able to resist Democracy and Socialism as well as separation (as regards Ireland).'[2]

After several days of discussion the Home Rule Bill was granted its first reading without a division. The explanations given by Trevelyan and Chamberlain for their resignations and the aggressive speeches made by Hartington and Goschen indicated that a very close vote could be expected on the crucial second reading. Goschen's detailed analysis of the contradictions in the bill was a fine example of his critical intelligence. There was, however, little that could be called constructive or that

[1] Goschen to Queen Victoria, 9 April 1886, RA D44/9.
[2] Queen Victoria to Goschen, 11 April 1886, RA B66/19.

showed any understanding of the demands of the majority of the Irish people. After noting potential areas of confusion, Goschen returned to the larger problem of political economy since Irish opinion was 'in marked contrast to all the economical literature of the Continent'. In what other country 'would a No-Rent Manifesto be issued?' Catholicism was another bogy to be conjured with. This bill would 'hand over the management of education to the Roman Catholic Bishops'.[1]

Now that the plan had been presented, the opposition, both Conservative and Liberal, could begin to function more effectively. This common resistance to Home Rule led to the gradual formation of the Unionist party, all the Conservatives plus Gladstone's Liberal opponents. In mid-April the first major joint rally of the anti-Home Rulers took place. Lord Cowper, a former Liberal Viceroy of Ireland, was chairman, and Salisbury, Hartington and Goschen denounced Gladstone and Parnell. But Joseph Chamberlain refused to participate. A happy Goschen, who saw his dreams for a coalition of Moderates nearing realisation, seconded Salisbury's resolution to petition Parliament to reject Home Rule. Goschen poured sarcasm on Gladstone's sudden discovery that justice must be given to Ireland. He suggested that the Prime Minister discovered Home Rule only when he realized his need for Irish votes after the recent election. And what of justice to the loyal citizens of Ulster who cherished the unity of the Empire? He did not distrust the Irish but obstacles existed which made Home Rule unworkable. Would the Irish resort to even greater violence than before if their wishes were denied? 'Well, if so, we shall make our wills and do our duty.'[2]

The Conservatives were jubilant with the success of the Opera House meeting and with having flushed out some Whigs and moderate Liberals. But many of the constituency Liberal organizations disliked seeing their representatives on the same platform as Conservatives. This made the formation of a distinctly Liberal group in opposition to Home Rule absolutely imperative and it

[1] *Hansard*, CCCIV (13 April 1886), 1458–82.
[2] George J. Goschen, 'The Cry of "Justice to Ireland" '. Goschen's speech was published by the Liberal Unionist Association.

was also the only possible way in which co-operation with Chamberlain might be possible. The vehicle decided upon was the Liberal Unionist Committee which was formed in April and which became the Liberal Unionist Association in May. Liberal Unionism was the means whereby many Whigs and moderate Liberals could gradually move into the Conservative party without feeling that they had betrayed their commitment to Liberalism. Not having heard from Goschen for a few days, the queen wrote to congratulate him on the success of the Opera House meeting and urged him to '*organize as many* such meetings, large and small, *all over* England and Scotland as you can'.[1]

Goschen plunged into the organization of the Liberal Unionists with the vigour of youth regained, greatly enjoying having parliamentary associates again after his years in the wilderness. He continued his main assignments, which were to keep Hartington pushed forward as the leader of the Liberal Unionists and to provide as much organizational and speaking support as possible. Three of Goschen's closest friends became the principal administrators and organizers of the Liberal Unionist Committee in April – Alfred Milner, Albert Grey and Alexander Craig Sellar. The work entrusted to Milner caused him much anxiety. He saw much-needed funds and victory slipping through their hands. It was essential for Hartington to be more aggressive. Goschen was urged to 'write to the Dukes and Bankers' for contributions and support.[2]

The queen was delighted with speeches delivered by Hartington, Derby and Bright but disturbed by Hartington's declaration that he wanted '*no* coalition with the Conservatives'. Her majesty's rugged practicality was appalled by the weirdly romantic notions of the politicians. Here was Hartington saying '*no other Liberal* government could be formed' while Lord Salisbury doubted 'the prudence of attempting a Conservative one' and Hartington objected 'to a Coalition'.[3]

Before the crucial second reading of the bill on 10 May,

[1] Queen Victoria to Goschen, 16 April 1886, RA B66/20.
[2] See Milner's letters to Goschen of 23 April and 25 April 1886, MP, Box 182.
[3] Queen Victoria to Goschen, 28 April 1886, RA B66/22.

Goschen made speeches at Edinburgh, Paisley, Glasgow and Preston. Nor was he unwilling – as were many Liberals – to attend meetings organized by the Irish Loyal and Patriotic Union which drew its main support from the Protestants of Ulster. The debate on the second reading lasted into the early morning of 8 June 1886 as Gladstone prolonged the debate while he searched for support. On 14 May a meeting was held at Hartington's London home, with more than sixty dissident Liberal M.P.s – including Chamberlain – in attendance. A few days before, the National Liberal Federation – the organization which Chamberlain had considered a major source of Radical strength and upon which he had lavished much time and effort – deserted him and pledged its support to Gladstone.

Goschen agreed with the queen that any additional delay such as the withdrawal of the bill and its later re-introduction would be unfortunate. It would mean a 'prolongation of the agitation' but Goschen feared 'that a large proportion of the Liberal party would eagerly grasp at such a solution, as most calculated to defer the dissolution of the party'. He was still confident that the bill would be defeated.[1] The queen regarded the 'odd alliance' of Hartington and Chamberlain as 'very undesirable'. How would Lord Salisbury respond to this new development? Lord Hartington must not 'pledge himself' to Mr Chamberlain. Chamberlain's views were so 'very extreme'. She wondered if Goschen would be able to 'join a government with Mr. Chamberlain whose views are all but Republican?'[2] Goschen implored the queen not to be 'over-anxious' about the co-operation between the Whigs and the Radicals. It was true that this introduced 'complications' but the queen should remember that 'no government could be formed without the good will of the Conservatives, who will far outnumber the Liberal dissentients'. While his differences with Chamberlain were very great, it might be necessary for them 'to *endeavour* to act together' in this grave crisis. It now appeared that Gladstone would ask for a dissolution of Parliament if the bill was defeated and this might be the wisest course to follow.

[1] Goschen to Queen Victoria, 13 May [1886] RA D44/22.
[2] Queen Victoria to Goschen, 13 and 15 May 1886, RA B66/25 and RA B66/26.

'In a new House of Commons the Conservatives would be in a different position and more able to take office if sufficiently numerous, while at the same time it would have become evident in what sense the Country would require a Government to act in respect to Ireland.'[1]

The shrewd Prime Minister had not yet played his last card and in a meeting with more than 200 of his supporters on 27 May he agreed to consider the possibility of allowing the Irish to retain some form of representation at Westminster. He proposed to delay the committee stage of the Home Rule Bill until the autumn or – as the Cabinet preferred – to reintroduce a slightly altered version of the present bill in the autumn. All this would depend, of course, on the second reading of the bill being passed and this would mean that the Commons had accepted the principle of Home Rule. But the conciliatory atmosphere engendered by Gladstone's concessions was destroyed on the following day when the Prime Minister allowed himself to be baited by Sir Michael Hicks Beach and Lord Randolph Churchill. He thundered at his interrogators that the bill as a whole was not to be reconstructed but only one particular clause. A few days later Goschen was able to send news which delighted the queen. Gladstone's attempt to detach some of Chamberlain's followers had failed. A meeting had just taken place between Chamberlain and some fifty of his friends. It was decided 'that almost all present would *vote against the Bill*. This ensures its defeat, as far as one can possibly judge. . . The result was in great part brought about by a letter from Mr Bright, in which he declared his intention to vote against the Second Reading.'[2]

Goschen led off the debate on the twelfth and final night of discussion on the Home Rule Bill. He reiterated all his old arguments – protection of minorities, Catholics and education, contradictions in the bill and the destruction of the empire. Gladstone was scored for his appeals to class prejudice and for having said that 'class and the dependents of class' were opposed to the bill. He entreated the democracy which was 'enthroned for the first

---

[1] Goschen to Queen Victoria, 15 and 17 May 1886, RA D44/25 and RA D44/26.
[2] Goschen to Queen Victoria, 31 May 1886, RA D44/34.

time' not to weaken the empire and to accept, instead, its great responsibilities.[1]

Gladstone's final speech was magnificent but it failed to sway the waverers. The alliance of Chamberlain and Hartington plus a solid Conservative vote had defeated Home Rule. Goschen was exhilarated when the tellers reported but the victory was a Pyrrhic one which was ultimately followed by more blood and more violence until an independent Ireland – though without most of Ulster – became inevitable. The bill was defeated by a vote of 343 to 313; 93 Liberals voted with the Conservatives.[2]

Gladstone asked the queen to dissolve Parliament and appealed to the people on the specific issue of Home Rule. The campaign was a short and bitter one and many friendships in the Liberal party were ruptured beyond repair. The Conservatives pledged themselves not to oppose Liberal Unionists as this would split the anti-Home Rule vote and might give the constituency to a Gladstonian. Agreement between Salisbury, Hartington, Goschen and Chamberlain was not a herculean task but the imposition of the arrangements on Conservative constituency parties who objected to voting for a Liberal, even if he called himself a Liberal Unionist, was a formidable assignment. Goschen thanked Salisbury for his efforts 'to smooth difficulties' but Conservative suggestions that Liberal Unionists and Conservatives should hold joint meetings were rejected as being 'very difficult' to arrange.[3] While Goschen – far ahead of most Liberal Unionists in the march towards Conservatism – was not averse to joint meetings, the majority of the Liberal Unionists preferred to consider themselves as the true Liberals who were simply waiting for Gladstone either to retire or to give up his Irish policy. Then, they argued, the Liberal party might be unified once again.

But the obstacles which faced the Conservatives and Liberal Unionists were overcome as they scored a decisive victory over the Gladstonian Liberals and the Irish Nationalists. When the

---

[1] *Hansard*, CCCVI (7 June 1886), 1145–68.
[2] A list of the Liberals who voted against Home Rule may be found in Elliot, vol. 2, Appendix II, pp. 280–3.
[3] SP, Goschen to Salisbury, 21 June 1886.

votes were tallied, the Liberal Unionists had 78 seats, the Conservatives went up from almost 250 to 316 while the Liberals dropped from more than 330 to 191 and the Irish Nationalists retained 85 seats. This gave the Unionists of both parties a combined majority of 118. It was estimated that 6 Liberal Unionists would follow either Salisbury or Hartington, 43 were followers of Hartington and 21 of Chamberlain while 8 wanted to return to Gladstone.[1] Chamberlain's prediction that Home Rule would not be a popular issue among the new electors in England was borne out by the returns. The Conservatives continued to increase their support in the English boroughs and they also reversed the trend in the English counties.

The Conservatives' victory in 1886 – though it left them some twenty votes short of an absolute majority – owed a great deal to their Liberal Unionist allies. Once the alliance had become a merger it would mean that the Conservatives had moved from minority to majority party. Gladstone's decision to battle for Home Rule also meant that the House of Commons would once again become the arena for two principal contending parties. The Liberal Unionists were committed to support the Conservatives until Gladstone repudiated Home Rule – an unlikely event – and the Parnellites were now aligned with the Liberals. No longer could they act as a guerilla force offering to throw their votes to the highest bidder as Parnell had so successfully done in 1885. It also provided further support for Parnell's moderate policy and enabled him to damp down the revolutionary ardour of the violent wing of the Irish Nationalist movement by arguing that Gladstone's acceptance of Home Rule meant that the great goal could be accomplished by peaceful means.

The joy which he felt at the defeat of Home Rule was soured for Goschen when his Edinburgh East constituents rejected him. He had reaffirmed those same principles which he had enunciated at the election of 1885. There were alternatives to the extremes of Home Rule or coercion. Why was no one willing to try 'large measures of decentralisation' for the entire United Kingdom? 'Justice to Ireland must not mean injustice to one-third of her

[1] Chilston, *Chief Whip*, pp. 81–4.

population.' Gladstone's Home Rule scheme was quite simply 'indefensible in principle, and unworkable in practice'.[1] Robert Wallace, Goschen's Liberal opponent, asserted that the Irish question could only be solved by a large grant of executive and legislative authority as Gladstone had urged. He expounded his belief in democracy and pointed to Goschen as a man who lacked faith in the people.

Polling took place in East Edinburgh on 5 July 1886. Wallace defeated Goschen by a vote of 3694 to 2253. In neither 1885 nor 1886 did the Conservatives run a candidate. Since the constituency remained in the hands of the Liberal party, at least until 1914, it seems fair to say that any normally attractive candidate who was granted the official designation by the Liberal party would win an election. Goschen's defeat was a source of unexpected light among dreary election returns for Gladstone and Granville.[2] The Queen, however, sent condolences to her faithful counsellor and correspondent of the past six months. The defeat was 'a *disgrace* to Edinburgh and Scotland' which could only be explained by their continued support 'of that really half deluded old man!'[3]

While it is unlikely that Goschen ever expected to return to his old party, Joseph Chamberlain and his followers thought that if Gladstone retired, the Liberal party could be reconstructed. Chamberlain advised Hartington that he would reject office in a coalition and warned that such a line of action would cause the Liberal Unionists to be absorbed by the Conservatives. Gladstone resigned on 20 July 1886 and at a meeting of the Liberal Unionists (Chamberlain was not present) on the same evening, the great majority opposed a coalition, but Goschen and a few others seemed to favour the idea.[4]

On the day of Gladstone's resignation, the queen was very busy. She wrote to Goschen that the Liberal Unionists must aid Salisbury in order to ensure governmental stability for a lengthy period of time. Gladstone was 'utterly unfit to become Prime

[1] George J. Goschen, 'Address to the Electors of the Eastern Division of Edinburgh', 17 June 1886, published by the Liberal Unionist Association.
[2] Ramm (ed.), *Correspondence of Gladstone and Granville*, vol. 2, pp. 455-7.
[3] Queen Victoria to Goschen, 6 July 1886, RA B66/38.
[4] Elliot Papers, diary entry for 20 July 1886, Book 11.

Minister again' and should 'retire'.[1] The queen wanted a Salisbury–Hartington coalition but Goschen pointed out that this was not the probable result of the crisis, though Salisbury would certainly receive massive support from the Liberal Unionists on almost all questions. Hartington's decision had nothing to do with 'personal' or 'mere party considerations' but with his conviction that the majority of Liberal Unionists would not follow him if he entered a coalition.[2]

Hartington realized that Goschen was more inclined to a coalition than the other Liberal Unionists and reminded Goschen that a 'separate offer' might be made. While the loss to the Liberal Unionists would be 'severe', Hartington thought it might improve communications between his group and the Conservatives. And if 'a total reconstruction of parties must come, you will only have preceded me a little'. Goschen replied two days later that he was 'aghast' – at the very proposal he would accept six months later.

I can fancy nothing more fearful than joining a Salisbury Government alone and what would my position be in their front bench. Fancy me between Beach and Churchill. But I do not fail to recognize the force of much that you urge; and I am glad you wrote, because it has forced me to think the matter out more fully.[3]

On the same day (24 July) that Goschen wrote to Hartington, Salisbury called on Hartington to urge him to form a government. The Conservative chief promised to enter such a Cabinet but was not entirely sure what his friends would do. He refused, however, to enter a government which included Chamberlain. Hartington concluded that Chamberlain's exclusion made a coalition impossible but pledged 'an independent but friendly support' to the prospective Salisbury government. Salisbury was not too crestfallen. The Conservatives were the largest party in the Commons and the great majority were eager for office. Akers-Douglas had counselled him on 17 July that the party would

[1] Copy letter Queen Victoria to Goschen, 20 July 1886, RA B66/39.
[2] Goschen to Queen Victoria, 23 July 1886, RA C38/15.
[3] Elliot, vol. 2, pp, 95–6 and DP, 24 July 1886, 340.2026.

insist on Salisbury being Prime Minister in a coalition but would prefer a purely Conservative administration.[1]

The Conservatives were deficient in debating strength in the House of Commons. Only Sir Michael Hicks Beach, who did not want the leadership again, and Lord Randolph Churchill had demonstrated sufficient dynamism and self-confidence in replying to Gladstone, Harcourt and John Morley. The thirty-seven-year-old Churchill was looking for his reward. He had been a brilliantly successful speaker against Home Rule throughout the country. Salisbury became convinced that Churchill must be Leader of the House of Commons and Chancellor of the Exchequer. The shrewd Prime Minister may also have reasoned that the youthful Churchill might guarantee his future as Salisbury's successor or, if given enough rope, hang himself. Goschen was 'staggered' by the appointment. Churchill would 'steady down; but as he imitated Dizzy at a distance, so men of even lower *moral* [sic] may imitate Churchill'.[2] And to Hartington, Goschen wrote: 'What a fearful miscue that Lord Randolph is to lead the Commons. It may put you sometimes in a very disagreeable position.'[3]

Although still without a seat, Goschen expected no trouble in finding one and therefore took part in the Liberal Unionist discussion as to where they should sit in the House of Commons. Again Goschen was ahead of his colleagues in wishing to sit on the government's side of the House but below the gangway. He hoped his suggestion would not be 'too compromising' but he warned Hartington 'not to let *your* men fuse too much with the Gladstonian opposition. I presume you will not sit on the front opposition bench?'[4] But this was exactly where the Privy Councillors among the Liberal Unionists decided to sit, and the remainder of the Liberal Unionists also sat on the opposition side of the House. In the long run this worked against Liberal reunification as feelings became greatly embittered when former

---

[1] Chilston, *Chief Whip*, p. 84.
[2] Elliot, vol. 2, p. 97.
[3] DP, [?] July 1886, 340.2027.
[4] *Ibid.*, Goschen to Hartington, [?] July 1886, 340.2028 and Goschen to Hartington, 1 August 1886, 340.2033.

Liberal colleagues took opposite stands on various pieces of legislation while sitting next to one another.

The new government met Parliament for a brief session which lasted from early August until late September and then adjourned until the new year. Churchill made a favourable impression upon some of his critics during this short meeting but many were still sceptical of his ability to frame a budget, while others worried about his weak health. His Dartford speech of 2 October conjured up the ghost of Disraeli's Tory Democracy and provoked rumblings of Conservative discontent. When the Cabinet commenced a series of meetings to draw up their legislative plans for the coming session of Parliament, the differences between Churchill and his colleagues became more acute. According to Lady Gwendolen Cecil, Salisbury began to prepare himself for a 'rupture' with Churchill in early November and sought 'to keep it within the limits of its individual origin'.[1]

Goschen, still without a seat, was as startled as everyone else when Lord Randolph's resignation appeared in *The Times* on the morning of 23 December 1886. But he had remarked to Mrs Goschen a few nights before, after having been to a dinner where both Salisbury and Churchill were present, that he could not 'understand how it is possible that these two men should be sitting in the same Cabinet'.[2] Churchill's decision to send off a letter to Salisbury on 20 December while a guest of the queen at Windsor Castle indicating that he would be unable to continue in the Cabinet unless the service estimates were reduced has been analysed at length. What finally emerges is the fact that Churchill's letter was meant to be the beginning of an exchange of views. Salisbury, seeing his chance to get 'rid of a boil on the back of his neck', decided to call Churchill's bluff and accept his letter as a letter of resignation.[3] Churchill, stung by Salisbury's answer, divulged the news to *The Times* and thus deeply offended the queen who had not been informed in advance. Churchill attempted to justify his miscalculation by implying that he had

---

[1] Cecil, *Life of Salisbury.* vol. 3, p, 324.
[2] Elliot, vol. 2, p. 102, footnote 1.
[3] Robert Rhodes James, *Lord Randolph Churchill* (London, 1959), p. 311.

hatched a brilliant scheme to seize power in the Cabinet. It was certain of success due to his own indispensability in the Commons when suddenly his plans were thwarted because he had 'forgotten Goschen', just as Napoleon had 'forgotten Blucher'. Lord George Hamilton, First Lord of the Admiralty, travelled to Windsor with Churchill on that fateful day and was nonchalantly informed by Churchill of his intentions. Hamilton was sure 'the fat was in the fire'. The Cabinet was 'groaning and creaking' as a result of Churchill's 'wayward and un-controlled language and action'. It was very likely that Salisbury would accept the resignation. Hamilton perceptively observed that when 'a man of Churchill's cleverness makes so terrible a blunder', he would naturally begin to advance 'all sorts of ingenious and plausible excuses to palliate or to explain away his mistake'. And so he invented the story of 'forgetting Goschen'.[1]

Salisbury picked his way carefully as the Cabinet was determined to find an acceptable solution without capitulating to Churchill. Hicks Beach, however, was very pessimistic and thought they might have to resign. But Akers-Douglas reported to Salisbury on 24 December that there was little support for Churchill within the Conservative party.[2] The Chief Whip was sure that the Conservatives would accept Hartington as Leader of the House of Commons but doubted they would accept him as Prime Minister. To be frank, the Conservative rank-and-file would rather have Hicks Beach or Smith as Leader. 'In any case and at all hazards a general election *must* be avoided, as we should certainly lose *many* seats.'[3]

A calculating Alfred Milner regarded the resignation of Churchill as 'a great blow to the Government and the country' but suggested that the only real solution to the crisis would be Goschen's acceptance of the Exchequer though without, as yet, a formal coalition.[4] Queen Victoria begged Goschen on 24 December to join Salisbury if Hartington were to refuse a

[1] Hamilton, *Parliamentary Reminiscences and Reflections*, vol. 2, pp. 49–51 and Sir Winston Churchill, *Lord Randolph Churchill* (London, 1951), pp. 603–4.
[2] SP, Akers-Douglas to Salisbury, 24 December 1886.
[3] Smith Papers, Akers-Douglas to Smith, 25 December 1886, PS9/205.
[4] MP, Milner to Goschen, 23 December 1886, Box 182.

coalition for the second time.[1] Goschen warned the queen that it might be dangerous for the future if Hartington and the moderate Liberals joined the Conservatives since it would leave the Liberal party permanently in the hands of the demagogues. If Hartington did not join Salisbury, he could not say what his own action would be until after he had consulted Hartington and other political friends.[2] The queen sent Goschen's letter to Salisbury, who replied on 30 December that he did not expect a 'satisfactory answer' from Hartington when they met on the following day.

If the answer is *not* affirmative it will be necessary to appeal to Mr Goschen. It certainly does seem absurd that he should shrink from calling himself a Conservative. All his opinions are those of the Conservatives. No Liberal constituency in the Kingdom will have him however much he may profess himself a Liberal. Any Conservative constituency would elect him at once if he called himself a Conservative.[3]

Lord Hartington did not arrive in London until 29 December and by that time the Conservative party had exhibited its unhappiness at Salisbury's apparent willingness to step aside for Hartington.[4] Goschen reported to Milner that the Conservatives were now 'recovering from their first stupor' and were boasting 'that they can get on without help'.

As for myself, you must admit that the only condition under which I could accept office, if at all, would be the very strongest call from the Conservative leaders and rank and file, and the heartiest desire on Hartington's part. Both seem indispensable. I think it quite possible that Hartington may wish me to join. I am more doubtful of the other point.

Another possibility would be for him to 'take the Exchequer without the leadership of the H. of C. . . . The leadership would probably follow very soon but the party would get accustomed to me first and the jealousy be infinitely less.'[5]

Goschen was apparently willing to go a very long way in order to avoid joining Salisbury by himself. One of Churchill's strongest supporters during the crisis was Sir Henry Drummond

[1] Queen Victoria to Goschen, 24 December 1886, RA B66/43.
[2] Goschen to Queen Victoria, 28 December 1886, RA C38/86. See also Alfred Austin, *The Autobiography of Alfred Austin* (London, 1911), vol. 2, pp. 248–53.
[3] Salisbury to Queen Victoria, RA C38/89.
[4] Chilston, *Chief Whip*, pp. 102–3.
[5] MP, Goschen to Milner, 29 December 1886, Box 184.

Wolff. He set out to get Churchill back into the Salisbury government or to arrange a broader coalition which would also include Lord Randolph. Wolff found Goschen lunching at the Athenaeum on 30 December and asked if 'it would be possible for Lord Hartington to form a government of which Lord Salisbury, Lord Randolph Churchill, Mr Goschen and Mr Chamberlain would form part'. According to Wolff, Goschen was 'enthusiastic' but wanted to know Chamberlain's reaction. Goschen authorized Wolff to tell Chamberlain that he was 'favourable to the project' considering the gravity of the crisis. When Wolff dined with Churchill and Chamberlain that evening, he tossed out the weird combination of names for discussion. Chamberlain instantly denounced it as 'ludicrous'.[1]

On the following day (31 December), Hartington rejected Salisbury's coalition proposals for much the same reasons he had advanced in July. But the Whig leader agreed to relay an offer from Salisbury to Goschen. Hartington urged Goschen to accept but was reluctantly forced to report to Salisbury on the same day that Goschen wanted time to think about the proposal since he was afraid of being 'isolated'. 'He would distinctly prefer the Chancellorship of the Exchequer without the leadership, if he accepts at all. I am afraid, however, that I cannot hold out to you any sanguine prospect that he will be induced to accept.'[2] But on the next day Hartington intimated success:

He would desire to be at liberty to state that in joining your Government, with or without one or two Liberal colleagues in the House of Lords, he had taken this step, not as having become a Conservative or ceasing to hold any of his Liberal opinions, but as a Unionist joining a Government which relies on the support of all shades of political opinion. If you think that such an interpretation of his action given by him would be resented by your party he would prefer to remain outside.

Next, he would wish to have a full consultation with you as to general policy, foreign, domestic, legislative, and financial, and satisfy himself that he would be able to act with you on all these questions, as he feels that any subsequent disagreement on them, leading to a possible separation, would materially aggravate the present difficulties.[3]

---

[1] See Churchill, *Randolph Churchill*, Appendix v, pp. 796–808.
[2] SP, Hartington to Salisbury, 31 December 1886.
[3] *Ibid.*, Hartington to Salisbury, 1 January 1887.

Goschen had conversations with Akers-Douglas about the possibility of a seat if he accepted office and about the way the Conservatives might receive him. Unhappy with so much speculation and publicity swirling about his head, he informed the Conservative's Chief Whip on 1 January that he was going out of town very briefly 'in view of the indiscreet pressure of the press to squeeze information out of me'. But he quickly returned and registered at the Coburg Hotel in London 'but have given no one the address so as not to be overrun by curious visitors'.[1] Akers-Douglas approved Goschen's decision not to lead the Commons. It 'will much facilitate his cordial reception by our party'.[2] Goschen had already sent for Milner to assist him 'in drawing up statements for the papers and in sundry other ways'.[3]

On 2 January 1887 when it was obvious that Goschen would enter the Cabinet, he reported to Hartington that Salisbury would permit him to bring two friends into the government. Goschen had leaped at this idea as it would 'increase the appearance of coalition rather than conversion'. He wanted Lord Lansdowne, then Governor General of Canada, and Lord Northbrook to enter the Cabinet as his Liberal Unionist colleagues. Goschen was pleased that Salisbury was going to be his own Foreign Secretary. The queen had sent him a telegram the evening before urging him to accept. 'Rather curious to send it without cypher in any attempt at confidentiality.'[4]

After several additional days of discussion, letters and telegrams, both Lansdowne and Northbrook declined to accept office and Goschen entered the Salisbury Cabinet alone. In a statement prepared for the public it was affirmed that Goschen had acted with Hartington's approval and that Hartington, while maintaining his independent position as leader of the Liberal Unionists, would provide such support as he could for Lord Salisbury. It was made clear that Goschen remained a Liberal Unionist. Lansdowne had been tempted but Canadian difficulties prevented his

[1] Chilston Papers, K.A.O. U564 C238/16 and C238/17.
[2] SP, Akers-Douglas to Salisbury, [1 January 1887].
[3] MP, Goschen to Milner, [1 January 1887], Box 182.
[4] DP, 340.2133.

accepting while Northbrook was simply not interested in joining the Cabinet.

W. H. Smith was appointed Leader of the House of Commons but Lord Iddesleigh, the former Foreign Secretary, was left without a place in the Cabinet. He died a few days later, very tragically, in Salisbury's office. Goschen played a major role in ousting Iddesleigh whom he regarded as a sick man and a weak Foreign Secretary. Salisbury informed Hicks Beach on 6 January 1887:

> To my extreme surprise, I found Goschen very strongly urging – almost insisting – that Iddesleigh should not stay at the Foreign Office. Bearing in mind your own strong view, I felt bound to give effect to this. Goschen wants this kept secret; and I do not know to what extent would have made it a *sine qua non*. But if it was to be done, it could only be done now, without brutally hurting Iddesleigh's feelings.[1]

Goschen's new colleagues rushed to congratulate him. In his home, all was joy. But Arthur Elliot was displeased as rumours reached him that Goschen might enter the Cabinet. When he received a final confirmation of this report he recorded that it was a 'great mistake'. It would weaken 'the independent position' of the Liberal Unionists. They must not be absorbed by the Conservatives but work instead for 'the reconstruction of the *Liberal* Party upon Unionist principles'.[2] Goschen summarized his reasons for accepting office to a sceptical Arthur Elliot and emphasized that 'Hartington urged it on me.'[3] But another Liberal Unionist, Leonard Courtney, saw matters somewhat differently. He was sure Goschen would 'slip into being a Conservative'. 'It is said he has joined under Hartington's pressure or command; perhaps it would be more correct to say Hartington's concurrence. One dominant consideration was that it was almost impossible to find him a seat anywhere.'[4]

Nor were the Conservatives over-sanguine about finding a constituency for Goschen. A vacancy, however, did exist in one

[1] St Aldwyn Papers, PCC/69. See Salisbury's 'Memorandum of Events' in the Smith Papers, PS12/24. It was written to assist Smith in placating Iddesleigh's angry elder son.
[2] Elliot Papers, diary entry for 3 January 1887, Book 11.
[3] Elliot, vol. 2, p. 107.
[4] Gooch, *Lord Courtney*, pp. 273–4.

of Liverpool's seven constituencies – the only one carried by a Gladstonian in 1886 – as a result of the death of its M.P. in late December. This constituency had been won by the Liberal nominee at the election by 2920 votes to 2750 for the Conservative.[1] It seemed to the Conservative leaders that Goschen might be able to add some Liberal votes to the solid Conservative bloc and thus win an additional seat. Goschen recognized the psychological importance of winning whichever seat he decided to contest but he apparently disliked the idea of taking a safe Conservative seat. That would tarnish the halo of Liberal Unionism which he hoped would brighten the Conservative cabinet and save him from the charge of political apostasy. So by 11 January he had made up his mind to contest the Exchange Division of Liverpool.

Goschen's electoral address was based almost entirely on opposition to Home Rule. The Exchange Division of Liverpool contained some commercial interests but it also included many Irish immigrants. A few of the shipping concerns had been angered when Randolph Churchill granted mail contracts to several German steamship companies.[2] T. P. O'Connor, an Irish Nationalist Member of Parliament, went to Liverpool to help in the struggle against Goschen. He worked almost without rest, 'made innumerable speeches, visited the sick and dying, and dragged some of them to the poll'.[3] Ralph Neville, the Liberal candidate, was a barrister who later became a judge. When the votes were counted on the evening of 26 January, Goschen was declared the loser by seven votes, 3217 to 3210. The best explanation for Goschen's defeat is that he lost a hard fight by a very close margin in an evenly balanced constituency. Neville was returned again in 1892 by 66 votes. The Constituency was

---

[1] In the election of 1885 the constituency had been won by the Conservatives by a vote of 2964 to 2907. The defeated Liberal was Captain W. H. O'Shea, the husband of Parnell's mistress.

[2] See Hamilton, *Reminiscences*, vol. 2, p. 56, and Henry S. Raikes, *The Life and Letters of Henry C. Raikes, late Her Majesty's Postmaster-General* (London, 1898), pp. 257–72.

[3] Thomas P. O'Connor, *Memoirs of an Old Parliamentarian* (London, 1929), vol. 2, p. 117.

then won by the Conservatives in 1895 (Neville was not a candidate) and 1900 but won back by the Liberals in 1906.

News of Goschen's defeat stunned the Conservatives and Liberal Unionists. They were still not sure that Lord Randolph would abide by his decision not to launch a full-scale attack on the government when he explained his resignation to Parliament Nor could the anti-Home Rulers be sure that the Round Table talks between Chamberlain, Trevelyan, Harcourt, Morley and Herschell would end in failure. On the day of the Liverpool election Hartington told Arthur Elliot that a setback for Goschen could be 'a fatal blow' to the government.[1] Eagerly awaiting news of Goschen's triumph, the Conservative Cabinet was dining with W. H. Smith. Then came the shattering report that Goschen had been defeated.[2] Liberal dreams of a Conservative collapse, however, were soon exploded.

Salisbury complained to Queen Victoria that this was all 'very annoying'. A seat could easily be obtained for Goschen but 'the difficulty is in satisfying his scruples – one might almost say his prudery – about his Liberal character. He will not have a distinctively Conservative seat but we can control no other.'[3] The intensity of Goschen's mortification was increased when he was obliged to accept the generous offer of Lord Algernon Percy to relinquish his solidly Conservative constituency at St George's, Hanover Square, in London. Goschen won this seat by a margin of more than three to one and was re-elected in 1892 and 1895 without opposition. He might well have wondered to what extent his opinions had failed to move with the times and to what degree the Conservatives had advanced into his old positions. Lord George Hamilton, now Goschen's colleague, could see no grounds for disagreement between the new Chancellor of the Exchequer and other members of the Cabinet. 'Upon questions of franchise, taxation, the maintenance of naval and military establishments and Home Rule he was heart and soul one of us.'[4]

---

[1] Elliot Papers, diary entry for 20 January 1887, Book 12.
[2] Hamilton, *Reminiscences*, vol. 2, p. 56.
[3] Salisbury to Queen Victoria, 27 January 1887, RA A65/33.
[4] Hamilton, *Reminiscences*, vol. 2, p. 54.

CHAPTER 9

BUDGETS, GOLD AND THE CONSERVATIVE LEADERSHIP

According to Sir Edward Hamilton, eventually a Permanent Secretary to the Treasury, 'The first qualifications of a Chancellor of the Exchequer are *character* and being a *gentleman*. Then comes influence and financial aptitude.'[1] Goschen satisfied these requirements and as he was also the only ex-director of the Bank of England to become Chancellor there were very close relations between the bank and the government while he was at the Exchequer.[2] It was also Goschen's good fortune to present his first four budgets during a time of prosperity. This enabled him to undertake the successful conversion of the national debt in 1888. Yet there remains a feeling that he failed to accomplish much of what needed to be done. The eloquent budget speeches and the carefully calculated statistical presentations leave one with the belief that he would have been a great success in the role which Gladstone played at the Exchequer in the 1850s and 1860s.[3]

The civil servants at the Treasury had been apprehensive at the prospect of 'Lord Randolph's descent among what he called a lot of d—d Gladstonians' but soon came to admire his original ideas. Algernon West, chairman of the Board of Inland Revenue, observed that Churchill and Goschen were very 'dissimilar'. Lord Randolph had been 'sharp, short and decisive' while Goschen 'loved minute criticisms, often criticizing his own criticisms; eager to persuade the person he was talking to, and fond of deferring decisions'.[4] Edward Hamilton agreed that Goschen had great

---

[1] HP, diary entry for 6 September 1900, Add. Mss 48677.

[2] Sir John H. Clapham, *The Bank of England* (Cambridge, 1944), vol. 2, p. 316.

[3] Goschen's budgets are discussed in Elliot, vol. 2, pp. 137–79 and more critically in Gardiner, *Sir William Harcourt*, vol. 2, pp. 118–25. The best discussion of Goschen's budgets is in Bernard Mallet, *The British Budgets 1887—88 to 1912–13* (London, 1913), pp. 1–68.

[4] Horace G. Hutchinson (ed.), *The Private Diaries of Sir Algernon West* (London, 1922), pp. 4–5.

critical gifts but wondered if he had 'real qualifications for con-struction and co-operation with others'.[1] Five weeks later Hamil-ton noted: 'Goschen cannot make up his mind what to do on the coming Budget. I am all for his doing nothing or doing a great deal. It is certainly very improving to work for him. He puts one on one's mettle.'[2]

Each of Goschen's six budgets provided him with a surplus. They brought in between £88 million and £91 million. He was one of the last Chancellors to deal with such small figures. By 1896 the revenue was £103 million and the Boer War brought it to £142 million in 1901. The revenue dropped to £131 million in 1909 but was up to £185 million in 1911.[3] Goschen dealt with a national debt which had been gradually reduced from £834,262,726 in 1815 to £649,770,091 in 1914. By 1920, as a result of the First World War, it had soared to £7,831,744,300.[4]

Goschen's first budget was introduced on 21 April 1887 and called for a one penny reduction in the pound on the income tax while, more controversially, the sinking fund (designed eventu-ally to pay off the national debt) was to be raided for £2 million and thereby reduced from £28 million to £26 million.[5] He also designated a number of areas in which reforms would have to be undertaken, such as currency and coinage, local taxation and death and stamp duties. Mallet observed that Goschen's speech showed 'an individuality of treatment and a technical mastery of his subject, such as only a lifelong experience of financial matters could explain'.[6] The budget pleased the majority of the House but Churchill and Gladstone were unhappy about the reduction in the sinking fund.

Goschen's most memorable achievement while at the Ex-chequer was his conversion of the national debt in 1888. It was 'the greatest of the century, and the last'. He was, as Clapham wrote, 'operating on the grand scale, dealing with nearly

[1] HP, diary entry for 11 February 1887, Add. Mss 48648.
[2] *Ibid.*, diary entry for 18 March 1887, Add. Mss 48648.
[3] Mallet, *Budgets*, pp. 364–407.
[4] E. L. Hargreaves, *The National Debt* (London, 1930), Table A, p. 291.
[5] *Hansard*, cccxiii (21 April 1887), 1418–59.
[6] Mallet, *Budgets*, pp. 1–8.

£600,000,000 of debt'.[1] Despite Lord Randolph Churchill's doubts, Goschen decided to plunge ahead. The proposals were generally well received, for they meant a saving to the entire nation, though parts of the financial world were not enthusiastic about a cut in the interest rate. The Chancellor of the Exchequer had been fully briefed on all previous conversions and sought to follow the successful conversion of 1844.[2] Gladstone and the Liberals also challenged the amount of the commission which was to be paid where holders had an option. The Treasury officials had insisted that an adequate commission be paid and it was eventually decided to allocate 1s 6d per £100. On 1 March 1888 Hamilton concluded: 'I see that the great difficulty we shall have is to induce him [Goschen] to accept the principle of a small brokerage which I believe in these days to be absolutely expected to insure success to that part of his scheme which is optional.' Almost a week later Hamilton recorded 'good progress with the Conversion scheme; though there is still not a little vacillation and timidity on the part of Mr Goschen'.[3]

Less than a week later the conversion plan was presented to Parliament and quickly approved. It simplified the nation's financial obligations by reducing three different types of 3 per cent government stock to one new denomination. The new stock would pay $2\frac{3}{4}$ per cent for fifteen years and then be reduced to $2\frac{1}{2}$ per cent for twenty years. This would mean a saving of £1 million the first year and of £1,400,000 for the following thirteen years. After 1904, Hamilton calculated that the yearly saving for the nation would exceed £2 million.

But Hamilton did not always find Goschen an ideal departmental head. When Goschen was grappling with plans for the budget and conversion in early February, Hamilton grumbled:

---

[1] Clapham, *Bank of England*, vol. 2, pp. 318–23. See the detailed explanation in Sir Edward Hamilton, *An Account of the Operations under the National Debt Conversion Act, 1888 and the National Debt Redemption Act*, 1889 (London, 1889).
[2] Secret 'Memorandum on National Debt Conversion', prepared by Edward Hamilton for the Cabinet, 28 February 1888, CAB. 37/21/4. CAB. 37 refers to the Cabinet Papers (1880–1914) which are in the Public Record Office. Extracts from Crown copyright records in the Public Record Office appear by permission of the Controller of Her Majesty's Stationery Office.
[3] HP, diary entries for 1 and 6 March 1888, Add. Mss 48648.

His critical powers make him a very improving man with whom to work;
but he is an unsatisfactory man in other respects to serve, by reason of his
inability to make up his mind and come to decisions, and of his want of
consideration towards those who have to be at his beck and call; for instead
of transacting his business with one straight away, he will often send for one
many times in the day, thus doing business by driblets and wasting the time
of himself and others.[1]

Goschen's second budget, which he introduced shortly after
his conversion plan had been made public, reduced the income
tax by another 1*d* to 6*d*.[2] His most important obligation was to
provide money for the new county councils. He decided to end
the system of grants-in-aid and to set aside certain imperial taxes
for the new local authorities. Some of his critics argued that
sufficient taxing power should be delegated to the new authorities. One item of Goschen's budget led to a considerable uproar.
He had proposed a wheel and van tax in order to force the users
of roads to pay for their upkeep. In the face of aroused public
opinion, Goschen capitulated. Bernard Mallet concluded that
stamp duties, death duties and the income tax were clearly in need
of 'careful reorganization, but none of these was treated in more
than a tentative and partial fashion'.[3]

In 1889 Goschen needed more money for the navy and for
local government. His scheme for a tax on ground-rent landlords
was rejected by the Cabinet but a proposal to place an estate
duty of 1 per cent on all real and personal estates valued at more
than £10,000 was accepted. It also agreed to increase the tax on
beer. Henry Chaplin, Britain's squire-in-chief, was opposed to
the estate duty and the increase in the beer tax. Goschen argued
that both taxes were reasonable. There was a connection between
them.

Pray consider that if we had proposed the Estate Duty alone, without a
corresponding addition to indirect taxation, we should have been setting a
very dangerous precedent to Radicals. The Government deliberately came
to the conclusion that, in the interest of Conservative finance, it was a duty

1 *Ibid.*, diary entry for 13 February 1888, Add. Mss 48648.
2 *Hansard*, CCCXXIV (26 March 1888), 267–365.
3 Mallet, *Budgets*, p. 21.

to find some share of the additional revenue required by having recourse to a tax on some article of consumption, and certainly the margin in the case of beer seemed to indicate that there lay the least obnoxious resource.[1]

Goschen was determined that all citizens – no matter how poor – must pay a portion of the national tax burden. In his budget speech he stressed the difficulty of finding 'new taxation' and concluded 'that it is better service to the State to increase the number of sources of revenue, than to attempt to find simplicity'. Rumbles of discontent were heard from the Liberal side of the Commons as Goschen broke with the Pitt–Peel–Gladstone tradition of simplification and consolidation in the tax structure of the nation.

If some of your great sources of revenue are breaking down under you, if you see a decline in them, and if on the other hand it is true that the income tax ought not be used for every emergency, then you must be looking about you for new means of meeting the new demands that are being constantly made.[2]

Goschen feared the drift away from indirect to direct taxation. This could lead to sophisticated methods of graduation and the redistribution of the nation's wealth. Paradoxically, Goschen regarded his estate tax as safe and reasonable. But Gladstone feared it as a novelty that might lead to graduation while Edward Hamilton had no doubt on the matter. 'The Estate Duty is the thin end of the wedge to a graduated system of taxation, which is pretty certain to be expanded in the future.'[3] And Bernard Mallet concluded that 'this measure by a Conservative government paved the way for Sir William Harcourt's drastic reform'.[4]

Goschen took his role of guardian of the public purse very seriously. He protested over the extravagance of some consuls who used the telegraph excessively. But he complained not only because of the money but because an excessive request for funds could lead 'to a supplementary estimate and general debate on

[1] See the Cabinet papers in CAB. 37/24/24 and 37/24/25.
[2] *Hansard*, cccxxxv (15 April 1889), 489–587.
[3] HP, diary entry for 16 April 1889, Add. Mss 48650.
[4] Mallet, *Budgets*, pp. 31–2.

foreign affairs for the sake of such telegrams'. When the queen asked for additional funds to entertain the Shah of Persia, Goschen grumbled that the money could be obtained from Parliament but the debate could turn to the character and actions of the ruler in question and 'give deep and lasting offence' as 'men do not scruple at anything'. They must be 'very careful in this respect'. In the summer of 1890 he wondered if it was wise for Sir Henry Drummond Wolff, then British Minister at Teheran, to come home via India at the expense of the public. It seemed to Goschen that Wolff had simply 'devised' a 'pleasant way' to 'come home at taxpayer's expense'. Nor did the Chancellor think much of a suggestion that the British government should provide 'financial and other aid' so that London might have a great international exhibition.[1]

As Goschen contemplated his fourth budget, he was determined to hold down military and naval estimates. He expected little trouble from the navy as the Naval Defence Act of 1889 was designed to run for five years and to add ten battleships and sixty cruisers to the British navy. The 'scare' of 1888–9 which led the public to believe that the British navy no longer maintained its superiority over any two other powers had been successful. Goschen now expected the army to pound at the doors of the Treasury. After some haggling an accommodation was finally achieved.[2] The most troublesome part of this budget came as the result of an attempt to deal with the 'rush to alcohol' which had provided him with a large part of his surplus from the previous year. On 28 March 1890, Hamilton recorded that the Cabinet had accepted Goschen's proposals 'en bloc'. The Chancellor proposed a tax on beer and spirits in order to establish a fund which would enable local authorities to buy up licences and thereby decrease the number of public-houses. Hamilton thought the compensation fund for the publicans to be 'rather an ingenious way of dealing with the vexed licensing question by a side-door'.[3]

But W. H. Smith began to have doubts about this plan before

[1] SP, Goschen to Salisbury, 5 May 1890, 2 January 1889, 1 August 1890, 22 December 1889.
[2] *Ibid.*, Goschen to Salisbury, 19 and 22 December 1889, and typed copy, Salisbury to Goschen, 20 December 1889.
[3] HP, diary entry for 28 March 1890, Add. Mss 48652.

the budget was formally introduced. His contacts with the brewers had convinced him that they wanted 'to be let alone. They think they have a fair claim for the remission of the additional beer duty and they are not willing that it should be used as a compensation fund.' Goschen refused to reconsider the Cabinet's decision. 'Besides there is the great sop to the Licensed Victuallers' interest of diminishing the number of licenses, a matter on which they have no inkling.'[1]

The Chancellor of the Exchequer promptly wrote to Salisbury in order to comment upon Smith's forebodings and to urge that they proceed with the original plan. Salisbury concurred but insisted 'that every enactment, except the mere power of levying the duty, be put into a Separate bill; so that if time fails they may be postponed without inconvenience'.[2] The Prime Minister's suggestion turned out to be a wise one. Edward Hamilton found the budget just short of 'masterly' when it was introduced.[3] There had been some grumbling from 'income-tax payers', from brewers and from extreme Temperance people'. But he did not expect trouble.[4] Hamilton was completely wrong. The temperance people were instantly up in arms. Meetings were organized throughout the country in an attempt to prevent the payment of compensation. While the temperance advocates wished to reduce the number of public-houses, they regarded compensation as a reward for evil-doing. As summer approached, the government found itself in a dangerous position. Its own followers were not very enthusiastic about the Irish Land Purchase Bill, the Tithe Bill or the Local Taxation Bill, the last of which embodied Goschen's temperance proposals. Goschen and C. T. Ritchie (Local Government Board) contemplated resignation if the compensation clauses were dropped. But eventually there was no other choice as government majorities declined and morale sagged.[5]

---

[1] SP, copy of letter, Smith to Goschen, 9 April 1890 and copy of letter, Goschen to Smith, 9 April 1890.

[2] *Ibid.*, Goschen to Salisbury, 10 April 1890 and Salisbury to Goschen, 12 April 1890.   [3] *Hansard*, CCCXLIII (17 April 1890), 692–791.

[4] HP, diary entry for 17 April 1890, Add. Mss 48652.

[5] See John Newton, *W. S. Caine* (London, 1907), pp. 207–31 and Timothy Healy, *Letters and Leaders of My Day* (London, 1928), vol. I, pp. 314–15.

In 1891 Goschen's budget was 'dull and humdrum as compared with those of previous years' but Hamilton regarded it as a splendid financial statement.[1] The major item of the budget was to make elementary education free. Salisbury and Goschen – fearful that the Liberals might tamper with the church schools – decided to establish a free system on lines which would protect the schools of the Established Church. Goschen's final budget in 1892 was introduced shortly before a general election was anticipated and contained little of a controversial nature.[2]

While Goschen deserves praise for his conversion of the national debt and the rugged honesty which he brought to the handling of the nation's finances, a final judgment on his career at the Exchequer must bring out numerous hesitancies and failures to act. He was adequate but, with his financial training, one expected much more.[3] A Conservative party member remarked when he surveyed Goschen's career that the Exchequer 'was the post for which he was least fitted'. Arthur A. Baumann went on to observe:

The truth was that Goschen's City training in a bill-acceptor's office, so useful to him in other ways, militated against his success at the Treasury. Goschen took broad and spirited views on everything except money. When money was in question, the old habit of dealing in fractions was strong upon him, and he became meticulous. Knowledge of the world, not close calculation, is what makes a good Chancellor of the Exchequer.[4]

Goschen's private secretary during his first three years at the Exchequer was Alfred Milner. In evaluating his old chief's career Milner stressed that, 'Criticism and analysis, sometimes carried to excess, were a delight to him. As a practical administrator he occasionally erred by taking too little for granted and by exhausting himself over the study of details.' In looking over Goschen's years at the Exchequer, Milner concluded that he had been a 'most competent and conscientious' Chancellor but

[1] HP, diary entry for 24 April 1891, Add. Mss 48655; *Hansard*, CCCLII (23 April 1891), 1176–214.
[2] *Hansard*, 4th series, III (11 April 1892), 1134–70.
[3] Mallet, *Budgets*, pp. 59–68. See also Sir Thomas H. F. Farrer, *Mr. Goschen's Finance 1887–1890* (London, 1891).
[4] Arthur A. Baumann, *Persons and Politics of the Transition* (London, 1916), pp. 7–10.

'the time was not favourable, nor was his own disposition, perhaps, very prone, to a policy of innovation'.[1]

Throughout Goschen's years as Chancellor of the Exchequer there were numerous departmental problems which had to be solved. The queen had disliked the Jubilee coinage and new patterns were being prepared. But the monarch was often difficult to please. Goschen submitted some designs to the queen who commented that 'the underlip projects too much and the chin though correct in shape is slightly too short and the eye is not good'. She insisted that 'Imp.' be added even if D.F. was dropped. The former was one of her 'proudest titles while the D.F. is really a most unnecessary one having been given to Henry VIII by the Pope'.[2] After protracted negotiations the queen finally had her way. Salisbury reported that the Cabinet had decided that the queen must never designate herself empress of England but she could certainly use the title with respect to India. It was agreed that she could have 'Ind. Imp.' or 'I. I.' on the new coins but they also suggested that 'D.F.' (Defender of the Faith) not be omitted.[3]

There were, however, more important problems for Goschen to deal with as Chancellor of the Exchequer. On 8 October 1890, Edward Hamilton dined with Nathan Rothschild 'who confessed to being very uneasy about the present state of things in the City'.[4] In mid-October the Chancellor went to the Bank of England and found things 'queer!' There were rumours that some of the best firms were in trouble over their excessive investments in Argentina. By the end of the month the speculation had 'quieted down'.[5]

But on Friday 7 November, Hamilton was at the bank and heard from the highly respected governor, William Lidderdale,

[1] Milner, 'George Joachim Goschen', pp. 359–64.
[2] Queen Victoria to Goschen, 10 June 1888, RA B66/50.
[3] Salisbury to Queen Victoria, 18 February 1892, CAB. 41/22/10. CAB. 41 refers to the photographic copies of Prime Ministers' letters (1868–1916) to the sovereign summarizing Cabinet meetings. The originals are in the Royal Archives but these copies are in the Public Record Office where they have been made available by the gracious permission of Her Majesty the Queen.
[4] HP, diary entry for 8 October 1890, Add. Mss 48654.
[5] Elliot, vol. 2, pp. 169–70.

that Murrieta's, an investment firm, was in trouble. A conversation with the Chancellor led Hamilton to record that Goschen 'does not like the state of things at all'.[1]

On Sunday 9 November, Goschen received a 'mysterious letter' from the governor of the bank which was 'very alarming'. Monday found Goschen at the bank where Lidderdale was 'in a dreadful state of anxiety. Barings in such danger that unless aid is given, they must stop.' The failure of this major company could have had catastrophic consequences. Goschen's conversion of the debt had released money for speculative purposes abroad and Barings had plunged heavily into Argentine stocks and bonds. Argentina was now in a state of economic turmoil and Barings could not meet its immediate obligations. The governor of the bank and other men prominent in the financial world insisted that the government must join a guarantee fund in order to avert disaster. It was estimated that Barings had liabilities which amounted to £20 million and immediately available assets of only £12 million. It appeared, however, that if time were granted, Barings could once again be solvent. Lidderdale told Goschen that Barings needed £4 million at once. The Bank of England would advance £1 million if the government would do the same. Then it would be necessary for the other great financial houses and banks to find the rest. But Goschen recalled that the great financial houses and banks of France had provided the needed guarantees without government aid when the Comptoir d'Escompte was in trouble the year before.

Goschen then visited several other prominent members of the financial community in the hope of getting them to assist Barings. Most were 'demoralised' and demanded government intervention. Goschen was told by the panic-stricken money men that he 'alone could save the situation'.

Lidderdale much more of a man and keeping his head though certainly he pressed me hard. I promised to consult Salisbury and Smith. I must say I felt overwhelmed with responsibility. If I do nothing and the crash comes I

---

[1] HP, diary entry for 7 November 1890. Add. Mss 48654. See L. S. Pressnell, 'Gold Reserves, Banking Reserves, and the Baring Crisis of 1890', in C. R. Whittlesey and J. S. G. Wilson (eds.), *Essays in Money and Banking* (Oxford, 1968), pp. 167–228.

should never be forgiven: if I act, and disaster never occurs Parliament would never forgive my having pledged the National credit to a private firm.

Steps were already being taken to buy time. Rothschild negotiated a £3 million gold loan from the Bank of France against Treasury bills and Lidderdale obtained half that sum from Russia.[1] Goschen did not get back to his office until after 3 p.m. and he told Hamilton that 'things were very bad indeed'. Hamilton was sure it was Murrieta's but Goschen replied that it was 'much worse than that: it is Barings!' It seemed to Hamilton that, 'The great crash of Overend and Gurney 24 years ago is nothing to the crash with which we are threatened.'[2] Goschen informed Salisbury of the crisis that evening just before the Lord Mayor's banquet. After an almost sleepless night, Goschen was again in the City the following morning. The demand was still for government assistance. But Goschen then saw W. H. Smith and the two politician-business men decided that the government could not provide special aid for Barings other than suspending the Bank Charter Act and employing its influence. Goschen sent a summary of his talks to Salisbury with the comment that 'things looked better'. The Chancellor and Smith were

agreed that any direct interposition on the part of the Government would be impossible under any circumstances . . . Tremendous pressure *may* be brought to bear on us as to help, but I think it will be absolutely necessary for *la haute finance* to find its own salvation. The Rothschilds are sure to put the screws on but it won't do, as Smith will explain.[3]

Salisbury saw the pessimistic Rothschild on the following day. The Cabinet now agreed that if the Bank of England violated its charter by lending to Barings 'on Argentine securities, we would join in a bill of indemnity *provided they obtained Gladstone's consent*'.[4]

Goschen was scheduled to speak in Dundee on Saturday and

[1] Elliot, vol. 2, pp. 172–4 and Appendix III, pp. 283–4 and Clapham, *Bank of England*, vol. 2, pp. 326–39. Pressnell, 'Baring Crisis', pp. 202–5, points out that Lidderdale believed the politicians had pledged more than they were later prepared to acknowledge.
[2] HP, diary entry for 10 November 1890, Add. Mss 48654.
[3] SP, [11 November 1890].
[4] *Ibid.*, typed copy, Salisbury to Goschen, 12 November 1890.

rather than add to the rumours, it was decided that he must not cancel his engagement. On Friday, the news of Barings' collapse had finally leaked to the public but the crisis was almost over. Two financial experts had been asked by Lidderdale to undertake a rapid survey of Barings' assets and liabilities. They reported to the governor on Friday that the firm was basically sound. Lidderdale then decided to recommend the establishment of a guarantee fund which could meet Barings' pressing liabilities of some £8 to £9 million. He saw Smith and Salisbury at 2 p.m. on Friday afternoon and eventually obtained an agreement with the politicians that the government would share all losses with the bank during the next twenty-four hours as he attempted to start the fund. The response was remarkable. The bank put up £1 million and by 5.30 Friday afternoon this had reached more than £3 million as the other important Houses came to the rescue of Barings. The five largest joint-stock banks were also contacted and they too provided an immense amount of money.

As Goschen sat down to lunch in Dundee on Saturday afternoon, he was delighted to receive a telegram from Smith informing him that the guarantee fund had reached £7 million and the crisis was over. The fund eventually totalled almost £18 million. Barings was reconstituted as a joint-stock company and by 1894 had paid back the advances made by the guarantee fund. Goschen had been absolutely correct when he insisted that the financial community could resolve the crisis without the introduction of public funds. The Chancellor had never wavered: 'we could not carry direct aid in Parliament even if we wished. How defend a supplemental estimate for a loss of half a million! And would not immediate application put the whole fat in the fire?'[1]

The Baring crisis convinced Goschen that it was necessary to provoke further discussion on the supply of gold available at times of emergency. The insufficiency of gold which could be quickly employed had been one of the more disturbing aspects of the Baring affair. There had long been an undercurrent of dissatisfaction with the Bank Charter Act of 1844 but majority

[1] See Elliot, vol. 2, pp. 172–4 and Appendix III, pp. 283–4, and Clapham *Bank of England*, vol. 2, pp. 326–39.

sentiment regarded it as sacred and virtually untouchable. Goschen was searching about for a means of increasing Britain's gold and banking reserves and on 28 January 1891 he presented a general outline of his ideas to the Leeds chamber of commerce. The banks were urged to publish their accounts more frequently and to keep larger cash reserves. He also advocated the substitution of £1 notes for the gold sovereign. As he later wrote:

I planned an attempt to give the public, of course entirely at their option, the opportunity of using £1 notes instead of the sovereign as part of the active circulation. Two-thirds of the gold thus set free were to be retained as security for the notes, but were to be kept as a separate reserve, augmenting the stock of gold in the vaults of the Bank of England. This separate reserve was to be utilized, in case of emergency, under the most stringent conditions as to rates of interest, in lieu of the very unsatisfactory expedient offered by the suspension of the Bank Charter Act.[1]

Goschen's speech led to a great deal of discussion and the publication of numerous pamphlets. The consensus, however, was clearly negative so Goschen modified his proposals. He wrote to Lidderdale in early July that the objections seemed rather weak but he conceded that the scheme would have to be withdrawn if the banking community was 'hostile'. The government had no desire to impose something which was not wanted. As Goschen amended his scheme, Lidderdale and the majority of the directors, though most had reservations of one kind or another, agreed that it would be useful in dealing with future crises.[2] But Goschen himself had doubts about the plan and was being pushed along by Lidderdale, Welby and Hamilton.

Goschen finally agreed to deliver a speech on 'Metallic Reserves' to the London chamber of commerce on 2 December 1891. Three days before, Lidderdale was deeply distressed at the Chancellor's hesitant attitude.[3] Though he had modified his Leeds generalizations so that they were now more sophisticated and precise, the heart of the programme remained the same – one-pound notes for gold sovereigns in order to enlarge the gold

[1] G. J. Goschen, 'Our Cash Reserves and Central Stock of Gold', *Essays and Addresses*, pp. 102–30. See also Clapham, *Bank of England*, vol. 2, pp. 340–50.
[2] Welby Papers, London School of Economics, R (S.R.) 1017, vol. 7, ff. 123–48.
[3] HP, diary entries for 19 November 1891 and 1 December 1891, Add. Mss 48656.

reserve. He warned the London chamber of commerce that his plan would not 'prevent panics' or 'check over-speculation'. The Chancellor was at pains to point out that legislative acts such as he was proposing were 'nothing compared to what bankers, merchants and all interested in industry may themselves exercise'. In a play for bimetallist support Goschen remarked that he had always been anxious to see the use of silver extended 'as far as it could be done compatibly with our general arrangements'.[1]

The Times supported the Chancellor of the Exchequer's plan but felt that his December speech had conceded too much to the opposition which had been aroused by his Leeds proposals. Goschen 'showed himself half-hearted in the matter – a characteristic which he has more than once exhibited in the course of his career'.[2] The attitude of the Liberals might be decisive. A few days later Hamilton discovered that Gladstone regarded it as a 'detestable' proposal. Gladstone thought it would encourage speculation and doubted there would be 'a single extra sovereign available in time of crisis'.[3] Within two weeks Goschen was forced to acknowledge defeat. The scheme had picked up very little support. One-pound and ten-shilling notes were not introduced until the beginning of the First World War compelled action.

The fears which many Conservatives and Liberal Unionists had entertained over the expected early demise of the Salisbury Cabinet were never fulfilled. Despite the temporary loss of Hicks Beach in 1887 due to his failing eyesight, the government pulled itself together and continued in office until 1892. Arthur Balfour distinguished himself when he replaced Hicks Beach as Chief Secretary for Ireland. W. H. Smith performed admirably as Leader of the House in his quiet, efficient way. Lord Randolph was left to sulk in his tent and to build castles in the air. Churchill did have some cause for hope in 1887 as Chamberlain was still a difficult ally for both Hartington and Salisbury. But Chamberlain's growing belief that Liberal reunion was impossible caused the Radical Unionist to revise his position. By 1889 he had

[1] G. J. Goschen, *The Metallic Reserve* (London, 1891).
[2] *The Times* (3 December 1891).
[3] HP, diary entry for 10 December 1891, Add. Mss 48656.

merged his National Radical Union with the general body of Liberal Unionists under Hartington. When Hartington became the eighth Duke of Devonshire in late 1891, it was Chamberlain who succeeded to the leadership of the Liberal Unionists in the Commons.

Unfortunately for the Conservatives, the health of W. H. Smith was a source of constant worry. After 1888 it became progressively worse and it reopened the whole question of the leadership of the House. Goschen often deputized for Smith when he was absent but the Conservatives were not always happy under his leadership. He was not yet one of them – being still a Liberal Unionist – and he had some distracting mannerisms which irritated a good number of Conservatives.

On 23 November 1888, Arthur Balfour expressed his 'uneasiness' about Smith's health in a draft letter to his Uncle Robert which he finally decided not to send.

If Smith goes, there are as I can see only two men on the Bench who can possibly succeed him – Goschen and myself. There are many very grave objections to the latter. But there is one which is insuperable. Goschen will certainly object, and be right in objecting, to serve under one who was not in Parliament when he first became a Cabinet Minister. Buckle sounded me on this point the other day and I gave him this answer: but I added that Goschen could hardly lead the Conservative Party in the House of C. unless he consented to call himself a Conservative and join the Carlton.

Even if, however, he consented to swallow the name, after having digested the principles, of the Tory party, there are objections to him. His fussiness drives Smith mad. It would, I hope, produce a less drastic effect on his other colleagues, but it would be trying. He cannot stay on the Bench, through mere fidgetiness, for ten minutes consecutively: – during these ten minutes his perpetual commentary on what is going on quite drowns the text – so that when one gets up to reply it is Goschen one feels inclined to reply to, as he is the only person one has heard! These however are small matters, and he is so able, loyal, good tempered and good natured, so obviously honest and so incapable of intrigue that, *faute de mieux*, he would, I believe, do very well both by his colleagues and the party.[1]

In early 1889 Smith offered his resignation to Salisbury but the Prime Minister refused to accept it. During the next two years,

[1] BP, draft letter Balfour to Salisbury, 23 November 1888, Add. Mss 49689, ff. 38–41.

Smith's health continued to deteriorate. His doctor warned him that it would be wise to step down but party loyalty and a sense of duty compelled him to continue. Nor did he appear very enthusiastic about Goschen succeeding him. The Chancellor of the Exchequer had not been overjoyed at losing his surplus so that elementary education would be made free. A grumble from Goschen led Smith to snap back. The Leader of the House regretted his sharp remark and apologized to Goschen. The latter replied in a hurt tone. Goschen conceded that Smith's remark had been 'heedlessly uttered' but it seemed to Goschen that it indicated what the Conservatives really thought of his budgets. It was clear, he wrote, that they had still not forgotten the parliamentary wrangling which had been caused by the Chancellor's wheel tax, his beer tax and his temperance proposals. 'What gave me pain, is not what you *said* but what I discovered you *thought*. . . . I am absolutely sure you meant nothing unkind, nor sarcastic. But sometimes one's feelings will out and a glimpse is given of what is latent in the mind.' After having rubbed Smith's nose in the dirt, Goschen concluded: 'Don't think any more of the incident.'[1]

By mid-July of 1891, however, Smith was so ill that Goschen once again became acting leader. In reviewing the parliamentary session which had concluded on 5 August, Edward Hamilton noted that Balfour had 'improved his position' as a result of the Irish Land Purchase Act which had just been passed. 'Goschen has not recovered from the shock which his Licensing proposals gave last year to his Parliamentary reputation; nor have further experiments in leading the House improved his chances of being Smith's successor.'[2] Smith's battered constitution finally succumbed on 6 October. Salisbury was on vacation in France but immediately wrote to Goschen that he would be back in a few days. Nothing was said about the leadership.[3]

There was growing feeling among both Conservatives and Liberal Unionists that Balfour must succeed Smith. But Goschen

---

[1] Smith Papers, Goschen to Smith, 7 March 1891, PS 16/17.
[2] HP, diary entry for 6 August 1891, Add. Mss 48656.
[3] SP, typed copy, Salisbury to Goschen, 7 October 1891.

harboured a strong feeling that an offer should be made to him. Unfortunately, the situation had changed dramatically since 1886. Goschen was still a Liberal Unionist and, more important, Arthur Balfour had demonstrated his great ability. Even the Liberal Unionist Chief Whip believed that Balfour must succeed Smith.[1] By 14 October, Salisbury was at his 'wit's end to know what emollients to apply to Goschen'.[2] And to Lady Salisbury he wrote: 'There is no help for it, – Arthur must take it. Beach was possible: Goschen is not. But I think it is bad for Arthur – and I do not feel certain how the experiment will end.'[3]

Goschen delivered a speech at Cambridge on 15 October which eased Salisbury's burden, for the Chancellor had acknowledged Balfour's great gifts and indicated that all Unionists would be prepared to serve under him if he were tapped for the leadership. But Goschen still entertained a slim hope that the mantle would fall on his shoulders. The Prime Minister now wrote to Goschen 'as tenderly' as he could in order to soothe the hurt pride of a man who had first entered a Cabinet twenty years before Balfour.[4] Goschen had, Salisbury acknowledged, 'all the qualities required for a House of Commons leader at this juncture, *except one*: that you are not a member of the political party which furnishes much the largest portion of the Unionist phalanx'.[5] Two days later Goschen replied that he understood why Salisbury had been 'compelled' to choose Balfour. He had felt 'during the last Session especially when I was acting for Smith that there was a growing uneasiness on the part of the Conservatives, lest I should be drifting into the leadership'.[6]

In an attempt to mollify him, Goschen was offered the 'Wardenship of the Cinque Ports' since it too had been held by Smith, but he promptly declined.[7] The new Leader also did his best to

---

[1] Chilston, *Chief Whip*, p. 221.
[2] BP, Salisbury to Balfour, 14 October 1891, Add. Mss 49689, ff. 137–8.
[3] Cecil, *Life of Salisbury*, vol. 4, p. 219, 14 October 1891.
[4] BP, Salisbury to Balfour, 18 October 1891, Add. Mss 49689, ff. 145–6.
[5] Elliot, vol. 2, pp. 186–8, Salisbury to Goschen, 17 October 1891.
[6] SP, Goschen to Salisbury, 19 October 1891. See also Austin, *Autobiography*, vol. 2, p. 254, Goschen to Austin, 17 October 1891.
[7] SP, Goschen to Salisbury, 22 October 1891, private. Walmer Castle in Kent was the official residence of the Lord Warden. After Goschen's refusal Lord Dufferin accepted the post.

ease Goschen's distress when he replied to the older man's letter of congratulation. Balfour only hoped that he might 'render half the services that you have done to the *Conservative* party!'[1] Goschen contained his anger and annoyance fairly well but he eventually unburdened his 'resentment' to Milner. His former private secretary had been Director-General of Accounts in Egypt since 1889.

I knew you would be greatly interested about the leadership business. Buckle told me you had once told him that you thought I should not consent to serve under Balfour, but that if he were made leader, I should retire, in good humour enough, but pleading that I had been an emergency man, that the emergency was passed as they now had a man of their own etc., etc. Buckle was immensely relieved when I told him the day before he pronounced for Balfour that I should not object to serve under him. . . Akers-Douglas and others have sworn by all their gods, that it was the fact of my not being a Carlton man, a real Conservative, which made a large portion of the party go strongly for Balfour and the friendly Conservative press took that line. But I never believed that that was the real reason.

The real reason was that 'Balfour had impressed the popular imagination.' Goschen 'did not want to be a leader with a luke-warm following, an opposition more personally hostile to me than to anyone else except perhaps Chamberlain, and in a moribund Parliament... The week or 10 days of public discussion as to our comparative merits was a most trying time and I was glad when at Cambridge I found the means of ending it at once.'[2] Milner answered Goschen in a very realistic vein. In his 'inmost heart', he had hoped Goschen would be selected. But he could understand that the Conservatives wanted '*their own man*'. It was, Milner concluded, 'just bad luck' for Goschen.[3]

Until 1890, it would have been almost impossible for Salisbury to have given the leadership to Balfour. If Smith had stepped down the only alternative to Goschen would have been Hicks Beach. And considering the revulsion which the vast majority of Conservatives had for a Liberal Unionist as their Leader, this might very well have been the solution. 'Black Michael's' health

[1] Elliot, vol. 2, pp. 188–9.
[2] MP, Goschen to Milner, 8 January 1892, Box 188.
[3] *Ibid.*, Milner to Goschen, 14 January 1892, Box 182.

improved after he left the Irish Office in early 1887 and in February 1888 he was appointed President of the Board of Trade. If Salisbury had attempted to by-pass Goschen for Balfour at any time prior to the temperance fiasco of 1890, the Chancellor of the Exchequer might well have resigned. The passage of the Irish Land Purchase Act just before Smith's death greatly increased Balfour's stature. And W. H. Smith had virtually given his life to keep Goschen out of the leadership. In 1911, just after Arthur Balfour resigned as Conservative leader, Sydney Buxton told Arthur Elliot that his physician had also treated W. H. Smith. The physician informed Buxton 'that in 1891 he had told W. H. Smith to retire as he had a dangerous if not incurable sickness. But W. H. Smith said he could not resign, as if he did, then Goschen would become leader. In another 6 months it would be Balfour which he earnestly desired.'[1]

---

[1] Elliot Papers; this is written in Arthur Elliot's personal copy of the *Life of George Joachim Goschen*, vol. 2, pp. 188–9.

CHAPTER 10

IMPERIALISM, IRELAND AND PERSONAL FINANCE

Sir Evelyn Baring, now the virtual ruler of Egypt though technically only British consul-general, had been delighted at Goschen's appointment as Chancellor of the Exchequer 'both on general grounds and because of your knowledge of Egyptian affairs'.[1] Goschen did not like the idea that both Egypt and the Suez Canal should be neutralized and internationalized if this meant that Britain would lose the dominant position she had gained by force of arms in 1882. He did not want Britain to be further tied by agreements with the continental powers if this meant that the problems which plagued international control of Egypt's finances were to be extended into other areas. On the other hand, as Chancellor of the Exchequer and a Gladstonian in finance, he did not wish to see huge sums of British money poured into Egypt.

Both Goschen and Baring agreed that the evacuation of Egypt could take place at some indefinite time in the future. But this would not be possible until the Egyptian economy had been improved, her debts paid off, and political stability permanently established. They agreed that the reconquest of the Sudan must be deferred as the cost would be much too high at that time. Their main point of difference was that Goschen wanted economies to satisfy the British Parliament and taxpayers while Baring requested additional funds for a variety of plans designed to help the Egyptians and to improve the British position in Egypt.

When Goschen arrived at the Exchequer, Sir Henry Drummond Wolff was in the process of bringing negotiations with the Turks and the Egyptians to a close. While it appears that Salisbury had little hope that the talks would succeed, they demonstrated to Europe, and especially to France, that Britain did not plan to

[1] CrP, Baring to Goschen, 7 February 1887, F.O. 633/5.

establish a permanent presence in Egypt. The Foreign Office made its attitude clear in a memorandum entitled, 'Suggestions for the Neutralization of Egypt under English Guardianship', which was presented to the Cabinet in early February 1887.[1] The title of the memorandum suggested that the problem was insoluble. For France would never accept a 'neutralization' under 'English Guardianship'. Goschen was not particularly sorry when the negotiations finally collapsed. In December 1886 he had admitted to Salisbury that the Egyptian 'difficulties are so immense that I would certainly not raise any unnecessary objections to any course leading to some kind of solution, but it costs me an effort to swallow neutralization'.[2] Britain never again paid any attention to Turkey's wishes with regard to Egypt even though Egypt would bedevil Anglo-French relations until 1904.

Even though he was not always able to get the sums of money he requested, Baring regarded 1887 as a turning point in Egyptian history and by December 1889 he was able to report 'real progress'.[3] Goschen received very favourable reports on Baring's activities from Milner once his former private secretary had taken up his new post. At the end of his first year in Egypt, Milner contentedly informed Goschen that England was 'doing some of her best work in the Valley of the Nile'. He was convinced that 'jingoism' was serving the cause of humanity.[4] Goschen recognized the fluid nature of the occupation when he objected to Salisbury's wish in May 1890 that the Bank of England inscribe a new Egyptian stock. The Rothschilds had been pushing this proposal very hard because it would 'make the public more confident'. Goschen pointed out that the value of Egyptian stock would decline rapidly if the British troops left. 'But though we may theorize as to a perpetual occupation I doubt its perpetuity. We shall not be perpetually in office.'[5]

The metamorphosis of Joseph Chamberlain continued at a striking pace. He visited Egypt during late 1889 and early 1890.

[1] CAB. 37/19/11.
[2] SP, Goschen to Salisbury, [?] December 1886.
[3] CrP, Baring to Goschen, 3 December 1889, F.O. 633/9.
[4] MP, Milner to Goschen, 2 November 1890, Box 182.
[5] SP, Goschen to Salisbury, private, [?] May 1890.

IMPERIALISM, IRELAND, PERSONAL FINANCE

Baring reported to Goschen on 19 January 1890 that Chamberlain saw 'that it is quite impossible for us to leave the country – at all events for a long time to come – as to which he is, without doubt, quite right'.[1] Baring had already sent Goschen an outline of Chamberlain's plans for social, political and economic reforms in Egypt. Goschen sent these ideas on to Salisbury on 29 January 1890 but without any enthusiasm. 'The enclosed from Baring will amuse and not bother you. Just like Chamberlain. Very large in his ideas.'[2] Goschen replied to Baring on 7 March 1890 with words of caution about over-extending and over-complicating British foreign policy commitments.

> But if the Government is loathe to abandon the idea of ultimate evacuation, it would, I think, be not so much on the ground that Egypt ought then to be left to herself, as on the ground that our occupation of the country would be a great military weakness to us in time of war. . . The Radicals, who never believe in international complications, and can look upon the matter from the philanthropic and social point of view, might under such circumstances, be more easily persuaded to abandon the idea of an evacuation than we.

Much had been done to improve the conditions of life in Egypt but it was unlikely that Chamberlain's grandiose dreams would ever be approved. The cost was much too great and the French would be outraged.[3]

As one of the senior members of the Cabinet, Goschen maintained a vigorous watch over Britain's foreign relations. Determined that Britain must be strong, powerful and respected, he was equally determined as protector of the public purse that all money spent must be put to proper use. No waste would be tolerated. Goschen generally supported Salisbury's foreign policy which he contrasted favourably to that of Gladstone; he had always advocated that Britain must pursue policies commensurate with her power in world affairs.

By the end of 1887, Salisbury had concluded an agreement with Austria and Italy to maintain the *status quo* in the Mediterranean. Aimed against France and Russia, the treaty had the hearty approval of the German Chancellor. Salisbury provided Goschen with the details of his German negotiations on 18 November

[1] CrP, private, F.O. 633/5.   [2] SP.   [3] CrP, F.O. 633/9.

1887. Goschen admitted he was 'perturbed about this Austro-Italian business, but not to the point of wishing to thwart' the Prime Minister's strong view, and 'the view of all or nearly all our colleagues'. Salisbury's arguments had been good and Goschen could see 'the dangers of the situation if we *do not* go forward'.[1]

There were a number of wrinkles which had to be ironed out with the Germans in Zanzibar and on the East Coast of Africa. An Arab rebellion in the German part of the coast of East Africa finally led to Britain joining a blockade which contained the rising as well as attempting to decrease further the slave-trade. Goschen found Salisbury's decision to join the blockade 'a very grave one'. There was no doubt that the Germans were in 'a frightful mess'.

> Is it not a fact that the German insolence with native races constitutes a very serious difficulty? Look at Samoa! I feel as if they had behaved disgracefully there. And would not the proposed partnership unless most carefully guarded expose *us* to some of the evil results of the German method of action? And have we not some evidence that there is a much better feeling towards us than there is toward the Germans on the Coast? Is it wise to sacrifice that feeling unless for some very potent advantage?[2]

Salisbury finally managed to convince the Cabinet that British participation would make it possible for them to influence German activity in a moderate direction.

A partial end to German-British bad feeling over parts of Africa was arranged in 1890. Britain agreed to give up the strategic North Sea Island of Heligoland in return for German recognition of British claims to East Africa and Zanzibar. There was some opposition in Britain and some regret that British territory was being ceded to another power. The queen also had a number of reservations. In order to soothe a somewhat aroused public opinion, Goschen urged Salisbury to amend his explanation of the deal 'so as to explain more fully to the common herd that we shall have exclusive power, and that all the foreign relations would be in our hands'.[3]

[1] SP, typed copy, Salisbury to Goschen, 18 November 1887 and Goschen to Salisbury, 20 November 1887.
[2] *Ibid.*, Goschen to Salisbury, 10 October 1888.
[3] *Ibid.*, Goschen to Salisbury, 16 June 1890.

Goschen never lost sight of Britain's paramount interest in the southern tip of Africa. A suggestion that the Cape Colony might be drifting into the orbit of the Transvaal led Goschen to write: 'I presume that the Cape Colony is unlike other colonies in this respect, that being indispensable to us, as the chief station on the road to the East we should not let the Colony go, if the Colonists desired to be independent.' Recognizing the potential danger in the Transvaal, Goschen concluded: 'I don't like the idea of giving the Boers access to the sea.'[1]

While Goschen advocated 'sensible' expansion and consolidation, he was not an advocate of expansion for its own sake. He did his best to deny, limit or modify assistance to missionaries, traders and adventurers in tropical Africa where the potential rewards seemed small. As Chancellor of the Exchequer he was always hesitant about employing public funds for the assistance of the chartered companies which were carving out their small empires in Africa. And he never forgot the doctrine of 'consolidation' which he and Milner had worked out. It led Goschen to worry about over-extension and the excessive commitments which might result.

In the spring of 1890, Goschen was 'rather disturbed' about the situation in East Africa where William Mackinnon's chartered company was engaged in conflict with the Germans.[2] And a year later it was Cecil Rhodes' British South Africa Company which was quarrelling with the Portuguese along the Zambesi River. On 31 March 1891 Goschen complained to Smith that he was 'uneasy about Portugal and all the more because I know so little'. It was essential that the Cabinet obtain more information from Salisbury. Goschen had heard that elements from Portugal's regular army were involved in addition to the volunteers. It appeared that 'the Chartered Police are very anxious for a brush with the Portuguese, and believe they can drive them into the sea'. Suppose, however, 'the mounted police were shot down . . . by Portuguese regulars'.

I think Salisbury contemplates fighting them as a possibility if the Portuguese are stubborn. Possibly he thinks he may leave it to the Company to

---

[1] *Ibid.*, Goschen to Salisbury, [?] December 1889.
[2] *Ibid.*, Goschen to Salisbury, 4 April 1890.

fight it out, but if they are beaten, we may be in for something big there before we know it. . .

As you know, I am uneasy altogether as to this Chartered Warlike Company.[1]

Salisbury was 'puzzled' by Goschen's complaint as Portuguese despatches had not been treated differently from any others. But he promptly provided Goschen with all the material he had requested.[2] The Prime Minister informed the queen on 4 April 1891 that the Cabinet had decided to prevent the Boers moving north into Mashonaland. 'The Portuguese are behaving very badly and it will probably be necessary to send some gunboats to protect British rights on the Portuguese African coast.'[3] Fortunately, within the next six weeks, Salisbury arranged an acceptable compromise with the Portuguese.[4]

The British East Africa Company was still bogged down in its attempt to construct a railway from Mombassa to Uganda. By late August 1891 it seemed to Goschen that the company was in a 'crisis' situation and he unburdened himself to the Prime Minister. The government had considered providing £20,000 for the railway survey while the company would make up the difference. It was imperative that the company recognize that it must be prepared to pay 'whatever it may be to *ensure the safety* of the survey expedition'. No further concessions should be made to the company unless new negotiations took place.[5]

Salisbury's reply included a solid blow at the tradition of 'Treasury control' which often irritated the Prime Minister. He suggested that Lugard, leader of the withdrawal operation in Uganda, should be placed in command of the survey expedition and provided with £25,000. If he exceeded that sum there would be no more money forthcoming. Once Goschen had obtained the funds from Parliament, the Treasury should 'make no conditions' and should only challenge 'obviously unreasonable' expenditure.

[1] Smith Papers, Goschen to Smith, 31 March 1891, PS 16/32.
[2] *Ibid.*, Salisbury to Smith, 6 April 1891, PS 16/37.
[3] CAB. 41/22/4.
[4] Cecil, *Life of Salisbury*, vol. 4, p. 275, Salisbury to Lord Harrowby, 15 May 1891.
[5] SP, Goschen to Salisbury, 26 August 1891.

In this case I have a great dread of the wisdom of Downing Street. It is rough Colonist's work – to be done by trusting well-chosen men – who will do the job as best they can – by hardihood, resource, and a quick eye – but often with irregularities in detail, against which you cannot guard without embarrassing them.[1]

On 15 September 1891, after reviewing the East Africa papers, Goschen commented that, 'The combination of philanthropy and finance creates a peculiar situation. We cannot contemplate the simple subsidizing of a commercial company.' Three days later Goschen complained that the 'Scotch Missionary party will move Heaven and earth to get us to subsidize not only the railway but the Company.' There seemed to be an attempt – joined by *The Scotsman* – to prove that 'the *Government*' was 'responsible for the retreat from Uganda'. It was essential that the government find out 'the precise financial position of the Company. What money they have still uncalled, if any, what prospects of a dividend, what assets, etc? They clamoured for territory, they were insatiable and now they retire.' But he did see a clever, partial cover for Lugard's retreat. Why not call it 'a temporary absence for the purpose of bringing up the survey party'. It was a pity there was so 'little resource or cleverness on the part of the East Africa Directors'. Goschen expressed his deep repugnance for expansion into areas which looked unlikely to attract private investment and which might end up as the responsibility of the British government when he exclaimed: 'It seems to me, if we are not extremely careful, that three administrations in the interior of Africa may be forced on us. Uganda, Johnston's empire in Nyasaland and Mashonaland.[2] The Prime Minister agreed that the East Africa Company was 'a very unsatisfactory company. It has many "illustrious" on its Board: but not many men of business. If you can get hold of Mackinnon and Mackenzie together you have the board; otherwise they will slip through your fingers.' It seemed to Salisbury that 'the only thing to be done is to let the survey go forward: reserving all decisions upon its results to a future time'.[3]

[1] *Ibid.*, typed copy, Salisbury to Goschen, 29 August 1891.
[2] *Ibid.*, Goschen to Salisbury, 15, 18 and 19 September 1891.
[3] *Ibid.*, typed copy, Salisbury to Goschen, 29 September 1891.

But once again, despite reservations, doubts and hesitations, the British government continued to move forward in Africa. The survey was completed in Uganda just before the Liberals returned to office in 1892. Lord Rosebery, Gladstone's Foreign Secretary, represented the imperialist wing of the Liberal party and there was no evacuation from either Uganda or Egypt. The two had become linked as a result of Cecil Rhodes' obsession for colouring the Cape-to-Cairo route red and because the strategical importance of Uganda in controlling the water of the Nile valley had been recognized.

In April 1892, Goschen met Cecil Rhodes at a dinner. He quickly advised Salisbury that the dynamic diamond king and Premier of Cape Colony was 'full of the idea that the *Cape Government* should approach Portugal with reference to buying Delagoa Bay, or leasing it if that would save the *amour propre* of the Portuguese'. Rhodes was worried that the gold-rich Transvaal might try to purchase the bay. Goschen told Rhodes that Salisbury believed the time was not opportune to approach the Portuguese and 'that possibly bankruptcy might be better for the dynasty, and order, than an alienation of Colonies'. While praising Salisbury, Rhodes wondered if it was 'not possible that the Portuguese Government might not object to be approached by the Cape Government though they would not treat with a great power. Would you *object* to their feeling their way?' Salisbury commented that he had, 'No Objection' to Rhodes' scheme.[1]

There were times when Salisbury worried about the economies demanded by his Chancellor of the Exchequer. Goschen recognized the Prime Minister's dislike for 'Treasury control' and pointed out that he did not enjoy vetoing his colleagues' demands for additional funds. Salisbury was not convinced and mentioned several specific cases – Scottish Office, consular service – to illustrate his view that the 'Treasury mind' as created by the permanent officials was often a cause of inefficiency in the working of the governmental machine.

[1] *Ibid.*, Goschen to Salisbury, 13 April 1892.

But, briefly, I believe that in public, as in private affairs, parsimony is a symptom of mismanagement. . . . This is the fault I find with the traditional Treasury system. They do not interpose their veto at the beginning of a policy, when they might prevent it, but at the tail of the policy, when they can only spoil it.[1]

Lord Randolph Churchill's departure from the Cabinet had meant the loss of a bright, clever politician interested in constructive legislation. His resignation signified that reforms would be conceded more grudgingly and with greater safeguards to protect vested interests. But the arrival of Goschen signalled a more harmonious Cabinet now that the gadfly was gone. Salisbury was not a domineering Prime Minister. Wishing to be left alone to guide foreign policy, he was usually delighted to grant considerable autonomy to his subordinates. But in the summer of 1890, Salisbury was angry with the members of the Cabinet from the Commons. Lack of time led them to abandon some major items of legislation despite Salisbury's objections.[2] With a massive majority behind him in the Lords the Prime Minister sometimes forgot the more heated atmosphere of the House of Commons and the necessity to concede something here in order to gain something there. The Cabinet had favoured a certain procedure in the handling of the Irish Land Bill and the Education Bill in 1891. When Goschen agreed to a modification on the floor of the Commons in an exchange with the Liberals, Salisbury complained that it was 'hardly fair' to the rest of the Cabinet.[3] But such discord seems to have been rare and when Salisbury wrote to Lord George Hamilton a few days after the Cabinet resigned in 1892, he agreed with the former First Lord of the Admiralty that 'the agreement and solidarity of our Cabinet have been quite remarkable – ever since Randolph left us'. It was their good fortune to have had 'a very "straight" set of men: so that intrigue in the Cabinet was unknown'.[4]

[1] *Ibid.*, Goschen to Salisbury, 26 May 1888 and typed copy, Salisbury to Goschen, 27 May 1888.
[2] Salisbury to Queen Victoria, 5 July 1890, CAB. 41/21/45.
[3] SP, Goschen to Salisbury, 4 June [1891], and typed copy, Goschen to Salisbury, 7 June 1891.
[4] *Ibid.*, typed copy, Salisbury to Hamilton, 16 August 1892.

In order to maintain his alliance with the Liberal Unionists, strong supporters of Free Trade, Salisbury found it necessary to criticize the National Union of Conservative Associations for endorsing Fair Trade – a return to protective tariffs – in November 1887. Salisbury was not, however, as completely pure in this matter as Goschen since he was prepared to employ retaliatory tariffs. Goschen could not agree and replied that most Free Traders would argue that retaliation 'hurts' the nation which employs it. While the critics of Free Trade were becoming more active, the great majority of the nation still identified Free Trade with prosperity and low food prices.[1]

As the only Liberal Unionist in the Cabinet, Goschen provided a link between the two branches of Unionism. He told Salisbury that the Scottish Liberal Unionists were unhappy about patronage but he added that this was not a complaint on his part and stressed his own view about appointments: 'A propos of your general argument I should never press you for a proportionate share of appointments to be given to Liberal Unionists. It would depend upon how many *fit men* they had among their numbers. And, too, where a man is specially fitted for a post.'[2] While guarding the interests of the Liberal Unionists, Goschen had only the loosest of connections with the wing of Liberal Unionism which was most likely to give trouble – the small Radical section led by Chamberlain. Goschen's position was made even more difficult when Chamberlain succeeded Hartington as Liberal Unionist leader in the Commons in early 1892.

In 1887 no one could have been certain that the Liberal split was permanent. The queen was concerned about the Round Table Conference which aimed at Liberal reunification. Goschen allayed her fears when he wrote that he did not believe the actions of Chamberlain and Trevelyan would affect the great bulk of the Liberal Unionists.[3] The queen continued to press Goschen for news of Chamberlain's 'views and doings'. She had found Hartington 'very gloomy the other day' as 'he feared a

[1] SP, typed copy, Salisbury to Goschen, 18 November 1887 and Goschen to Salisbury, 20 November 1887.
[2] *Ibid.*, Goschen to Salisbury, 20 October 1888.
[3] Goschen to Queen Victoria, 3 February 1887, RA C38/150.

deadlock in Ireland'. Hartington had told her he would continue
to support Salisbury and the present government 'as long as they
kept out Mr Gladstone and Home Rule and this *must be done*.
Goschen had done a fine job in keeping Hartington 'up to the
mark' and she hoped he would 'be able to *keep* him *right* and
straight now. And three days later, the queen wrote that Hartington was 'not a very *strong* man and requires *constant* keeping
up'.[1]

Arthur Balfour made his reputation as Chief Secretary for
Ireland but in 1887 he was only just beginning to show the
parliamentary skill which eventually brought him the grudging
praise of even the Irish Nationalists. Much of the sharp give-and
take of parliamentary debate was left to Goschen as he far excelled
Smith and the other members of the government front bench
until Balfour had proved himself. There were often fierce exchanges between Goschen and the Liberals though they paled in
comparison with the hatred hurled at Chamberlain by Gladstonians and Irish Nationalists. On 4 July 1887, Goschen's old friend,
Sir William Harcourt, now one of Gladstone's chief lieutenants,
roared at Goschen: 'You have gone from this bench as a deserter
and we will take care you don't return to it as a spy.' In the
following year, Harcourt was indignant when Goschen referred
to him as a 'soldier of fortune'.[2]

The extensive use of the 'guillotine' had so limited parliamentary obstruction that a new Coercion Bill for Ireland became
law in July 1887. This was to be the cornerstone of the Cabinet's
commitment to ensure that the law was obeyed. But it was
recognized that strong government must be just and fair and
while no Conservative regime could ever forget the landlords, the
brutal facts of an oppressed Irish peasantry cried out for a solution.
Not even a Conservative government had any use for such
reactionary absentee landlords as Lord Clanricarde. The Liberal
Unionists were still sufficiently liberal to be hostile to coercion
unlesss it was linked to conciliation, and Chamberlain of course
still wished to go far beyond conciliation and into that hazy land

[1] Queen Victoria to Goschen, 7 and 10 March 1887, RA B66/47 and RA B66/48.
[2] Gardiner, *Sir William Harcourt*, vol. 2, pp. 45, 61–3.

of federalism on the lines of the Canadian model – which, however, he insisted was not Home Rule as conceived by Gladstone and Parnell.

Balfour's Coercion Bill was coupled with a Land Bill designed to aid distressed tenants in Ireland and its final provisions caused alarm in the Tory right wing. The Cabinet's decision to tamper with judicial rents led Lord Cranbrook to protest.[1] Salisbury's need to pacify his Tory followers was made more difficult by Chamberlain's need to demonstrate that he was forcing a Conservative cabinet to adopt radical policies. On 15 April 1887, Salisbury had written to Hicks Beach that the Irish landlords were 'crying out lustily'. He was 'sorry to see that Chamberlain is praising us'.[2]

Goschen bombarded Balfour with suggestions about Ireland. As Chancellor of the Exchequer, he was not always happy about the attitude of the Irish landlords. Lord Lansdowne, now Viceroy of India, had failed to pay taxes on the extensive estates he owned in Ireland. The Irish landlords argued that they could not pay their taxes because their tenants were paying rent to Parnell's emissaries under the plan of campaign. Goschen wrote to Balfour on 25 January 1889 that he had 'been in daily terror lest the Irish Party should bring up the question of landlord arrears'. It was essential that the arrears be reduced. Lansdowne's position was 'exceptional' and he 'should be made to pay up'.[3]

Balfour agreed that the arrears must be reduced but the plan of campaign and other Irish tactics made it difficult for the landlords to collect their rent. 'Indulgence' would certainly be required in some cases.[4] Before the arrival of Balfour's letter, Goschen wrote again on this topic. 'Think of the case of individuals: if they have Lansdowne or other men of that kind up, and show what they would call culpable leniency on our part while we are strict with poor defaulting tenants.'[5] Balfour still urged indulgence since

[1] Alfred E. Gathorne-Hardy (ed.), *The Diary and Correspondence of the First Earl of Cranbrook* (London, 1910), vol. 2, p. 285, diary entry for 20 July 1887.
[2] St Aldwyn Papers, Salisbury to Hicks Beach, 15 April 1887, PCC/69.
[3] BP, Goschen to Balfour, 25 January 1889, Add. Mss 49706, ff. 30–4.
[4] Goschen Papers, copy Balfour to Goschen, 29 January 1889, Dep. C, 183, f. 21.
[5] BP, 29–30 January 1889, Add. Mss 49706, ff. 22–9.

the landlords were unable to collect their rents because of 'something very like default on the part of the Government'.[1]

The Cabinet had cause for alarm in 1889. By-election results had been going against the government and little of a constructive nature had been introduced for Ireland. Parnell was vindicated before a commission set up to investigate accusations brought against him in *The Times*: they turned out to be based upon a forgery. The public felt that he had been badly treated. It seemed as though the tide had turned and that Gladstone might win a large majority at the next election. Then came the O'Shea divorce case in 1890 and Parnell's refusal to step down as leader of the Irish Nationalists. Goschen wrote in his diary that, 'The Gladstonians began by saying that character had nothing to do with politics, but the Dissenters soon made a tremendous fuss.'[2] Parnell's brilliantly organized party broke in two and Parnell died the following year. The Cabinet could now face the prospect of an election during which the Irish would be quarrelling among themselves. Writing just after the Irish Party tore itself to pieces Edward Hamilton reflected:

In the present uncertain circumstances, one thing is pretty clear and that is, that if Home Rule has to be laid on one side not a single Liberal Unionist will return to the Gladstonian fold – which if it comes about will be pretty clear proof that it was not Home Rule that really determined them to break away from the Liberal party; but they had used it as a plank on which to beat a retreat from radicalism in the air.[3]

In 1891 Balfour's ambitious Irish Land Purchase Bill finally became law though it turned out to be less effective in buying out the landlords and in creating independent Irish farmers than the Chief Secretary had hoped. It was much too complicated and contained far too many safeguards designed to protect the landlord. Balfour's abortive Irish Local Government Bill of 1892 was characterized once again by safeguards rather than generosity and

[1] Goschen Papers, copy, Balfour to Goschen, 31 January 1889, Dep. C. 183, f. 21. For Goschen's 'Memorandum on the Claims of Irish Landlords for Relief in respect of Public Charges on their Estates' of 26 February 1889, see CAB. 37/23/6.
[2] Elliot, vol. 2, pp. 176–7.
[3] HP, diary entry for 1 December 1890, Add. Mss 48654.

it deviated in numerous retrogressive ways from the Local Government Act of 1888 which had been passed for England and Wales. The Congested Districts Board which was set up under the provisions of the Land Act of 1891 was, however, a sensible and intelligent attempt to improve and to diversify the Irish economy.

The unemployed, radical and Irish protest meetings in Trafalgar Square in 1887 aroused Goschen's ire and he pressed for a firmer policy. On 21 October 1887 he wondered why Henry Matthews, the Home Secretary, and Sir Charles Warren, Chief Commissioner of Police, were not taking more effective action. He admitted that the London meetings had been 'well-managed' but they seemed 'not to come to an end and the London public will become extremely vexed at the continual interruption both of business and of free movement'. The government should show more of an interest in what was happening. Some of the speeches had 'been so incendiary that the leaders and speakers, notwithstanding previous failures, should have been arrested'. Goschen admitted to the Prime Minister that there was 'no danger of any kind'. But he doubted 'whether we as a Government ought not to show ourselves alive to the fact that a large portion of the Metropolis is suffering grievous annoyance and sometimes alarm'.[1]

Salisbury agreed with Goschen and urged the Home Secretary to prosecute 'all speakers who incited to any breach of the law. I also told him I thought it would be necessary to rail in Trafalgar Square – with gates of course which should be ordinarily left open. But on consideration I thought it better to reserve the order for this for a Cabinet.'[2] The Cabinet's decision to close Trafalgar Square to public meetings in early November led directly to Bloody Sunday (13 November) and many cracked skulls. Economic recovery and a decrease in unemployment helped to bring the radical agitation under control.

Goschen wished to show that he still had liberal convictions and that he was not unaware of what were called 'social problems'.

---

[1] SP, Goschen to Salisbury, 21 October 1887.
[2] *Ibid.*, typed copy, Salisbury to Goschen, 24 October 1887.

In 1889 he was intensely annoyed and 'did not think it quite wise or fair for Beach to tell a big audience that I found the Cabinet too democratic'.[1] Two years later he urged Salisbury to add the following phrase to the queen's speech: 'and the measures dealing with the laws relating to Factories and Workshops, Savings Banks, and Public Health will, I hope, promote the comfort and well-being of my people'.[2]

In 1888 Goschen had been required to find funds for the county councils and the London County Council which were to be set up under the terms of the Local Government Act of that year. After the Third Reform Act of 1884 which had extended household suffrage to the counties, it was impossible not to reform local government in these areas. The Cabinet was being urged to go forward slowly by the Tory squires while Chamberlain was pushing for a democratic measure. It was finally decided that the control which the landowners had exercised in the counties through the Justices of the Peace must be reduced. The Local Government Act of 1888, although more democratic, was not as ambitious in some areas as the one prepared by Goschen in 1871 and the parishes were not granted self-government until the Parish Councils Act of 1894. Goschen and the Conservatives were careful to see that the Poor Law was kept out of the hands of these new democratic bodies whose powers were narrowly circumscribed and whose right to levy taxes was severely limited.

Joseph Chamberlain had been encouraging the Salisbury Cabinet to bring in a new Employers Liability Bill which would end the practice of permitting employers to 'contract out'. Sir John Eldon Gorst, now Financial Secretary to the Treasury, prepared a memorandum advocating an Employers Liability Bill along the lines suggested by Chamberlain. Salisbury stated his objections to Gorst's scheme in a letter to Goschen on 25 March 1892 which Goschen sent on to Balfour.

Treating this purely as a question of electoral architecture – I think you would lose more by the wrath of the employers than you would gain by the gratitude of the men. If both of those two parties were from the outset in

[1] *Ibid.*, Goschen to Salisbury, [?] November 1889.
[2] *Ibid.*, Goschen to Salisbury, 28 November [1891],

an impartial frame of mind towards us – the favour of the workmen might be the best investment of the two. But the favour of the employers if we do not adopt Gorst's suggestion is much more to be counted on than the favour of the men if we do. Gorst's proposed investment would therefore be rash.

I speak as an opportunist.[1]

Two months before, Salisbury had indicated that he had 'no objection to Gorst's scheme', so it would appear that the forthcoming election had convinced him that this was not the moment to go forward.[2]

The Liberals, having lost so many of their aristocratic and upper-middle-class supporters, now turned to the lower classes and the Celtic fringe in their search for votes. The Newcastle programme of October 1891 called for Irish Home Rule and church disestablishment in Wales. It was hoped that a pledge to reform the land laws would win the agricultural labourers while the trade unionists were promised an Employers Liability Bill. Hazy promises were also made about minimum hours for workers and payment for members of the House of Commons. This programme attracted many votes but it also antagonized a good portion of the middle class.

The Chancellor of the Exchequer scorned proposals of this nature. Prosperity, a better life and a higher standard of living were already characteristics of an increased number of Englishmen every year. He denounced proposals for state intervention when he spoke to the Statistical Society on 6 December 1887. Fifteen years later he felt that his position was still valid. There were those who demanded 'the artificial reconstruction of society on a Socialistic basis'. They did not see that Britain's wealth was becoming more equitably distributed each year.

No violent specifics have been applied to produce it. The steady working of economic laws, under a system of commercial and industrial reform, is bringing about the result I have described. We see it most clearly in the case of the middle class. We see it clearly, though not quite so clearly, in the aristocracy of the working-class. The influence is permeating society downwards. May we not hope – nay, confidently reckon – that that progress will continue, and will ultimately affect even that vast mass of the labouring

[1] BP, Salisbury to Goschen, 25 March 1892, Add. Mss 49706, ff. 124–9.
[2] Ibid., Salisbury to Balfour, 24 January 1892, Add. Mss 49690.

population whom, it may be admitted, it has not yet reached, and who, if their position has somewhat improved, as it certainly has, have been benefited not by obtaining a share in accumulated wealth, but by the greater cheapness of what they buy with their wages. And the best of this automatic Socialism is that it appears to operate even in a time of depression. Despite the complaint of absence of profit and of bad times generally, despite want of work and the irregularity in the employment even of those who have work, the great central body of society is strengthening its economic position.[1]

In 1893 Goschen delivered the presidential address to the British Economic Association and he ridiculed the 'popular fallacy that in the affairs of actual social life, social emotionalism is altruistic and Political Economy the reverse'. It was true that public opinion would no longer accept the doctrines of political economy which had seemed impregnable in 1850 since the public did not 'understand analysis and hypothesis' and rejected the idea of 'economic man'. But it was not true that political economy or the 'science of Wealth' neglected either 'the moral habits of a people' or 'the development of its intelligence'. The main problem now was neither the 'sentimentalist' nor the 'philanthropist' but the 'emotionalist'. The work of the economist had produced the Poor Law which had arrested

demoralization and the weakening of self-dependence. The ultimate result of the uncalculated generosity of the emotionalist may be infinitely more disastrous than the evil which in his generosity he tries to cure. . . If tender treatment of an individual pauper, and if an administration of the Poor-Law, founded on ethical consideration alone, should diminish the efforts of self-help, a whole class may suffer ultimately from action taken towards individuals. . . It is called hard, but it is wise, and it serves the general interest.[2]

Nor did Goschen see anything wrong with the competitive economic system in Britain. When queried about the 'alarming growth' of monopolies and asked to set up a committee to investigate, he replied that competition in Britain was 'so great'

---

[1] Goschen, 'The Increase of Moderate Incomes', *Essays and Addresses*, pp. 217–81.
[2] 'Ethics and Economics', *ibid.*, pp. 328–41. He admitted that trade unions ('an ethical revolt against unrestricted competition') might become excessive in their demands but 'economic doctrine does not necessarily condemn this movement'.

that he did not believe it was 'possible for any length of time to control the markets'. He was sure 'that the attempt to do so would meet with the failure which it would certainly deserve'.[1]

The Chancellor of the Exchequer was also worried about his own financial condition. On 2 February 1890 he wrote to his brother Charles – the head of Fruhling and Goschen – in order to discover the exact sources of his income. 'I must go over my investments with you. They are certainly tremendously sub-divided. I cannot understand half their names but they seem to me very South Americanish.' He concluded that he had about £90,000 invested in Fruhling and Goschen and about £46,000 elsewhere. After making some additions and subtractions, it appeared that he had about £115,000 of interest-producing capital. Adding up the approximate returns, he thought they would produce £6800 a year. This did not include Ambalema, his salary and Lucy's £500 a year. He agreed that Fruhling and Goschen was generous to allow him 6 per cent on his holdings with them and he made about 5 per cent on the other £46,000 – a large part of which was in Alliance Fire. But if the interest went down to a safe 4 per cent, he would only be able to '*safely*' calculate on £5,000 a year. As Chancellor of the Exchequer he received £5,000 a year. During the past three years his total income had averaged between £12,000 and £13,000 while his expenses had been about £10,000. He estimated that his home at Portland Place was worth more than £20,000 while Seacox Heath was valued at £100,000.

Charles Goschen replied two days later with a 'counter statement: which is about what you make it also'. His brother could count on £8,000 a year. If he retained high office for a number of years, Charles thought that George could arrange his budget on the basis of a yearly income of £11,000. Charles listed the Chancellor of the Exchequer's investments which went from Uruguay and Argentina by way of Mexico to Minnesota and the Atcheson and Topeka Railroad. After complex negotiations which lasted through the month of February, it was finally arranged – short of the collapse of the London money market –

---

[1] *Hansard*, CCCLIII (11 May 1891), 491.

that Goschen would have a guaranteed income from his investments and holdings of about £9,000 a year.[1]

It was while he was at the Exchequer that Goschen's eldest daughter, Lucy Maude, married a clergyman whose parish was in Ireland. Lucy Maude was thirty when she married in 1888 and Alice was thirty-two when she left the family in 1900. The two youngest, Beatrice Mary and Fanny Evelyn, never married. Just as William Henry Goschen had worried over the marriage of George Joachim Goschen in the 1850s, so too did George Joachim Goschen become distressed over the marriage plans of his eldest son, young George. He wished to marry the youngest daughter of Lord Cranbrook, Evelyn Gathorne-Hardy, but as George was only in his early twenties and the lady, whom the Goschens liked, was eight years older, it was decided that George should become private secretary to Lord Jersey, the Governor of New South Wales. This would mean an absence of two years (1890–2). New South Wales was to take the place of Ambalema. George turned out to be as faithful as his father had been forty years before. He returned to England after his service in Australia and married Miss Gathorne-Hardy.

One of Goschen's great disappointments was the loss of his private secretary in late 1889. Goschen understood that Milner – now thirty-five years of age – was entitled to move into a post which would provide greater scope for his abilities. Having turned down an offer to become private secretary to the new Viceroy of India, Lord Lansdowne, in 1888, he decided to accept an appointment to the Egyptian civil service late in 1889. R. E. Welby, Permanent Secretary at the Treasury, and Algernon West, Chairman of the Board of Inland Revenue, wanted to find a position for Milner in the British civil service. They had seen evidence of his administrative ability and were unwilling to lose him to a career abroad. An opening at the Board of Inland Revenue in 1889 looked promising but Milner was passed over. West did not think Goschen applied sufficient pressure. The Chancellor had seen, however, that Milner was leaning towards the idea of service in Egypt. Political patronage was also involved.

[1] D. C. Goschen Papers.

W. H. Smith agreed that Milner was a 'clever fellow' but would it be wise 'to give him a post which has generally been bestowed as a reward for great party services'.[1]

West and Welby continued to work for Milner's return to England and when West decided to retire in 1892, he was determined that Milner should succeed him. There were some problems in shouldering aside several other aspirants but by the spring of 1892 they had succeeded. While Milner still preferred foreign service, he did not think it possible to refuse the chairmanship of the Board of Inland Revenue. Goschen speculated on the anticipated general election when he wrote to congratulate Milner.

I wonder how much time I shall have to work with you? Possibly only the month of the election. The Unionists, a very impressionable folk, are in better health than usual just at present, but personally I neither think nor hope that we shall win. What I should like would be that our opponents should come in with a very small majority. I think that would be best for the country. Their policy and their promises ought to be tested.[2]

[1] Chilston Papers, Smith to Akers-Douglas, 17 October 1889, K.A.O. U564 C25/94.
[2] MP, Goschen to Milner, 6 May [1892], Box 188.

CHAPTER 11

THE 'FIFTH WHEEL' RETURNS TO THE ADMIRALTY

In the elections of July 1892 the Liberals were victorious but Gladstone and his Irish allies had a majority of only forty. This was not the decisive margin for which he had yearned. After careful consideration, the Salisbury government decided to meet Parliament before resigning. It was now necessary for Goschen to decide whether to sit in opposition with his Conservative colleagues or with the small band of forty-six Liberal Unionists now under the leadership of Chamberlain. He had little difficulty in reaching a decision. On 8 January 1893 he advised the Duke of Devonshire that he was going to join the Carlton Club. 'As to opinions there is little difference between the Conservatives, and that wing of the Liberal Unionists to which I have belonged, and I am certainly as Conservative in that respect, as a very large portion of the Conservative Party.'[1] Devonshire concurred and noted that Chamberlain would probably 'be more at ease when he knows of your decision'.[2] Salisbury sponsored Goschen and Balfour seconded him for membership of the club.

Goschen took part in the struggle against the second Home Rule Bill with flowery oratory in defence of the Union and searching criticism of the contradictions which he saw in Gladstone's revised scheme for Ireland.[3] Gladstone's tremendous parliamentary skill finally brought the Home Rule Bill through its third reading on 1 September. One week later it was rejected in the House of Lords by a massive vote. Gladstone's defeat on this issue, his opposition to demands for more money for the navy and his age, finally induced him to retire in March 1894. The queen asked Lord Rosebery to become Prime Minister: Sir

---

[1] DP, Chatsworth, 340.2506.
[2] Elliot, vol. 2, p. 197.
[3] *Hansard*, VIII (17 February 1893), 1803–22 and *Hansard*, XI (17 April 1893), 461–84.

William Harcourt never fully adjusted himself to being passed over in favour of the young nobleman.

Harcourt remained Chancellor of the Exchequer and Goschen continued his remorseless analyses of Harcourt's budgets. His first budget annoyed Goschen; his second left Goschen numb and barely able to recover from such revolutionary audacity.[1] In 1889 Goschen had placed a 1 per cent tax on estates valued at more than £10,000 but had refrained from completely remodelling death duties. The feeling had grown that realty must no longer be treated more gently than personalty. Public opinion also insisted on the introduction of a sophisticated system of graduation. Harcourt's civil servants, Edward Hamilton and Alfred Milner, gave him strong support and sound advice. Money was needed to pay for the navy and this was one way to get a good portion of what was required. Harcourt wanted a single tax (replacing current probate and estate duties) on the principal value of all property when the owner died whether it was settled or unsettled, real or personal. In addition to this major job of simplification, Harcourt proposed the first serious system of graduation in British financial history. The tax was to range from 1 per cent for estates between £100 and £500 to 8 per cent for estates exceeding £1 million.

For Goschen, this was a tax which could be forced higher and higher until it might be employed for the socialistic purpose of attempting to redistribute wealth. He denied that his 1 per cent duty of 1889 had anything to do with graduation since it had been 'based on the same principle as the exemption below a certain point in the Income Tax'.

I pay Socialistic literature on the subject, of which there is a good deal, the compliment of reading it; I think it ought to be read; people ought to know and appreciate more than they do the aims of some very capable literary men who are guiding the Socialistic movement. And what is one of the main doctrines by which by peaceful means they think they may secure for a certain portion of the population a greater share of the wealth and property of the nation? It is by means of graduated Death Duties. The Chancellor of

---

[1] *Hansard* (16 April 1894), 469–509. See also Henry W. Lucy, *A Diary of the Home Rule Parliament 1892–1895* (London, 1896), pp. 340–5.

the Exchequer might have quoted the essays of the Fabian Society as express-
ing the views of the economists who are in favour of these measures.

Harcourt was providing machinery for 'a strong form of fiscal
robbery'. By opposing graduated death duties, Goschen knew he
would be criticized for defending the special privileges of capital,
wealth and property but this was not really so.

I am looking at the matter simply from the point of view of national interest.
We cannot realise what would be the condition of the country without large
accumulations of capital in the ordinary forms of business. It would be a
disaster that capital in those forms should be dispersed. . . I protest against
these enormously high duties – and 8 per cent is a very high duty – because
they will frustrate the object aimed at. It is bad finance to set any tax so high
that everybody sets about thinking how to evade it.[1]

When the Finance Bill went into Committee, Goschen urged
Salisbury and Balfour to get the Conservative party prepared for
immediate action since, 'The first clause raises almost every
question' and they were going to find themselves 'in the midst of
controversy at once'.[2] By the time the Finance Bill came up for its
third reading in mid-July, the Conservatives had only succeeded
in wringing minor amendments out of Harcourt. Goschen had
already admitted that the game was lost. Salisbury fought the
new tax with great restraint in the Lords, remembering that the
money was needed for the navy. 'In short, it is unjust,' wrote
Salisbury, 'but it is an injustice which may be excused by the
serious need.'[3] Even Gladstone regretted Harcourt's graduated
death duties which he regarded as very extreme. But none of the
Conservative Chancellors of the Exchequer who followed Harcourt ever considered repealing this excruciatingly effective
instrument for raising additional funds.

Almost twenty-five years after Goschen had attempted to re-
invigorate parish life, H. H. Fowler, president of the Local
Government Board, moved to democratize the parishes. Goschen
was placed in an uncomfortable position for his seemingly radical

---

[1] *Hansard*, xxiv (8 May 1894), 626–45.
[2] BP, Goschen to Salisbury, 15 May 1894, Add. Mss 49690, ff. 86–9.
[3] Salisbury Papers, unpublished and uncompleted manuscript of vol. 5 of Lady
Gwendolen Cecil's biography of Lord Salisbury, pp. 13–16. The manuscript
comes to an end in 1897.

proposals of 1871 had now been made inadequate by the rapid changes which had transformed British life. Fowler proposed to establish parish meetings composed of all ratepayers in the smaller parishes while the larger parishes were to elect councils with all ratepaying inhabitants having the vote. Cumulative voting for the Boards of Guardians was abolished along with *ex-officio* Guardians and the property qualifications for office. Goschen's fears were instantly aroused for he could again see the nightmare which haunted him – the poor controlling the Poor Law.

At the first reading of the bill, Goschen rose to say that it vindicated his own 1871 plans when everyone had said he was foolish to try to revive parish life. But he warned that care must be taken not to give too much power to these new bodies.[1] The titanic struggle over Home Rule delayed the second reading of the Parish Councils Bill for England and Wales until early November. Goschen now began to elaborate upon his reservations to Fowler's comprehensive plan. 'Here is a Bill which goes beyond the Parish Council, which deals to a certain extent with Boards of Guardians, with rating and with other matters on the fringe of the question.' It would be wise to delete the parts of the bill which dealt with the Poor Law as this made the bill too complicated. Excessive complications had been one of the major weaknesses of his own bills in 1871.[2] The lengthy committee stage of the bill enabled Goschen and the Conservatives to introduce numerous amendments designed to limit the scope of the new bodies. He hammered away at the theme that the proposed Poor Law change was an 'immense one'. Goschen also objected to the removal of nominated Guardians. When Fowler interrupted to say that there were only 23 nominated Guardians in London in comparison to 705 who were elected, Goschen retorted that 'the 23 might exercise an extremely good influence in the parishes where they were now'.[3]

Fowler's liberal provisions about female suffrage and female office-holding led Goschen to thunder that he was 'a consistent

[1] *Hansard*, x (21 March 1893), 716–20.
[2] *Ibid.*, xviii (7 November 1893), 430–44.
[3] *Ibid.*, xx (21 December 1893), 139–40.

opponent of female suffrage in any direction. I am thoroughly opposed to it.'[1] The bill finally passed its third reading in the Commons but Goschen and the Conservatives warned that they were not satisfied with the Poor Law provisions and several other areas of the bill. They confidently expected these differences to be modified to their satisfaction in the House of Lords.

The Conservatives knew they could not antagonize the great majority of the voters and they considered carefully the extent to which they might modify or kill various Liberal measures. On 20 January 1894, Balfour informed Goschen that he had been analysing 'the electoral effect likely to be produced by the action of the House of Lords in the most important matters now pending'. He thought that they would gain more than they would lose if they insisted on putting a contracting-out clause in the Employers Liability Bill. 'The Agricultural labourers care more for the Poor Law Clause than for the allotment clause in the Parish Councils Bill. But the former is very unpopular with our best men among the farmers and small squires. Electorally it may be difficult to strike a balance of loss or gain.'[2]

Goschen was distressed, however, when it appeared that Salisbury and the Lords were prepared to allow the Poor Law clauses to remain in Fowler's bill. It seemed to Goschen that this meant he had been wasting his time in putting up such a fierce fight in the Commons. Still he hoped it might not be too late to exclude London from the provisions of the bill as it related to the Poor Law. He worried that the Boards of Guardians in London would be 'handed over to the Progressives and Mr. Sidney Webb and his Socialists'. He urged Salisbury to work for the deletion of London even if he decided not to fight for the total exclusion of the Poor Law clauses.[3] Goschen wrote to Balfour on the same day to express his disappointment.

I myself can't help believing that the working classes generally, though a portion would remain with us, may voice an infinitely angrier storm if the Employers Liability Bill is wrecked than the Agricultural labourers would on

[1] *Ibid.*, xx (12 January 1894), 1537–8.
[2] Goschen Papers, Balfour to Goschen, 20 January 1894, Dep. C. 183, f. 42.
[3] SP, Goschen to Salisbury, 28 January 1894.

account of the excision of the Poor Law Clauses, even if it endangered the Bill which I don't believe it would. I have always thought our course on the Employers Liabilities dangerous but when you, Salisbury and Chamberlain are of one mind, who shall prevail against you?[1]

Salisbury had no intention of changing his course at Goschen's request and even became rather annoyed at some of his remarks. The Lords eventually imposed some modifications on the Parish Councils Bill before it finally passed into law but did not go so far as Goschen desired. They went too far for Gladstone and Fowler but the Liberals decided to accept the amendments in order to keep the bill from being dropped.

Divisions within Rosebery's Cabinet led the Conservatives and Liberal Unionists to believe they would soon be back in power. They began to plot various ways to accomplish this object. Chamberlain advocated an amendment to the queen's speech urging a new conference on bimetallism. This might detach some of the government's supporters, especially men from Lancashire. He asked Goschen (17 January 1895) for the attitude of the financial community.

I imagine that it depends very much upon you. From your previous utterances I gather that you incline to an experiment although you are not enthusiastic. I understand that Lord Rothschild is much in the same mind. If you declared openly in favour of a Conference I suppose the City would follow.[2]

Goschen had already admitted that he was not 'so *absolutely* sound on the question myself as to think everyone a fool or a lunatic who is not a monometallist'.[3] But he was not impressed by Chamberlain's scheme which he sent along to Balfour.

It reminded me of politics and re-called the fact to my notice that 'the usual channels of information' had occasionally contained speeches and articles setting out how the 'quartette' [Salisbury, Balfour, Devonshire and Chamberlain] who control the destinies of the Unionist party was practically agreed on a social programme of a fairly extensive character, and which would not fail to interest any future Chancellor of the Exchequer.

---

[1] BP, Goschen to Balfour, 28 January 1894, Add. Mss 49706, ff. 156–7.
[2] BP, Chamberlain to Goschen, 17 January 1895, Add. Mss 49706, f. 160.
[3] St Aldwyn Papers, Goschen to Hicks Beach, 23 September 1889, PCC/83.

I wonder what you and Salisbury will think of adding bi-metallism to it. As on this question, I have been asked my opinion, I have given it fully and frankly. You will observe that I see many disadvantages in it, tactical disadvantages, but I know too little of your general intentions as to the coming campaign and of what are fair possibilities to form a valuable opinion.[1]

Goschen obviously resented the fact that the 'quartette' was not a 'quintette'. In his reply to Chamberlain he listed a number of objections to a bimetallic resolution. If it succeeded in defeating Rosebery, they 'would come into office pledged to a bi-metallic policy – I will not say absolutely bi-metallism'. This would be a bad issue on which to fight an election since bimetallism would mean an increase in food prices which was 'why Chaplin and Co. are so strenuous for it'. If they failed with Chamberlain's amendment, it would be quite damaging so early in the session. The difficulty in the City of London was that within the financial community the monometallists were 'fanatically' attached to their view. Almost all the London newspapers, *The Statist* and *The Economist* were against bimetallism. 'The London press is almost foolish on the subject . . . The discussion of the cotton duties could scarcely be kept out of the debate and I know no more ticklish subject. I have a very strong bias myself to the Indian side of the question. I should fear that a debate in which Indian finances were discussed, would be full of pit-falls.'[2]

Balfour judged Goschen's reply to Chamberlain 'very strong' but not 'absolutely conclusive'. If there was a chance to turn out the government, it might be worth trying. Balfour acknowledged his own support of bimetallism but conceded that Goschen held 'the key of the position'.[3] Goschen expressed the same opinion to Salisbury a few days before Parliament reconvened. 'I do not relish the idea of a general election in which bimetallism would be hung round our necks but you would think it a chain of honour.'[4] Balfour had sent on Goschen's letters to Salisbury and the Prime Minister commented upon the strong element of reserve in Goschen's general attitude.

[1] BP, Goschen to Balfour, 21 January 1895, Add. Mss 49706, ff. 158–9.
[2] ChP, Goschen to Chamberlain, 21 January 1895, JC 4/7.
[3] Goschen Papers, Balfour to Goschen, 25 January 1895, Dep. C. 183, f. 44.
[4] SP, Goschen to Salisbury, 31 January 1895.

Goschen is undeniably cool. We asked them for today about three weeks
ago, but they returned us an answer which we both thought decidedly stiff.

I am inclined to agree with Goschen about the effect of a bi-metallism
amendment. I think that on the whole it would lose more votes than it
would gain.[1]

Eventually nothing of consequence emerged from these discussions on bimetallism though the sympathy evinced by some
members of the Conservative party is of interest. They felt that
something had to be done to aid a depressed economy at home
and a collapsing silver standard in India where it had been
necessary to stop the free coinage of silver in 1893. The scarcity
of gold, however, came to an end at just this time with the
discovery of new sources of supply in South Africa, Colorado,
the Yukon and Australia. During Salisbury's last ministry the
gold standard emerged triumphant as Russia, Japan and India
adhered to it while only China, among the more important
countries, remained aloof.

On 1 February 1895 Balfour suggested several additional
areas in which the government might be challenged. Among the
most important were the depressed state of agriculture, Indian
Cotton Duties and their effect on Lancashire, and the failure
of the Liberals to state their precise proposals on the reform of the
House of Lords.[2] In the first days of the reassembled Parliament,
the small Liberal majority held together exceptionally well. The
Conservative and Liberal Unionist leaders finally decided to
do something about the Indian Cotton Duties. In March 1894 the
Indian government had found itself in financial trouble and
decided to establish a general 5 per cent duty on imports. Pressure
from the British government – fearful of demonstrations in
Lancashire – led to the exemption of cotton goods from the new
import duty. By the end of 1894, the new duty had been extended
to the importation of cotton goods and Lancashire was in arms
even though the Indians were forced to place an excise tax on
their own cotton products.[3]

[1] BP, Salisbury to Balfour, 26 January 1895, Add. Mss 49690, ff. 99–102.
[2] Goschen Papers, Balfour to Goschen, 1 February 1895, Dep. C. 183, f. 45.
[3] See P. Harnetty, 'The Indian Cotton Duties Controversy, 1894–1896', *The
English Historical Review*, LXXVII (October 1962), 684–702.

Goschen was completely opposed to a motion which criticized the Indian Cotton Duties. He thought that all Members of Parliament must represent the Indians since they had no representatives of their own at Westminster. A disinterested view was essential. It may have been easier for Goschen to take such an attitude because he never fully appreciated the British manufacturers' point of view. In this instance it could be argued that the Indian duties were for revenue and not for protection. The general view of most British politicians was that British needs took precedence over Indian interests despite all the pious talk of obligations to 'the lesser breeds'. In this particular case, however, H. H. Fowler, now Indian Secretary, scored a stunning triumph when Sir Henry James – second to Chamberlain in the ranks of the Liberal Unionists in the Commons – introduced his hostile motion on 21 February 1895.

Sir William Harcourt reported the debate to Queen Victoria with relish. James's speech had been 'feeble' while Fowler's statement, delivered with great 'moral weight', had 'absolutely paralysed and discomfited the opposition, which began to dissolve'. Goschen gave 'a patriotic speech deprecating the action of Sir H. James as dangerous and injurious to our Indian Empire'.[1] Alfred Milner also congratulated Goschen for his fine speech. The latter replied in a letter which demonstrated his general unhappiness at the way in which he was being elbowed aside by Salisbury, Balfour, Devonshire and Chamberlain.

The foolish venture of an official attack on the Government under James's banner, was really contemplated, and all but carried out with the connivance and instigation of the four leaders, the quartette, I call them, and only I stood out and refused point blank to take any part in such a policy or indeed to be silent. I insisted on taking my own line, and have thereby saved the situation.

When I had announced my intention, Chamberlain characteristically said, 'Perhaps it is quite as well that Goschen should represent what is called the conscience of the nation.'

Salisbury denounced such 'altruism' at the expense of a British industry. It is astounding how he misreads public sentiment sometimes. He prophesied that few people would take my view.

[1] Buckle (ed.), *Letters of Queen Victoria*, 3rd series, vol. 2, pp. 479–81.

After all, it was only for 'black men' that sympathy was to be expressed. As to any agitation in India, it was pooh-poohed altogether, 'a mere ripple on the ocean'.[1]

The Rosebery Cabinet continued to stagger along. On Friday, 21 June 1895, the Liberal government did not expect trouble. Sir Henry Campbell-Bannerman, Secretary of State for War, was about to announce that the Duke of Cambridge had finally been coerced into giving up the post of Commander-in-Chief. One obstacle to military reform had been removed. But a vote of censure on the lack of cordite supplies in the army was brought against Campbell-Bannerman and to the surprise of both sides of the House, the Liberals were defeated by seven votes. Goschen had wound up the debate for the Conservatives and though he had received rousing cheers from his own side, his speech did not seem to contemplate victory in what was basically an unfair attack on Campbell-Bannerman. Rosebery and Harcourt convinced the Cabinet that they must resign immediately.

The queen accepted Lord Rosebery's resignation and Salisbury agreed to form a Cabinet. He indicated that after he had formed a government, there would be an immediate general election. Chamberlain and Devonshire met on the morning of Monday, 24 June, and at noon went to Salisbury's house where they were joined by Arthur Balfour. Salisbury was to see the queen at Windsor later in the afternoon. The 'quartette' was in session to decide upon the shape of a Conservative – Liberal Unionist coalition government. The 'fifth wheel' was no longer as essential as he had been after Lord Randolph Churchill's resignation nine years before. A melancholy presence lingering over the discussions must have been the memory of Lord Randolph, dead at the age of forty-five in January.

When Salisbury, Balfour, Devonshire and Chamberlain met to discuss appointments, Chamberlain was told that 'the whole field was open to him'. He turned down both the Home Office and the Exchequer in order to become Secretary of State for the Colonies. When Balfour suggested the Exchequer, Chamberlain said that he had told Goschen he would not claim that post. Devonshire

[1] MP, Goschen to Milner, 23 February 1895, Box 189.

declined the Foreign Office and Salisbury once again combined that office with the premiership while Devonshire became Lord President of the Council. Balfour was again First Lord of the Treasury and Leader of the House of Commons.[1]

When the meeting adjourned, it seemed to have been accepted that Goschen would probably ask to return to the Exchequer. But Goschen surprised the 'quartette' by insisting that he go to the Admiralty. Considering Goschen's refusal of the Exchequer, it is clear that he was not trying to keep the post for himself when he discussed this appointment with Chamberlain and received the latter's pledge not to claim it. It would appear that Goschen was prepared to take the Exchequer if the choice had been between Chamberlain and himself, and this had been the only way to keep Chamberlain out. With Chamberlain safely in the Colonial Office, Goschen could step aside knowing that Sir Michael Hicks Beach would probably be offered the Exchequer.

Goschen, almost sixty-four and with fond memories of his previous sojourn at the Admiralty, insisted that he be appointed First Lord. He probably realized too, that with Chamberlain and Devonshire in the Cabinet, he would not be able to play the commanding role he had enjoyed from 1887 until 1892. Lord George Hamilton was surprised when he read of Goschen's appointment in the Gazette. Hamilton had been First Lord of the Admiralty from 1886 until 1892 and the Chief Conservative spokesman on naval matters during the past three years. Salisbury explained to Hamilton that Goschen had declined all offices except the Admiralty and he therefore offered Hamilton the India Office. Hamilton thought that Goschen 'foresaw . . . a row between Chamberlain and the Birmingham fiscal school and the free-trade policy of the Treasury' and did not wish to be a 'protagonist in this coming controversy'.[2]

Lord George seems to have read too much of the tariff reform struggle of 1903 back into this earlier period. The opinion of Edward Hamilton at the Treasury is more accurate and contains

[1] J. L. Garvin and Julian Amery, Life of Joseph Chamberlain (London, 1932–70), vol. 3, pp. 4–6.
[2] Hamilton, Reminiscences, vol. 2, pp. 251–2.

one of the factors which undoubtedly influenced Goschen's final decision.

I am sorry not to have Goschen back again at the Treasury; though, until lately, I had long been under the belief that Goschen would prefer another place. I know that he had the refusal of the Chancellorship; and I expect the reason why he declined the offer was that he feels that a reduction of the Sinking Fund is inevitable, that his reputation as a financier had already suffered from the reduction which he made in 1887, and that he could not be responsible for proposing a further reduction himself.[1]

There was opposition to Goschen's appointment from an area which must have caused him grievous personal distress if he became aware of it. The queen forgot her old ally of 1886 and remarked to Salisbury that Goschen had not been 'altogether popular' at the Admiralty twenty years before. She praised the work of Lord Spencer at the Admiralty since 1892 and appeared to have forgiven him for his support of Home Rule. Spencer's years as First Lord of the Admiralty had been meritorious not only because he was a good administrator, 'but from his personal and social position, which had lent prestige to what is our national service'.[2] Victoria wanted an aristocrat and not a successful merchant banker turned politician. Salisbury replied that he had already informed Goschen that the Admiralty was his since he did not wish to return to the Exchequer and no government could be formed without him.[3] The queen made no further objections. Salisbury and his Cabinet had decided upon an immediate dissolution and won a massive victory in the July elections.

Milner had quickly congratulated Goschen on his return to the Admiralty. A few days later, Milner wrote again to praise the important ideas about naval and military reorganization which had been advocated by Spenser Wilkinson. Wilkinson wished to be considered for the position of secretary to the Committee of Defence which was to be set up under the chairmanship of Devonshire.[4] But Goschen was not impressed and his reply demonstrated the basic conservatism which led him to oppose

[1] HP, diary entry for 26 June 1895, Add. Mss 48667.
[2] Queen Victoria to Salisbury, 26 June 1895, RA C40/30.
[3] Salisbury to Queen Victoria, 26 June 1895, RA C40/36.
[4] MP, Milner to Goschen, 25 and 29 June 1895, Box 182.

many suggested naval reforms. To Goschen, Wilkinson was a 'gad-fly' and an 'enthusiast'.

These enthusiasts always capture you, – to your honour be it said.

All I can say is, and this you cannot report to Wilkinson, that if the Defence Committee was what he would like to make it, and with him as Secretary, judging from your description, I would not continue as First Lord of the Admiralty. The position would be intolerable.

The Admiralty will be administered precisely as before, but such matters, few in number, as went to the Cabinet, questions as touching war and navy together: or such a piece of work as the Naval Defence Act or Naval Works Bill (perhaps), questions of the large character, would go to the Defence Committee or a Cabinet Committee.

Spenser Wilkinson's great ability must be exercised in forming our minds. Such men (vide Gordon) are too great to put into harness.[1]

The key phrase in Goschen's letter was his commitment to administering the navy 'precisely as before'. He was unwilling to consider the radical changes which might be required if Britain was to be adequately prepared to defend her great empire. One could be sure that Goschen would be ruthlessly honest in his handling of the Admiralty but one could be equally certain that he would not move very far from the generally conservative and orthodox views of his naval advisers who wanted no interference from the War Office, the Prime Minister or the newly created Defence Committee of the Cabinet. Salisbury, Balfour, Dilke and a few other politicians and theorists had long recognized that the British defence establishment was in need of reform if it was to reach the standards of the continental states, which now had conscription and proper military planning staffs. There seemed to be a lack of co-ordination between various departments and an inability to look at the requirements of the empire as a whole.

Shortly before leaving office in 1892, Salisbury had sent Goschen a lengthy letter on the reform of the Admiralty but during his five years as naval chief the latter did not act on these suggestions. Salisbury had written that he was 'really puzzled' as to what should be done with the Admiralty as it was 'given up to pedantry of the worst kind'. He doubted that the First Lord

[1] *Ibid.*, Goschen to Milner, 30 June 1895, Box 189.

'could do much unless he was a man of very exceptional mould'. Salisbury thought the only 'remedy' was 'to convert the First Lord into a Secretary of State'. If they returned to power again, he thought that this should be considered along with the substitution of a lump sum to the departments instead of estimates. And he thought it would be wise to establish 'a tribunal of three or five Cabinet Ministers to determine all questions at issue between the Departments'.[1] The germ of the idea for a Committee of Imperial Defence had been in the air for some time. Publicists like Wilkinson and politicians such as Sir Charles Dilke had been advocating the establishment of a committee charged with considering the defence needs of the entire empire. They hoped that it might break down departmental jealousies and provide a body under the chairmanship of the Prime Minister which would contain other key Cabinet members and their professional advisors as well as being able to call in experts when necessary for their opinion and advice.[2]

The Hartington Commission of 1888–90 had already suggested the establishment of a Naval and Military Council, presided over by the Prime Minister, to discuss service estimates and to consider and decide upon matters of interest to both army and navy. By 1895, little had been done to implement the report of this commission though a Joint Naval and Military Defence Committee composed of experts had been established. It was finally decided to make Devonshire (formerly Lord Hartington) the head of a new Defence Committee of the Cabinet.

Before the end of 1895, Balfour, Salisbury, Devonshire, Goschen and Lansdowne had prepared minutes which contained their views on the new Committee of Defence.[3] Balfour's minute of 24 August 1895 was designed to provoke discussion. He suggested that the President of the Council should be the permanent chairman of this committee of the Cabinet. The Secretary for War and First Lord of the Admiralty were to be

---

[1] SP, typed copy, Salisbury to Goschen, 10 February 1892.
[2] See Franklyn Arthur Johnson, *Defence by Committee* (London, 1960).
[3] All five minutes are contained in the confidential Cabinet memorandum, 'Committee of Defence', CAB. 37/40/64.

permanent members and to be assisted by whatever experts they needed. Other members of the Cabinet might be invited to attend. The President of the Council would have 'no authority to intervene in the departmental work, either of the War Office or of the Admiralty' nor would he 'have the right either to send for or to give orders *directly* to the officials of either department'. Records of decisions were to be kept in duplicate at the War Office and Admiralty. Balfour then went on to the most important area of controversy – what exactly was the committee to do? It should 'decide all questions of importance connected with Imperial Defence, which involve the co-operation of Army and Navy'. The committee could only be really effective if a 'very wide interpretation' of its functions was accepted.

Salisbury did not formally present his views until October. He thought that the normal size of the committee should be kept as small as possible. The only regular members should be the President, Secretary for War, Commander-in-Chief, First Lord of the Admiralty and First Naval Lord. Others were to be called in as required.

The great question which the Committee has to decide is *what is the work for which the Army and Navy have to be fitted, and how are they to be* fitted for it? This question will include the normal condition of home defences; troops, fortifications, floating batteries or stationary ships, and the Channel squadron, harbour, and torpedo boats in the Channel, and precautions against torpedoes on the other side. It will further include the service of the Mediterranean and the China Seas, in which large questions of policy must necessarily be touched. What are to be the functions of the Mediterranean Fleet? Is it merely to watch and mask Toulon; or is it to be used as occasion may serve to reinforce diplomatic operations in the Turkish Empire, in Greece, in Morocco, or in Egypt? And for these purposes, when determined, what should be its numbers and constitution? In the China Seas other questions of policy must be dealt with. Is the British force to be capable of coping in the open sea with the combined forces maintained there by Russia and by France? Or is its duty to keep vessels of the size and numbers required for the purpose of aiding the action of diplomacy in China? Or is it to be so constituted that it will be able to discharge both these functions?

He went on to mention British problems in the Indian Ocean, Africa and South America.

Devonshire's minute of 3 November emphasized the information he would need if Lord Salisbury's suggestions were to be carried out. For the army he would need information on establishments, fortifications and barracks, material and mobilization plans. He conceded that he had 'little experience' of the way in which the navy was administered but thought the Admiralty should be able to supply information on 'how far the Navy is sufficient, or otherwise, to defend vital points and vital interests, and next how far its establishments are, or ought to be fixed, with reference to other less essential and more local duties'. The work of the committee would compel the two departments 'to face more directly than they need do now, the question of what it is which they undertake to do, and what are their resources for doing it'.

When Goschen submitted his minute on 22 November, he reached the surprising conclusion that he preferred Balfour's proposals. This was undoubtedly because of the lack of detail in Balfour's minute, since Balfour actually wanted to go far beyond anything Goschen was willing to concede in the way of establishing a genuinely effective and powerful Committee of Defence. Goschen's minute provides an important insight into both the strategic and administrative aspects of his mind. He regarded the 'programmes' suggested by Devonshire and Salisbury as 'so vast' that 'the work they would entail on those who are to be the principal members of the Committee, would be beyond their strength, and beyond the time which they could possibly devote to it consistently with the performance of their ordinary duties'. How could he possibly 'assist in overhauling the estimates of the War Office as well as . . . expound my own?' Goschen irritated the Prime Minister and the Foreign Office when he observed:

Further, it seems obvious generally that if the Admiralty and the War Office are to be thus called on to defend or justify every portion of their system, and if, continuously, the highest questions of naval and military strategy are to be considered, the proceedings of the Foreign Office would similarly have to be reviewed, so as to enable the Committee to judge whether or not they were conformable with the means of enforcement at the disposal of the nation, and to what degree it would be necessary to mould the policy of defence accordingly.

The Admiralty knew its tasks and was performing them with great ability. Goschen denied the Prime Minister's charge that a tug-of-war between various departments determined 'the distribution of our strength'. The essential idea behind the formation of the committee, argued Goschen, was not to call 'the Admiralty and War Office to account for their general proceedings' but to enable the army and navy to deal more effectively with 'joint problems' and to concentrate 'the attention and influence of Cabinet Ministers of high rank on these questions'. He agreed that the Defence Committee might be an excellent body to reconcile 'conflicting views between the spending departments and the Secretaries of State for India and the Colonies, and the Chancellor of the Exchequer. In a word the Committee would discharge duties which a large Cabinet cannot perform adequately yet the responsibility for which must in part be placed on Ministers outside the War Office and the Admiralty.' It would be a good idea to bring the 'broadest features of the estimates' before the Defence Committee before they went on to the Cabinet. As an example of the 'practical and urgent' subjects which the committee might try to resolve, Goschen suggested a discussion of the conflict between the Admiralty and the Colonial Office over the dockyard at Hong Kong. A meeting about some difficulties in Gibraltar might also be useful.

Lord Lansdowne at the War Office agreed that the committee might be useful but he too had some reservations. The suggestions made by Salisbury and Devonshire were 'too vast for practical purposes'. He wondered if the committee would ever be able to 'digest 'the vast amount of material which Devonshire wanted from the War Office. Much might be accomplished, however, if the committee limited itself to 'new proposals' advocated by the War Office and the Admiralty which concentrated upon 'concrete questions as they arise'. The Admiralty's obstructive attitude to the new Defence Committee is illustrated by some of the correspondence which passed between Devonshire and Goschen. The Duke's rugged and solid qualities were not those needed to trample down the negativism of the service departments. Balfour soon realized that it would be necessary to have the Prime

Minister preside over the committee if it was to function effectively. In late 1903 when Devonshire resigned from the Cabinet, Balfour – now Prime Minister – assumed the chairmanship of what had been called the Committee of Imperial Defence since 1902.

But in 1895 Goschen was eager to scuttle the project. He had not known it but there was already a Joint Naval and Military Defence Committee made up of professional officers which seemed to be doing the type of work tentatively assigned to the new Defence Committee. Devonshire was informed of this on 28 August.

They discuss such questions as garrisoning St. Helena and the defence of all our ports, distribution of duties between army and navy in that defence, defence of rivers, torpedo arrangements, guns, besides even larger questions. . .

Here is the basis, the nucleus for the Council. We can be an upper Chamber to this Committee and deal with the conclusions at which they have arrived, *or*, we might simply add the Secretary for War, and myself to the Committee and you preside under the present arrangement. At all events, this organization, made *after* the report of your Commission, carried out its spirit and we can easily graft something upon it.[1]

Salisbury, however, 'pooh-poohed' Goschen's suggestion.[2] The Prime Minister warned Devonshire that Goschen was 'jealous' of the new Defence Committee and would require 'delicate treatment'.[3]

A year later, Goschen became quite excited over one of Devonshire's speeches which some newspapers took to herald 'a sensational new departure in Naval Policy'. Goschen knew nothing of any such 'new departure'.[4] In March of 1898 the First Lord of the Admiralty grumbled when Devonshire called a meeting of the Defence Committee. What was to be discussed? Was the Defence Committee to become 'an Aulic Council for the discussion of campaigns?' Would he 'be cross-examined as to what the fleet can or ought to do? Are the members of the Committee to suggest plans of operation?' He would strenuously

[1] DP, 340.2644.
[2] *Ibid.*, Goschen to Devonshire, 6 September 1895, 340.2657.
[3] *Ibid.*, Salisbury to Devonshire, 17 October 1895, 340.2657.
[4] *Ibid.*, Goschen to Devonshire, 31 December 1896, 340.2713.

object 'to any *desultory* strategic conversation'.[1] The normally phlegmatic Devonshire was annoyed by this letter. Chamberlain had asked for a meeting of the committee without specifying a particular problem. It might have to do with West Africa or China. If a crisis were to develop, rapid decisions would be required. Devonshire doubted that most members of the Cabinet had sufficient information to discuss sensibly 'the proposals which you and Landsdowne might have to make' and it could be very helpful if 'a few members of the Government at least should be acquainted with the main conditions of the question we should have to face'. Devonshire wondered if Cabinet discussions might not be 'desultory' if no one knew what was going on.[2]

Devonshire's sharp rejoinder did not succeed. The First Lord of the Admiralty returned to the fray a week later.

Lansdowne has sent me your paper with questions, etc., covering as it seems to me almost the whole field of Admiralty administration. (I say nothing about the W. O.) We had better have a meeting to clear up our respective responsibilities, and the extent to which the Committee of Defence is to exercise surveillance over us, and our preparations.[3]

Once again Devonshire's imperturbability was shaken. 'I really do not think however that a meeting is necessary merely to *clear up our respective responsibilities and the extent to which the Committee on Defence is to exercise surveillance over you and your preparations.*' He had attempted to show Goschen in his letter of 12 March what the committee might discuss.

I can describe it more shortly by saying that the discussion would be an anticipation, in what I think would be a more convenient way, of the discussion which would take place in the Cabinet when the crisis becomes a little more acute. . . If there is to be a Defence Committee at all, I think there must be something for it to consider, when war with France seems at least possible, if not with France and Russia.[4]

The inadequacies of the Defence Committee of the Cabinet were revealed to the public when British strategy and planning proved so defective during the Boer War.

[1] *Ibid.*, Goschen to Devonshire, 12 March 1898, 340.2759.
[2] *Ibid.*, copy Devonshire to Goschen, 12 March 1898, 340.2760.
[3] *Ibid.*, Goschen to Devonshire, 20 March 1898, 340.2761.
[4] *Ibid.*, copy Devonshire to Goschen, 23 March 1898, 340.2762.

The Boer War, the elections of October 1900, the retirement of Goschen and Lansdowne's move from the War Office to the Foreign Office convinced Devonshire that the status of the Defence Committee should be thrown open to discussion.[1] Once again the essential conservatism of the Admiralty and the War Office was revealed. They intended to give up none of their prerogatives without a fight. Devonshire's minute of 2 November 1900 began the discussion.

> The Committee has not been, I think, altogether without its use, but it has been nothing more than an informal Committee of the Cabinet, occasionally calling into Council the Commander-in-Chief, the First Naval Lord, or other professional advisers, and it certainly has not occupied that place in naval and military administration which the Royal Commission, of which I was Chairman, had in view, or which, I think was intended when it was instituted at the beginning of the present Government.

If it was decided to keep the committee in existence Devonshire proposed that 'it should meet at certain definite intervals, that it should have a Secretary or Joint Secretaries, and that agenda for its meetings should be prepared, as well as Minutes of its proceedings kept'.

Lansdowne favoured the retention of the committee. It was necessary 'considering the great size of the Cabinet. . . As to its functions and composition, my opinions are very much what they were in 1895.' On 9 November 1900, Goschen submitted his views and despite the Boer War they had changed little since 1895. He still wanted the Defence Committee to limit its activities to the most menial chores. While having no objection to the preparation of a regular agenda, he doubted the need for regularly scheduled meetings. Meetings should be called when they were required. He voiced grave reservations, however, about keeping minutes. 'A short summary might not be amiss' but this should be done only by the naval and military directors of intelligence. 'I urgently deprecate the introduction of any outsider.' The appointment of someone such as Spencer Wilkinson to the post of secretary of the committee would be 'out of the question'. Goschen attached a copy of his minute of 1895 and concluded that he saw 'no reason

[1] Confidential Cabinet memorandum, 'Committee of Defence', CAB. 37/53/71.

to modify in any degree the views which I have there expressed'.

The Board of Admiralty had been only slightly changed since Goschen's Order in Council in 1872. What had changed, how-ever, was the size of the navy itself. In 1871, when Goschen was first sent to the Admiralty, there were 61,000 seamen, boys and Royal Marines while the estimates were just under £10 million. In 1895 there were 85,000 men and the estimates had climbed to almost £19 million. By 1900, the year of Goschen's retirement, the number of men had jumped to 112,000 and the estimates to £29 million.[1] Goschen seemed to be facing one crisis after another and the formerly parsimonious Chancellor of the Exchequer found himself, as he had in 1871–4, demanding larger and larger amounts of money for the navy. It was now Goschen's turn to become upset as Sir Michael Hicks Beach, in Goschen's former post at the Exchequer, insisted upon economies. Salisbury and his Cabinet struggled to maintain Britain's non-alignment in what seemed an increasingly hostile world. Britain's major antagonists were regarded as France and Russia. France was making trouble throughout Africa and in other parts of the world, but especially about Egypt. Russia had always been a problem – in the Ottoman Empire, on India's frontiers and in the Far East. Britain had no important quarrels with Austria and Italy and had, indeed, co-operated with these states in arranging the standstill agreements for the Mediterranean in 1887. The accession of William II in 1888 and the deposition of Bismark in 1890 had led to an uncertain element in German foreign policy. In 1895, however, there still seemed to be no fundamental differences between Germany and Britain as there were between Britain and France, and Russia and Britain. But the massacre of the Armenians in the Ottoman Empire presented the Cabinet with a grave crisis. Public opinion in Great Britain was scandalized by the crimes being committed by the Turks. Salisbury wished, if possible, to aid the Armenians but he had also to consider the possibility that the Russians might take advantage of the situation and attempt to seize Constan-tinople. Gladstone had emerged from retirement and demanded

[1] Sir William Laird Clowes, *The Royal Navy: A History from the Earliest Times to the Death of Queen Victoria* (London, 1897–1903), vol. 7, pp. 8–11.

intervention even if Britain had to act on her own. But the Cabinet, led by Goschen, strenuously opposed sending the fleet to Constantinople; they feared it would mean war with Russia. Salisbury had a high regard for Sir Philip Currie, British Ambassador to Constantinople, and wished to give him authority to bring the fleet to Constantinople. Goschen opposed such a wide delegation of authority and carried the Cabinet with him.[1]

The Prime Minister was convinced that the Ambassador should be able to call up the fleet on his own initiative if it was required. The Cabinet's refusal

to give carte blanche to Currie, means, or at least may mean, the surrender of Constantinople to Russia. If Russia gets there much before we do, so as to be able to man the Dardanelles forts with her own men, I take it that the place is impregnable. On the other hand if we get there first we are a good deal the strongest and our voice will be at all events very weighty in the ultimate arrangements that are made.

Salisbury did not know whether the Russians would move on Constantinople but he found the activity of the Black Sea fleet very 'suspicious'. While the Prime Minister thought the Crimean War had been a 'mistake', it was a fact that 'the keeping of Constantinople out of Russian hands has . . . been made a vital article of our political creed'. 'Meanwhile the world at large, including everybody, except the circle round the Admiralty, believe that the Straits can under the Turk be easily forced: and that if we are distanced in the race for Constantinople it will be only due to our neglect.'[2] Goschen had, in effect, conceded the Admiralty's lack of planning when he wrote to Salisbury on 24 November that he felt he did not 'know enough about the Dardanelles, the preparation at the forts, torpedoes &c. Would the expenditure of a little secret service money there not be advisable?'[3] But now he hastened to defend the Admiralty.

[1] SP, Cecil, unpublished vol. 5 of *Life of Salisbury*, pp. 83–5 and J. A. S. Grenville, *Lord Salisbury and Foreign Policy* (London, 1964), pp. 50–3. The letters which passed between Goschen and Salisbury during October and November of 1895 are in the Salisbury Papers.
[2] *Ibid.*, Salisbury to Goschen, 3 December 1895.
[3] *Ibid.*, Goschen to Salisbury, 24 and 27 November 1895.

I will only say that I hold you to be in error in saying that the world at large – everybody *outside the circle of the Admiralty* – believes that the Straits can easily be forced. You might more correctly say that everybody who knows nothing of the defences, the geography and the torpedoes of the Dardanelles is of that opinion. I know scores of naval officers quite outside the Admiralty circle including Commanders-in-Chief who would be responsible for the operation, who quite disbelieve in it being an *easy* operation, though of course it can be done.[1]

Salisbury lost the debate on forcing the straits and it took some time for his annoyance to abate. When Goschen circulated several papers on the naval estimates for 1896 in mid-December, Salisbury grumbled:

The papers you have circulated make me unhappy. Their is something, if I may put it so, theological in the absolute confidence of the counsels given by your advisers . . .

The Eastern question may be summed up thus. It is impossible to mend the lot of the Armenians without coercing or deposing the Sultan. It is impossible to get at the Sultan without quarrelling with Russia, Turkey, France and (now) Austria. So there is *no* practical course open at present. I suppose the American conflagration will fizzle away.

Salisbury's letter was written the day after President Grover Cleveland issued an ultimatum which supported Venezuela in her boundary dispute with British Guiana. Goschen was delighted to hear that Salisbury was not too worried since he had 'feared it might become very serious'. He wondered if Salisbury wanted any ships moved about in American waters because of the hostile attitude of the United States.[2] But the Prime Minister had sent a report to the queen on the same day stating that Britain should 'remain quiet'.[3] Salisbury regarded Cleveland's message as an 'electioneering dodge'.[4]

Goschen agreed that 'the Yankee business will probably . . . come to nothing', but it was still necessary to have plans for the possible ways in which the navy might be employed. 'Our weakest point, perhaps our only weak point is Vancouver Island,

[1] *Ibid.*, Goschen to Salisbury, 7 December 1895.
[2] *Ibid.*, Salisbury to Goschen, 18 December 1895 and Goschen to Salisbury, 19 December 1895.
[3] Salisbury to Queen Victoria, 19 December 1895, CAB. 41/23/41.
[4] SP, Salisbury to Goschen, 23 December 1895.

for our squadron in the Pacific is weak compared with the American force at San Francisco.' The China fleet of the United States must be watched since the British Pacific squadron was 'very much scattered at present'.[1]

A new complication developed with Dr Jameson's raid into the Transvaal on 29 December. Two days later Goschen wondered if the British ships in America should not be strengthened. It might be wise to organize a 'flying squadron'. It could be kept in the Channel and would be prepared to move immediately to a danger zone.

> It would create remarks, but looking at the situation generally, are we not justified in rather strong steps.
>
> The outlook seems to me very bad in many directions, not the least in that of Germany who now seems inclined to protect the Boers as the Americans protect Venezuela.[2]

The presence of German ships off the Portuguese port at Delagoa Bay in Mozambique was disturbing. It increased the fear that Germany might try to aid the Boers by sending reinforcements from German East Africa through the Portuguese colony to the Transvaal. On 2 January 1896, Salisbury agreed with Goschen 'that two at least out of the three Zanzibar ships should go to Delagoa Bay'.[3] A few days later Goschen reported that, 'The ships for the Flying Squadron have been selected, six in number, captains chosen, and orders given for the commissioning of the ships.' Later the same day, after having read the 'Lisbon telegrams about the German pressure on the Portuguese', Goschen moved vigorously.

> I think as the Portuguese have been staunch, we ought *at once* to send the nearest ships we have to Delagoa Bay . . . without a day's delay. I expect you will wish to assure the Portuguese of our practical support . . .
>
> On receipt of the telegram I wrote to Chamberlain suggesting sending our nearest ships to Delagoa Bay at once, and he cordially approved.[4]

The Germans backed down before Britain's firm stand in South Africa. But the Cabinet was so worried about the extensive

---

[1] *Ibid.*, Goschen to Salisbury, 22 December 1895.
[2] *Ibid.*, Goschen to Salisbury, 31 December 1895.
[3] *Ibid.*, Salisbury to Goschen, 2 January 1896.
[4] *Ibid.*, Goschen to Salisbury, 7 January 1896.

trouble spots in which Britain was involved that it decided to reject Salisbury's strong line with the United States and to press for negotiations and a compromise. This time Goschen was in the minority supporting the Prime Minister. Unfortunately, 'the apparent feeling of the Cabinet is that we are to stand anything from the Americans'.[1]

[1] SP, Goschen to Salisbury, 13 January 1896.

CHAPTER 12

FOREIGN AFFAIRS, BOERS AND RETIREMENT

The unsettled conditions which existed in Armenia, the Transvaal, China and the United States made it possible for Goschen to increase the Admiralty estimates in 1896 by more than £3 million and to plan for five new battleships and four new first-class cruisers. Britain's lack of allies encouraged a debate shortly after the kaiser's telegram to Kruger on whether her 'isolation' was 'splendid' or 'dangerous'. Goschen evaluated British foreign policy in a speech he delivered at Lewes on 26 February 1896. He distinguished between 'the isolation of those who are weak and who therefore are not courted because they can contribute nothing, and . . . the isolation of those who do not wish to be entangled in any complication and will therefore hold themselves free in every respect'. Britain's isolation was 'not an isolation of weakness, or of contempt for ourselves, it is deliberately chosen, the freedom to act as we choose in any circumstances that may arise'. Goschen was sure 'that we have but to hold up our hand and our isolation will terminate, and we shall receive a welcome into several groups of other Powers'.[1]

In 1896, Goschen celebrated his sixty-fifth birthday. The 'Fortunate Youth' was becoming an old man. In 1895 young George had been elected to Parliament. Only eleven M.P.s had been in the Commons before 1865. Among them were Goschen and Hicks Beach.[2] About this time the Prime Minister and the First Lord of the Admiralty were embroiled in a sharp controversy about the role of the navy. Salisbury was convinced that the Admiralty kept too many ships in the Western Mediterranean prowling about before the French fleet at Toulon. Earlier in the

[1] See Christopher Howard, 'The Policy of Isolation', *The Historical Journal*, x (1967), 77–88 and Elliot, vol. 2, pp. 206–8.
[2] Henry W. Lucy, *A Diary of the Unionist Parliament 1895–1900* (Bristol, 1901), p. 90.

year, Goschen had objected to the number and the size of the ships which Salisbury wished to send to East Africa when the Germans acted in a quarrelsome manner. British irritation with the Germans was increased when a German-backed candidate for the sultanship of Zanzibar was spirited away by a German gunboat. On 22 December, Goschen defended the Admiralty's assessment of the situation. The German naval force off the East African coast was not really very large.

When you ask me to send a battleship to Zanzibar, I feel much as I believe you would feel if being Foreign Minister, you were desired by the Prime Minister to send one of your great Ambassadors, with all the paraphernalia of a great European Embassy, to the court of some petty African potentate in order to impress him.[1]

On the following day Goschen acknowledged that some of his 'differences of opinion' with the Prime Minister were 'very deep-seated'. 'For instance, you want ships in the belief that they will "over-awe", but I feel that the main duty of our fleet is to ensure the safety of the country and to be prepared to fight if necessary.' Salisbury's suggestion that the 'large force' he wanted for East Africa could be back in the Mediterranean in less than three weeks was rejected by Goschen. The Prime Minister should 'remember that a Coastal Merchant ship or two conveniently run aground in the Canal might cause serious delay: and most emphatically, no chance must be allowed to the French to join two great fleets.' He was sure that Salisbury only wished to '*reduce*' and not to remove the Mediterranean fleet.[2]

Once the Cabinet decided to reconquer the Sudan, Salisbury had hoped to make minor concessions to France in other parts of the world. This might pacify her as the British consolidated their position in the Nile Valley. But Chamberlain was only willing to agree to the smallest adjustments in West Africa. In early September 1897, Goschen had questioned Salisbury about the 'ugly situation in the Niger area. Salisbury thought that the Russo-French alliance had some advantage for Britain since it was 'a decided check' to Germany. He did not expect France to

[1] SP, Goschen to Salisbury, 22 December 1896.
[2] *Ibid.*, Goschen to Salisbury, 23 December 1896.

be 'disagreeable' over Egypt. The Niger was disturbing and gunboats would be needed.[1] On 19 September Goschen admitted 'the
necessity of holding our own against the local French encroachments' but he wondered if Chamberlain was not too aggressive.
It might be wise, Goschen thought, to have a Cabinet meeting on
this 'vital issue' if there was a real diagreement between Salisbury
and Chamberlain.

Salisbury replied that Chamberlain did not want war. But he
was urging tactics upon Salisbury that were 'diplomatically
impossible' since they would humiliate the French. 'No French
Minister would dare to withdraw his troops on a summons from
us, from a place which he had occupied as rightful French
territory.' The Prime Minister thought that the 'proofs of ownership' were 'weak' on both sides. Goschen's gunboats, he hoped,
would have a 'salutary effect'.[2] An agreement was finally reached
in June of the following year.

Goschen had now to turn his eyes towards the Far East. France,
Russia and Germany had combined to limit Japanese gains after
the Sino-Japanese War of 1894-5. Britain had dominated Chinese
trade and commerce but the other Great Powers and Japan were
now determined to obtain their share of the spoils. The Germans
sent troops into Kiao-chow in November 1897 and early in 1898
obtained a long-term lease. The Russians demanded compensation
as did France, Britain and Japan while the United States wanted to
be sure that China would not be closed to her merchants and
traders. The Inspector-General of the Chinese Customs service was
Sir Robert Hart. His retirement could lead to trouble if he was replaced by a non-Briton. On 20 December 1897, Goschen remarked:

If the Russians were to 'occupy' Port Arthur in a serious sense, Japan
would, I presume, have something to say, having been turned out of it herself. You will remember that Japan is navally very strong, and it would
become a question whether she might not be useful, and be utilized in some
way, but I hope that Russia is not going to be foolish.[3]

[1] *Ibid.*, Goschen to Salisbury, 4 and 10 September 1897, and unpublished vol. 5 of
Life of Salisbury, p. 239.
[2] *Ibid.*, Goschen to Salisbury, 19 September 1897 and unpublished vol. 5 of *Life
of Salisbury*, pp. 239–40.
[3] *Ibid.*, Goschen to Salisbury, 10 and 20 December 1897.

Ten days later, Goschen informed Salisbury that he was 'prepared for very vigorous action' if an attempt was made to replace Hart by a Russian. 'I attribute more importance to this point commercially than to almost anything else.'[1]

Salisbury proposed a deal to the Russians in late January which would have enabled Russia and Britain to co-operate in the exploitation of China. The Russians were not interested, believing they could get more on their own. At about the same time (February 1898), Lucy Goschen died. It was a terrible blow to the First Lord of the Admiralty but he immediately informed Salisbury that he 'must now throw myself into my work again, and not let my sorrow distract me from my public duties.'[2]

Balfour reported to Goschen that the Cabinet had decided it could not prevent the Russian lease of Port Arthur and Talienwan since Britain had not protested when the Germans obtained a long lease on Kiao-chow. But they had, of course, insisted that the Most Favoured Nation Treaties be kept in force with respect to China.[3] Now that Germany and Russia had grabbed part of China, the British felt they had no alternative but to seize a bone for themselves – Wei-hai-wei. Once they had decided upon Wei-hai-wei, Goschen wanted even more. He wondered if Sir Claude MacDonald, British Minister at Peking, should not be sent instructions to ask for additional concessions in the Yangtze Valley and the Hong Kong area. MacDonald

ought to make it plain that Wei-hai-wei, the railway, etc. are intended as compensation for Port Arthur and Talienwan but that if a port or anything of that kind is given to France we must have Kowloon and Chusan.

Don't let us be too late. The fleet *cannot* return without good results in its pocket. We could not stand its coming 'empty away' under any circumstances.[4]

Eventually the British obtained concessions in both Wei-hai-wei and Kowloon.

[1] *Ibid.*, Goschen to Salisbury, 31 December 1897.
[2] *Ibid.*, Goschen to Salisbury, 24 February 1898.
[3] BP, copy Balfour to Goschen, 26 February 1898, Add. Mss 49706, ff. 172–5.
[4] BP, Goschen to Balfour, late March or early April 1898, Add. Mss 49706, ff. 181–2.

The First Lord of the Admiralty assessed the confrontation
with Russia for Milner:

The Russians have lied perfectly abnormally; and certainly did take us by
surprise at the end by an unexpected move in the middle of friendly negotiations. . . Never was there a more difficult problem than what to do. There
was the possibility of war, but it was thought Port Arthur was too narrow a
shelf on which to rest so tremendous a decision. And how do we stand as
regards war? Thus: we can fight France and Russia together, but without
much margin. We cannot do more. If Japan were to join them we should be
in a *very* difficult position. On the other hand, I am not sure whether we
are likely to be in a better position for fighting than we are now.[1]

Goschen had submitted his estimates and shipbuilding programme for 1898-9 to the Cabinet on 17 February 1898. He
proposed more men, more ships and, of course, more money.
Justifying the need for three new battleships he observed that
Britain must carefully watch the fleets of Germany, the United
States and Japan as well as those of France and Russia. When he
presented his estimates to the House of Commons on 10 March
1898 he acknowledged that he was asking for 'a colossal sum'.[2]
In June, however, Goschen was disturbed by reports of massive
naval construction in Russia and he brought this new information
before the Cabinet for 'more serious and urgent consideration'.[3]
The Cabinet finally decided to authorize a supplementary estimate
which would enable Goschen to lay down four more battleships.
Hicks Beach, the Chancellor of the Exchequer, was continually
aghast at the sums Goschen was demanding.[4]

1898 also witnessed the reconquest of the Sudan, the meeting
of Kitchener and Marchand at Fashoda and the Spanish–
American War. The blockades established by the United States
made it necessary to consult the Crown's legal advisers in order
to be absolutely clear on the rights of neutrals. Goschen reminded
Balfour that 'Spain must be treated as a civilized power and not as

---

[1] MP, 14 April 1898, Box 31.
[2] CAB. 37/46/20; *Hansard*, LIV (10 March 1898), 1252–77.
[3] Confidential Cabinet memorandum, 'Russian Naval Construction', CAB.
37/47/39.
[4] See the letters which passed between Goschen and Hicks Beach in the St
Aldwyn Papers, PCC/83.

South American Republics'.[1] The Spaniards had been annoyed at Britain's failure to aid them diplomatically. They also argued that new fortifications were required near the Queen of Spain's Chair at Algeciras in order to repel the armed forces of the United States. This was a deliberately provocative act so far as Goschen and the Admiralty were concerned and led to a serious diplomatic crisis.[2] The guns at the Queen of Spain's Chair would be able to fire directly across the bay into Gibraltar. Goschen was even more aroused than some of his Admirals. On 11 July 1898 Goschen asked Balfour if the British Ambassador to Spain, Sir Henry Drummond Wolff – Balfour's old crony from 'Fourth Party' days – appreciated 'the extreme gravity' of the situation. British public opinion might very well regard this as a 'causus belli'. 'The Spanish Minister may plead that the course pursued is within the Sovereign rights of Spain. So it may be. But there are certain sovereign rights, the exercise of which is incompatible with the friendly relations with neighbouring powers.' It was imperative that Wolff 'be instructed that we cannot in the last resort, permit the erection of batteries which would render Gibraltar waters impassable and that his task must be to let the Spaniards understand this in as friendly a way as possible'.[3]

A week later Goschen informed Salisbury that the situation in Algeciras was still 'serious'. The Admiralty had always considered that 'any attempt to fortify those heights would have to be protested against, *effectively* at once'.[4] The Spaniards were overwhelmed by the United States and an armistice was arranged in mid-August. Goschen, however, was still concerned about the fortifications going up on the Queen of Spain's Chair. Balfour was acting Foreign Secretary during most of August and Goschen returned to the subject in the middle of the month. He did not 'care much about forts on the bay, for we can get at them with our ships, but we can't get at the Queen of Spain's Chair'.[5]

[1] BP, Goschen to Balfour, 25 April 1898, Add. Mss 49706, ff. 188–90.
[2] Grenville, *Salisbury and Foreign Policy*, p. 217.
[3] BP, Goschen to Balfour, 11 July 1898, Add. Mss 49706, ff. 195–7.
[4] SP, Goschen to Salisbury, 17 July 1898.
[5] BP, Goschen to Balfour, 14 August 1898, Add. Mss 49706, ff. 199–200.

Salisbury agreed that there might be 'trouble'. 'I suppose we shall have to blockade Algeciras.'[1]

The First Naval Lord, Admiral Richards, was not yet too worried as the fortifications seemed to be primarily defensive. But if Spain were to put up permanent military works which threatened Gibraltar and then refused to demolish them, 'the answer (in my opinion) would be the prompt despatch of a military expedition . . . before France could interfere'.[2] Goschen disagreed with Richards and called for immediate action.[3] Balfour agreed.

> If the telegram I sent yesterday to Wolff fails I think that we shall have to send an ultimatum to the Spanish Government in the shape of a demand that one of our Officers shall be allowed to inspect the works at Algeciras, etc. If this is refused, I see nothing for it but to withdraw Wolff and blockade some Spanish port.

Considering the attitude of Admiral Richards, Balfour thought it wise for Goschen to come up to London and take over personal supervision at the Admiralty. Rothschild had been told to refuse any new loans to Spain. The War Office wanted to wait until Khartoum had been taken but Balfour believed that they were 'quite strong enough at sea to do what we want without the aid of the other branch of the Service'.[4] On the same day, Balfour informed Salisbury of his decision and confessed that he hated 'taking strong measures against a nation in its extremity but if they drive us to it, what can we do?'[5]

Salisbury agreed with Balfour that Spain was a problem but he opposed immediate action, feeling that the Spaniards would back down. To the Prime Minister, the 'present crisis' had been produced by a 'sharp collision of Jingoes' and the fact that the Admiralty was 'wild over the danger of bombardment from the Queen of Spain's Chair – though the actual danger does not seem large'. It was impossible, however, to ignore the Admiralty's concern. 'On the other hand I have no doubt that Wolff is right:

[1] *Ibid.*, Salisbury to Balfour, 22 August 1898, Add. Mss 49691, ff. 24–7.
[2] SP, Richards to Balfour, 25 August 1898, A/93.
[3] BP, Goschen to Balfour, 26 August 1898, Add. Mss 49706, f. 203.
[4] *Ibid.*, copy, Balfour to Goschen, 30 August 1898, Add. Mss 49706, ff. 205–6.
[5] *Ibid.*, copy, Balfour to Salisbury, 30 August 1898, Add. Mss 49691, ff. 28–32.

and that the idea that they had surrendered the right to protect Algeciras from their own soil, in obedience to our demands would be fatal to any Spanish Government.'[1]

Balfour had volunteered to remain at the Foreign Office for an additional ten days but Salisbury rejected the offer.

We seem to be moving pretty straight towards war; and I do not think I can devolve upon any other member of the Cabinet the responsibilities arising out of that situation. I think I am bound to satisfy myself in that matter: and I of course know nothing except the very fragmentary information I can collect from the telegrams. Some little time must elapse before I can inform myself – and probably some further communication with the Spanish Government must be necessary. And then if any serious step has to be taken a Cabinet must be summoned which of course will bring me home.[2]

The Prime Minister was obviously hoping to gain time and to prevent an unnecessary war.

Lansdowne informed Salisbury on 7 September that there would be no difficulty in landing 'a very formidable little force at Ceuta or Algeciras if the Spaniards drive us to extremities'.[3] An anxious Goschen also wrote to Salisbury on 7 September and expressed his concern over Salisbury's view that 'less pressure' might be a wiser course for the moment.

In this minute, I seem to see a totally different attitude from Balfour's, but one for which I was not totally unprepared, as from the first, (as I remember from a remark you made at the Cabinet) I gathered you yourself were not impressed very seriously with the gravity of the situation but fell in more or less with the views of your colleagues.

But can we go back now, or halt, or let things drift? I think it is impossible.

The 'facts' were clear and when it came to 'sovereign rights', it must be remembered that Gibraltar was 'a question which we must discuss on grounds of national safety'. Goschen conceded that Salisbury was

the best judge whether or not it is wise to let a little more time slip by, so as to give the Spaniard some door of retreat or concession, but I must frankly

---

[1] *Ibid.*, Salisbury to Balfour, 31 August 1898, Add. Mss 49691, ff. 33–6.
[2] *Ibid.*, Salisbury to Balfour, [?] September 1898, Add. Mss 49691, ff. 37–8.
[3] SP, Lansdowne to Salisbury, 7 September 1898.

say that I could not remain responsible for naval defence if Spain is allowed to erect the fortifications apparently contemplated, or for the continuation of the works at Gibraltar under an increasing force of Spanish guns, with Spain open to the French.[1]

Goschen complained to Balfour on the following day (8 September) that Salisbury's minute was

disastrous: it is totally out of keeping with all you had done. It is just as I feared when this ticklish business which may bring on a war, was passed in the middle from one hand to another, the latter being the hand of a man who did not believe your policy. Salisbury ought to have stopped your action, or to have continued in it. Now he asks a number of questions, most of which have been answered before, and all of which, if asked ought to have been . . . answered before we telegraphed that we could not 'tolerate' Spain's action, or words to that effect. Now, Salisbury evidently shrinks from the job.

It was deplorable that Salisbury, Curzon and Lansdowne were all out of town at this critical moment.[2]

A month later Balfour admitted that he did not agree with Salisbury's conciliatory approach to Spain. He rejected Salisbury's view that the Spaniards were good soldiers and doubted that British intervention would lead to hard fighting and a prolonged occupation. It seemed to Balfour that the withdrawal of the British Ambassador plus a blockade of either Cadiz or Barcelona with perhaps a raid on the works at Algeciras would have done the trick. But the matter was complicated and Salisbury might be right.[3] Even after the Cabinet had committed itself to Salisbury's policy, Goschen continued to worry about the constructions which were still being raised at Algeciras.[4] By the end of the year, however, Salisbury's sensible amalgam of firmness allied with courtesy had succeeded in enabling the Spaniards to back down without feeling they had been humiliated.

The Spanish embroglio has been overshadowed by the Fashoda incident when it looked as though fire-eaters in both London and Paris might provoke a war. General Kitchener had routed the Khalifa at Omdurman in the first days of September and had then marched on to Fashoda where he confronted Captain Marchand

[1] *Ibid.*, Goschen to Salisbury, 7 September 1898.
[2] BP, Goschen to Balfour, 8 September 1898, Mss 49706, ff. 207–9.
[3] *Ibid.*, copy, Balfour to Goschen, 11 October 1898, Add. Mss 49706, ff. 215–21.
[4] SP, Goschen to Salisbury, 1 December 1898.

on 19 September. Fortunately the moderates in both camps
prevailed and war was averted. But for six weeks, the tension was
intense. On 4 October 1898 Goschen asked the Prime Minister
for information. 'Fashoda! – Shall we have to mobilize? Or wait
quietly and see Marchand starved out?' It seemed to Goschen
'that we must be much nearer war than we were during the Niger
negotiations'.[1]

Late in October the British Ambassador in Paris began to report
significant military and naval preparations which alarmed the
Cabinet. The French were also doing their best to create the
impression that the Russians were prepared to assist them.
Goschen found the reports

> *very* serious. If the Russians join, we shall have a Herculean task: and we
> ought not to forget this in our present preparations.
>
> Ought we not to mobilize? We ought to be in an immediate position to
> face the possible action of the two powers.
>
> A terrible scramble would be so inadvisable, and it must be a scramble if
> we don't act before war breaks out.[2]

The Admiralty had already started to prepare the reserve squadron
on 24 October and three days later it was decided to have the
fleet ready for war. But the French were not prepared for a
conflict and in the first days of November, the French acknowledged the inevitable and recalled Marchand.

French and Russian naval construction remained Goschen's
greatest worry. Hicks Beach had already warned Salisbury on
27 January 1899 that the demands of the army and navy would
lead to increased taxation if they were granted.[3] Goschen submitted his detailed proposals to the Cabinet on 31 January and
regretted that the estimates were of 'unprecedented magnitude,
exceeding by a very large sum the swollen Estimates of last year'.
But he concluded that 'the excess is unavoidable' if Britain was to
retain her naval supremacy before the French and Russian
challenge.[4] On 19 March 1899 Goschen informed the Commons

---

[1] *Ibid.*, Goschen to Salisbury, 4 October 1898, and [October 1898].
[2] *Ibid.*, Goschen to Salisbury, [October 1898].
[3] Hicks Beach, *Life of Hicks Beach*, vol. 2, pp. 90–2.
[4] CAB. 37/49/7, confidential Cabinet memorandum, 'Navy Estimates, 1899–
1900'.

that the additional £3 million which would raise the naval estimates to almost £27 million was absolutely essential in the critical times in which they lived.[1]

Despite the darkening horizon in South Africa, Goschen was optimistic about the possibility of cutting naval expenditure within a few years. He warned Hicks Beach that the estimates for 1900–1901 would still be high but he expected a large cut in 1901–2 when present programmes finally reached completion.[2] By the summer of 1899, however, the First Lord of the Admiralty was once again badgering the Chancellor of the Exchequer for more money. He insisted that a naval depot was needed in the Falkland Islands 'in case of war with the United States'. It would serve 'as a station from which to watch for American reinforcements coming round from the Pacific to reinforce the Atlantic Squadron'.[3] There were other more ominous problems than possible wars with the United States. Britain's relations with the Transvaal and the Orange Free State were rapidly deteriorating. Goschen had, of course, followed the complex negotiations with President Kruger very carefully. He had felt a special interest since 1897 as Chamberlain had appointed Alfred Milner Governor of Cape Colony and High Commissioner for South Africa. This was a magnificent opportunity for Milner after five years as chairman of the Board of Inland Revenue. Goschen was one of the speakers at a banquet given for Milner on 2 April 1897 and the First Lord of the Admiralty was carried away by the occasion. Referring to the recent victories won by Admiral Rawson at Benin, in what is now Nigeria, Goschen reminded Milner that if he ever needed help he would find more than enough at the great British base at Simon's Town. Britain was determined to remain supreme in the southern part of Africa.[4]

On 14 July 1897 Milner sent off a lengthy report to his old chief. He regretted that Sir Gordon Sprigg, the Prime Minister of Cape Colony, had probably gone beyond what Cape public opinion would accept when he offered £1 million towards the

[1] *Hansard*, LXVI (9 March 1899), 306–25.
[2] St Aldwyn Papers, Goschen to Hicks Beach, 4 February 1899, PCC/83.
[3] *Ibid.*, Goschen to Hicks Beach, 4 July 1899, PCC/83.
[4] Cecil Headlam (ed.), *The Milner Papers* (London, 1931–3), vol. 1, p. 34.

construction of a battleship at the Queen's Diamond Jubilee.[1] Goschen had not been impressed by the colonial Premiers when they were in London.

Chamberlain raised a Frankenstein which almost devoured him. I did not like them. I thought most of them, with the exception of the Canadian, rude and over-bearing, quite without tact, very ordinary men, their wives very common, and they were exacting to the last degree. They enjoyed immensely driving about in the Queen's landaus with scarlet footmen on the box.

The annual session of Parliament was due to end on the following day and Goschen confessed that he 'felt a perfect nausea for the House lately'. He was doing well at the Admiralty 'though with never-ending anxieties'. The Commons itself had 'been intolerably dull and wearisome'.[2] Milner's message of sympathy at the time of Lucy Goschen's death led Goschen to reply at great length since it provided an outlet for repressed emotions and was addressed to a correspondent in whom Goschen had the utmost confidence.

Apart from my home life, I now live exclusively for my administrative work and foreign politics with which it is intertwined. All domestic legislation pulls on me, and to be quite candid to an old friend, I am sick of the House of Commons except on naval questions. It could not well be otherwise. Everything is so changed, methods, tone, subjects, men, principles, appreciations.[3]

On 28 July 1899, Goschen told Milner why he had not written sooner. He did not want his letters to differ from Chamberlain's instructions to the younger man. Goschen acknowledged that he and the Colonial Secretary had 'not always seen "eye to eye" ... in this business, though on the broad lines we have been agreed'. British public opinion seemed prepared to agree that war might be 'inevitable'.[4] Goschen's letter was sent just after Milner's intransigent attitude had scuttled the Bloemfontein Conference in early June. Chamberlain, however, was still trying to work out a compromise. It is clear that the British government did not want

[1] *Ibid.*, vol. 1, pp. 76–7.
[2] MP, Goschen to Milner, [summer] 1897, Box 4.
[3] *Ibid.*, Goschen to Milner, 14 April 1898, Box 31.
[4] MP, Box 31.

a war with the Boers but it was determined to assert British supremacy in South Africa. The British were reasonably confident that the Boers would back down but if they did not, the Cabinet was prepared to move forward. The area was considered too vital for the defence of the entire empire to permit any further nonsense from the Boers. On 13 August 1899 Goschen advised Hicks Beach that 'things were taking a turn which would make it a scandal if matters were not peacefully arranged'.[1] But the Cabinet realized that war was a distinct possibility. This meant that the British forces in South Africa must be reinforced. Goschen agreed and sent to the Prime Minister some material on the harbour at Durban together with his view on the troops to be moved to Cape Colony. He was unhappy about the War Office's decision to send reinforcements from Egypt rather than from England. It seemed 'to emphasize the paucity and the poor quality of the troops at home'.[2] On 23 August Goschen expressed his shock to Salisbury:

> The War Office paper about the number of men necessary for a Transvaal war, and of the time which preparations would take, is a sickening document: and if the Boers knew of its contents, they might really think it best to make a dash at Natal etc., during the many months before the mass of the expedition will arrive. I must look into the question of landing the troops at Durban. I cannot believe that the landing could not be effected much quicker.

Goschen confessed his distress at the hostile manner adopted by Milner towards the recent Boer proposals and approved Chamberlain's reply

> rather snubbing Milner (deservedly) and telling him not to throw cold water on the new suggestions in advance. I must say, the advance was very great and, as Chamberlain said, went beyond Milner's Bloemfontein proposals. Looking not only at what is fair and generally expedient, but specially at the War Office plans and their endless delays, it would be madness in my judgment rashly to reject any fresh concession.[3]

By 5 September, however, Goschen agreed with Chamberlain 'that the attitude of the Boers now looks as if they are prepared

---

[1] St Aldwyn Papers, Goschen to Hicks Beach, 13 August 1899, PCC/83.
[2] SP, Goschen to Salisbury, [mid-August] 1899.
[3] *Ibid.*, Goschen to Salisbury, 23 August 1899.

for war'.[1] Goschen was now thinking of every possibility as both sides prepared their ultimatums and fighting broke out. His primary tasks were to see that the British troops were transported to South Africa as quickly as possible and to prevent the Boers from obtaining supplies through the Portuguese port of Lourenço Marques at Delagoa Bay in Mozambique. In the early months of hostilities it was also necessary to send Blue Jackets and marines to the assistance of the small British army, which had not yet been properly reinforced for the task before it.

As they began to pour troops into South Africa, the British became acutely conscious of their 'isolation' and of their exposed position at home. France and Russia were far from friendly: it was therefore essential to retain Germany's friendship. Fortunately, William II was in one of his conciliatory moods. He had urged Kruger to come to terms with the British and in the autumn of 1899 he was preparing for a trip to London. However, he could not resist the opportunity to squeeze the British a bit and seized the chance to further German interests in Samoa.

On 26 October Goschen objected to Salisbury's directive that food-supplies destined for the Boer troops must be seized as contraband of war. Goschen's recollection was that the Cabinet had agreed 'to search and seize as little as possible and to trust the Portuguese at Delagoa Bay, and to our authorities at other places to detain munitions of war'. It was acceptable to deny food to

a fortress or beleaguered post, but generally, this country should surely not set the example or follow an example, if example there be, of hampering the importation of food. Our interests are entirely the other way. You reply that whatever we do or not do, our enemies will act precisely as they please. But this view carries us very far and is not justified by history.

Much 'friction' would be created with neutral states and numerous conflicts would emerge in the prize courts. 'It is different with ammunition and guns which are clearly for warlike purposes, but with food supplies the questions would be endless.'[2] Goschen lost this debate to the Prime Minister. It was decided to prevent

[1] ChP, JC 4/7. The Orange Free State pledged its support to the Transvaal in the last days of September.
[2] SP, Goschen to Salisbury, 26 October 1899.

the import of food into Delagoa Bay if it was obviously destined for the Boer armies. On 15 December 1899 Goschen informed Salisbury that British ships on duty at Delagoa Bay were boarding all vessels outside territorial waters, examining the papers, and searching suspicious cargoes.[1]

William II had been pleased by the settlement of the Samoan controversy with Britain in Germany's favour early in November and later in the month he arrived for his first visit since 1895. Chamberlain used the visit to push his scheme for an Anglo-German alliance. The Colonial Secretary's speech in Leicester on 30 November was made immediately after the kaiser's departure and led to a minor diplomatic crisis. It went far beyond the general wishes of political leaders and public opinion in Britain, Germany and the United States by calling for an alliance, or an understanding, between the three great Teutonic powers. On top of Chamberlain's speech came news of continued British ineffectiveness in South Africa as General Sir Redvers Buller seemed unable to wrest the initiative from the Boers.

Goschen poured out the anger and irritation which he felt to Balfour on 5 December 1899: 'Did you ever see a story of imbecility and futility more striking than the enclosures to Buller's printed letters?' They indicated that a large British force had surrendered to a smaller Boer unit. The whole affair had been 'pitiable'. Buller seemed to have given in to 'helpless pessimism' and Milner was 'not much better'. 'Why don't they arm every Englishman and fall on the Dutch farmer rebels. Apparently nothing but despair. We send him division after division, and he feels nothing but extreme anxiety, no confidence in himself or anybody.' Goschen could not understand why the British troops had failed to go on the offensive. He then turned to Chamberlain's 'extraordinary' speech. It was apparent to Goschen the moment he had seen a report of the speech that it 'would undo much of the good of the Emperor's visit. I thought nothing could be more injudicious than using the word "alliance". The States and Germany of course repudiated the term.' Chamberlain's action was unfair to the entire Cabinet. 'Why, at this moment irritate the

[1] *Ibid.*, Goschen to Salisbury, 15 December 1899.

French? I really believe Chamberlain thinks, that with American good-will we can flout all the powers with impunity. But we can't. He habitually over-estimates our power.'[1]

By mid-December Goschen had a new type of contraband with which to contend – contraband in men. He informed Salisbury of his concern 'about the officers and men proceeding to the Trans-vaal openly'. The Admiral in command in South Africa was 'yearning to stop them'. Goschen had been investigating the precedents.[2] Many of these officers and men were Germans, eager to aid President Kruger. On 24 December Goschen reported that the German vessel, *Herzog*, was sailing to Delagoa Bay with 'military officers engaged for the Transvaal'. Goschen could not decide whether or not it would be wise to bring the vessel into a Prize court. '*Our* law books would justify us, but as you know, I would avoid a quarrel with Germany.'[3] Almost a week later Goschen advised the Prime Minister that, 'The fun(?) has begun. A cruiser has taken the "Bundesrath", sister ship to the Herzog into Durban... Now we shall see what happens. It could not be avoided if there was to be a real search.'[4]

The German government protested strenuously but was soon calmed down. Goschen continued to be bothered by French and German ships carrying contraband to Delagoa Bay but as Lord Roberts turned the tide of battle in the early months of 1900, these supplies became of much less importance. The Transvaal and the Orange Free State were in the process of disappearing as organized states though their citizens were determined to continue the struggle. By the summer of 1900, Britain had formally annexed the Boer republics.

The queen wondered if the fleet should not be mobilized but Goschen and the Cabinet refused to be panicked. Goschen in-formed Sir Arthur Bigge, the queen's secretary, on 30 January 1900 that he kept 'this eventuality in view and immediate mobilization could take place at any moment'. But this decision 'would inevitably lead to counter-steps on the part of other

[1] BP, Goschen to Balfour, 5 December 1899, Add. Mss 49706, ff. 222–5.
[2] SP, Goschen to Salisbury, 15 December 1899.
[3] *Ibid.*, Goschen to Salisbury, 24 December 1899.
[4] *Ibid.*, Goschen to Salisbury, 30 December 1899.

powers, whose governments at present are not menacing us navally in any way'.[1] The hostilities in South Africa meant that Goschen would require more money for the navy. Hicks Beach braced himself for the expected onslaught from the Admiralty and the War Office. On 19 January 1900 Goschen explained some of the details of his proposed estimates to Hicks Beach and conceded that they were 'almost appallingly high'.[2] Salisbury came to the aid of his service chiefs in their struggle with the Treasury and implied that the Treasury was impeding the war effort. Hicks Beach retorted angrily and insisted that there had been no real Treasury control since the Boer War began.[3]

Goschen's persistence succeeded, for on 26 February 1900, he introduced naval estimates which called for almost £1 million more than he had requested in 1899. The estimates had now increased by 50 per cent during his five years at the Admiralty. Goschen informed the House of Commons that he still saw no need for mobilization as Britain was 'not menaced by any naval Power'. Europe already knew that Britain had a large number of ships. For the first time he spoke of the 'appalling' sums which Germany was spending on her naval programme whereas he had previously concentrated on France and Russia. In South Africa, the navy had accomplished a great deal. 'Since the beginning of July, 181 transports and freight ships have been engaged in the conveyance to South Africa of a force of 132,000 officers and men, 23,000 horses, and 23,600 mules.'[4]

Immediately after Goschen's speech a large Boer force under General Cronje was taken prisoner and the siege of Ladysmith was raised. Goschen chortled to Milner:

What a week we have had! Cronje's surrender, and Ladysmith relieved. I have spent 3 or 4 miserable months about Ladysmith. It was too awful to think of our force of 10,000 British troops surrendering to or captured by Boers! It would have been a disaster to my mind exceeding in humiliation anything in our history.[5]

[1] RA E55/1119.
[2] St Aldwyn Papers, PCC/83.
[3] SP, Hicks Beach to Salisbury, 1 February 1900.
[4] *Hansard*, LXXIX (26 February 1900), 1111–32.
[5] MP, Goschen to Milner, 3 March 1900, Box 29.

Two weeks later Goschen thanked Milner for a lengthy letter about the extent of 'Dutch disloyalty' in South Africa. But the First Lord of the Admiralty was still in a jubilant – though tired – mood. 'What a change in the whole situation. I can go to a Club now where foreigners congregate, which I was not able to do for three months.' Goschen was happy to hear that Milner could work fourteen hours every day but confessed that he could not, 'I work away and do nothing else, though I loathe the sight of the piles of Admiralty papers. I am sick of it and nearly five years is enough of it at my age. And always endless bothers and terrible anxieties.'[1]

Optimism over the course of the Boer War reached new heights in mid-May when the siege of Mafeking was lifted but Goschen now found himself burdened with additional anxieties in China. While initially Salisbury was unworried about the Boxer Rebellion, it soon became obvious to the British Minister in Peking, Sir Claude MacDonald, that the danger to the foreign legations was much greater than originally thought. While Salisbury did order Goschen to redistribute the Far Eastern fleet, the Prime Minister was fearful that an international force sent in to aid the besieged legations might lead to the partition of China. By the middle of June the majority of the Cabinet – including Goschen – were determined to force the Prime Minister's hand. They were convinced that it was essential to get an international relief army organized as rapidly as possible even if it meant the participation of Russians, Japanese and Americans. The pressure which they exerted on Salisbury succeeded, for on 18 June 1900, Goschen advised the Prime Minister that he was

strongly of opinion that the policy of sending more troops to Tientsin and Peking having been accepted, it would be advisable to send more troops from India *at once*, without waiting for further developments. It appears that other nations are sending large detachments, (vide telegrams from Petersburg) and we had better act quickly too, and be prepared for further emergencies.

It appeared that Peking might 'be in great danger for some time and there may be a catastrophe'.[2]

[1] *Ibid.*, Goschen to Milner, 17 March 1900, Box 29.
[2] SP, Goschen to Salisbury, 18 June 1900, private, A/93. See also the report prepared by the Admiralty on the strength of the various states in China waters, CAB. 37/53/56.

Catastrophe was averted, however, as the international force succeeded in entering Peking on 14 August. It now seemed to Goschen that the time was right to strike a bargain with Germany. The kaiser wanted some assurance from Britain that the Open Door would remain in effect in the Yangtze Valley. He also wished to keep the international army in existence until its German commander arrived and objected to the Russian view that the foreign troops must be removed as quickly as possible. It was, Goschen argued, a marvellous opportunity to cement friendly relations with Germany. The Prime Minister disagreed, feeling that there was little to be gained from pushing forward too rapidly in pursuit of the confusing and conflicting statements which William II had uttered. Goschen could see no reason why Germany should not be given assurances about the Open Door in China. The Japanese were worried about Germany's actions and Goschen thought it would be wise 'to keep in touch and on the best terms with Japan, if we are compelled to keep all other Powers at arms length'.[1]

Salisbury – on holiday in the Vosges mountains – was not convinced by Goschen's reasoning. Together with Lansdowne and Lord George Hamilton, Goschen had been left in charge of China policy when the Prime Minister left London. They were later helped by Chamberlain and Balfour. The situation was further complicated when the Prince of Wales and Lascelles, the British Ambassador to Germany, met William II towards the end of August. The kaiser stressed Germany's interest in the Yangtze area and her fear that Britain might attempt to secure a monopoly in that region. The Prime Minister was unimpressed. He still objected to giving any 'special assurances' to the Germans and informed Goschen that the policy of the British government could not be based 'on so slender a basis as the half dozen words which Lascelles has reported from the German Emperor'. The kaiser had made it clear that he wanted a 'formal' statement from the British on the Open Door in China. Salisbury remarked: 'When you formally contract international obligations some precision of language is desirable.' The Prime Minister was unable to

[1] *Ibid.*, Goschen to Salisbury, 17 August 1900.

comprehend the meaning of such terms as 'policy of the open door' and having 'Germany on our side'. The latter was to be

the consideration we are to receive for announcing our adherence to the policy 'of the open door'. These vague utterances may indicate the basis of a future understanding but they certainly do not furnish it. This language might be more intelligible if we had shown the slightest inclination to depart from the policy of not seeking preferential tariff privileges, which we have pursued all over the world.[1]

Goschen sent a copy of this letter to Balfour and commented: 'I have in vain tried to induce Salisbury to meet the German Emperor's advance or suggestion halfway with what success the enclosed copy of a letter in reply to one from me on the subject will show. – Most characteristic.'[2]

On the same date, Goschen informed Chamberlain that Salisbury's attitude was causing Britain to lose a splendid opportunity to exchange ideas with the Germans.[3] On the following day, Goschen complained to Chamberlain that 'Absolute isolation is playing the devil.'[4] Salisbury's opponents, led by Goschen, met at the Admiralty on 4 September and agreed that Goschen should telegraph the Prime Minister urging him to keep the British troops in Peking and to reject the Russian proposal for withdrawal. This was the perfect opportunity to establish better relations with Germany. Salisbury agreed to keep the British contingent in Peking but Goschen was still not satisfied. He complained to Chamberlain that Salisbury had not used the troop issue to open up talks with the kaiser.[5] Goschen wrote to Salisbury and referred to 'the constant antagonism of Russia and of France' which made him hope they 'could keep Germany fairly cordial'.[6] The pressure from his colleagues finally forced Salisbury to give way. He opened negotiations with the Germans and reached agreement over China issues on 16 October 1900. While Chamberlain expressed his satisfaction with this treaty,

[1] BP, copy, Salisbury to Goschen, 29 August 1900, Add. Mss 49706, ff. 257–8.
[2] *Ibid.*, Goschen to Balfour, 1 September 1900, Add. Mss 49706, f. 259.
[3] Amery, *Life of Chamberlain*, vol. 4, pp. 138–9, 1 September 1900.
[4] ChP, typed copy, Goschen to Chamberlain, 2 September 1900.
[5] Garvin and Amery, *Life of Chamberlain*, vol. 4, p. 139, 4 September 1900.
[6] SP, 4 September 1900.

Salisbury regarded it, correctly, as of little permanent value since the terms were drawn so vaguely.

By this time the khaki election of early October had taken place and George Joachim Goschen had decided to end his long career in the House of Commons and at the same time to give up his Cabinet post. Since the death of his wife he had grown ever more tired of the give-and-take in the House of Commons. The huge administrative tasks which the Boer War had imposed upon him increased his desire to retire while he was still in good health. Before informing the Prime Minister, Goschen advised the Duke of Devonshire of his plans to retire. The Cabinet's decision to hold elections in early October had forced Goschen to clarify his thoughts about his political future.[1] On the following day he informed Salisbury that thirty-seven years was 'enough, and more than enough of the House of Commons'. He also wished to resign from the Admiralty. Confident of another victory for the Unionists, Goschen urged the Prime Minister to reconstruct his Cabinet in the public interest. He hoped that their colleagues in the Cabinet would 'place their offices at your disposal and leave you a perfectly free hand'.[2]

Salisbury was not as confident about the election as Goschen and suggested that Goschen keep his seat at the general election and then retire. Goschen strenuously protested. It would be 'unfair' to his constituency.

And suppose what you expect, should take place, namely that we are beaten at the polls. How should I stand before the public, if, having sought re-election in the belief that we should have a majority, I threw up the seat as soon as I found that we should be in a minority, and that as would be said, I could no longer hold office. It would not be decent.[3]

But Goschen had no intention of giving up the Admiralty immediately. He expected to remain there until the elections were over and assuming he had a majority, Salisbury began to 'recast' his ministry.[4]

[1] DP, Goschen to Devonshire, 6 August 1900, 340.2831.
[2] SP, 7 August 1900.
[3] *Ibid.*, Goschen to Salisbury, 13 September 1900.
[4] *Ibid.*, Goschen to Salisbury, 15 September 1900.

The queen was also told of his decision.[1] She would have liked him to remain in office but appreciated his desire to retire and only wished that she too could take a rest.[2] Salisbury had already informed the queen that he 'grieved' at Goschen's retirement since he was 'a very valuable colleague'. He had attempted to change Goschen's mind, 'but quite in vain'. It seemed to Salisbury that Goschen 'would accept a peerage' and the Prime Minister could not think of 'a fitter occasion' for the use of the queen's prerogative.[3]

But Goschen was not absolutely certain that he wished to go to the House of Lords. He confided to Salisbury on 28 September that he had not really 'thought out the alternatives' and wished to discuss it further with his family.[4] In the general election, the Unionists were again returned with a large majority. Goschen then informed Salisbury that he had decided to accept a peerage. He was still undecided as to the name he would choose and used this excuse to seek out information about his new status. 'It would facilitate my decision if I knew what rank in the peerage the Queen contemplates bestowing on me. You have so far simply spoken of a peerage.' He hoped he was not 'indiscreet' in asking and was also disturbed at the thought that his peerage might be announced as 'one of a "batch" '.[5]

Salisbury disliked the term 'one of a "batch" ' for Goschen wrote to the Prime Minister on 31 October 1900:

As to the 'batch', I think you misapprehended my meaning. I knew, of course, that a certain number of peers would be made as usual after an election, but I had not realized that I myself should be included as an item of the batch. As many of my political friends and part of the public were interested to know whether I intended to accept a peerage so as to retain opportunities for some fragment of political life, and as my case was different from that of men given peerages for party services, &c &c, I thought that the announcement of my transfer to the Lords would probably be treated separately. . .

[1] RA B5 1/99.
[2] Queen Victoria to Goschen, 19 September 1900, RA B66/61.
[3] 17 September 1900, RA A76/34.
[4] SP, Goschen, to Salisbury, 28 September 1900.
[5] *Ibid.*, Goschen to Salisbury, 12 and 18 October 1900.

As to the rank, no one knows precedents better than the Queen. When Cabinet Ministers are shunted (euphemistically promoted) they are consoled by the title of Viscount. If another title just passed through my mind as a possibility, I was thinking of length of service and a number of high posts occupied, but this could only be a momentary feeling.

On the rear of the letter, Salisbury's secretary put the matter rather more succinctly: 'Accepts Viscountcy: would have liked an Earldom.' Nor had Goschen been informed that the Prime Minister's son-in-law, Lord Selborne, was to succeed him, since Goschen concluded his letter by observing:

You did not mention my successor in your letter, but Selborne came to me yesterday. I can most sincerely say that you could not have appointed anyone whose selection for the post could have given me so much pleasure. . . . I need not say that I shall be ready to help him to the best of my ability.[1]

His wish not to be 'one of a batch' was conceded. Salisbury informed Devonshire on 15 November 1900 that the list of honours for retiring ministers would be sent in immediately. 'This is the more necessary as Goschen objects to being one of a "batch" '.[2] On that very same day Goschen left the Admiralty and the Cabinet career of the 'Fortunate Youth' which had begun more than thirty years before had finally come to an end. He was created Viscount Goschen of Hawkhurst.

Goschen explained the reasons for his resignation to Milner on 26 October 1900:

There has been a singular unanimity in the way both my friends and the press have accepted what I have done: there has been scarcely a word of censure as to my withdrawing myself from my old sphere and my work. Indeed I have had the most satisfactory letters from all sides. Only some of my own family have murmured and asked me whether my action was patriotic. I feel no qualms on that score. I am sure I have done right, though I can understand without being vain that many people think it may be rather difficult to fill my place at the Admiralty. But there is one advantage to the public to which I attribute great importance: viz. that the Government must be more or less reconstructed and that an example has been set, which it may be difficult for others, on occasions, to avoid following, of Ministers retiring spontaneously when they approach or pass 70 and when younger men

[1] *Ibid.*, Goschen to Salisbury, 31 October 1900.
[2] DP, 340.2850.

ought to come on. Again a change ought to take place in *comparatively* peaceful times, if it is possible that the older men would break down under the pressure of a war, so that new men know the ropes, and have gained some experience.

It seemed to Goschen that the Cabinet had been getting a little 'stale'. He reported that Seacox Heath was 'looking very beautiful now, but alas! only two daughters! We all miss Alice extremely.'[1]

Goschen was intensely interested in the partial reconstruction of the Cabinet which took place. Lord Selborne succeeded Goschen at the Admiralty, Salisbury gave up the Foreign Office to Lansdowne while remaining Prime Minister and St John Brodrick replaced Lansdowne at the War Office. Sir Matthew White Ridley and Henry Chaplin were sacked by Salisbury while Lord James of Hereford remained as Chancellor of the Duchy of Lancaster even though Salisbury and Balfour had hoped he might voluntarily step down. James had already informed Goschen in the summer that he was opposed to the entire Cabinet placing their offices at the disposal of Salisbury and Goschen had concluded that the seventy-two-year-old James wished to retain his position. Not until the last days of December did Arthur Balfour finally find time to write Goschen about the Cabinet changes. It had been 'abominable work' and there were many 'sorenesses which are not likely soon to be healed'. The Cabinet was a 'good one' but only time and events would show if it was a 'strong one'.[2]

Goschen was delighted that Balfour had treated him as if they were still Cabinet colleagues. He hoped that their political relationship might remain as close as it had been. The former First Lord of the Admiralty felt considerable sympathy for Henry Chaplin and thought that James ought to have resigned. The reconstruction had not been made public in a very satisfactory manner. 'It concentrated attention on each single case unduly. Piecemeal announcements were perhaps unavoidable but prolonged the agony, kept men in expectation and made disappointments more acute.' The appointment of Salisbury's son to a

[1] MP, Box 29.
[2] Goschen Papers, Balfour to Goschen, [?] December 1900, Dep. C 183, f. 49.

position in the ministry was also a 'strong order' but a 'father's services are always allowed to count in favour of the son'. Having mentioned the advantages which a father can obtain for his son, Goschen raised a family issue which Balfour had ignored in his letter. Goschen had asked that young George be considered for an appointment as Whip but the post had gone to Victor Cavendish instead.

I am bound to say that it came round to me from many people that the idea was very current that they thought *I* had a fair claim to that kind of recognition of services of the father in favour of the sons and nephews, when they are otherwise eligible; but I myself was very reticent about it, not wishing it to be known that I had approached you on the subject in case of non-success. *I* quite admit that Victor Cavendish had a prior claim. . . Shall I confess that the fact of your leaving my letter so long unanswered made me think that the idea was being entertained?[1]

Although distressed at being unable to obtain the post for his son, Goschen, nevertheless, was looking forward to his well-earned retirement.

It is clear that Goschen embodied many of the finest values of the nineteenth-century middle class: hard work, honesty, industry, morality. But he never liberated himself from one of the more deplorable bourgeois attitudes: a tendency to place personal blame on those who had failed to rise up the ladder to worldly success. He could not grasp the possibility that the economic and social system might be responsible for poverty, misery and unemployment. Nor did Goschen realize that by asking for special favours for his son, he was attacking the central ethical value of *laissez-faire* liberalism: equality of opportunity for everyone. He failed to comprehend that he had, himself, started life far more equal than many others because of his father's great wealth.

An absolutely honest and dedicated politician and public servant, Goschen was wrong on the two greatest issues of his active political career: the extension of the vote and Ireland. As he grew older, he tended to look backward rather than forward. There was both an ideological failure and a failure of imagination.

[1] BP, Goschen to Balfour, 1 January 1901, Add. Mss 49706, ff. 262–4.

This is, of course, not uncommon. Bold and dynamic leaders who understand the past, dominate the present, and partially control the movement to the future are never in abundance. This may not be a total misfortune. But it is apparent that Goschen's reach never exceeded his grasp.

CHAPTER 13

'JOE' AGAIN 1900—1907

The death of Queen Victoria in 1901 and the retirement of Salisbury in 1902 seemed to herald the dawn of a new age. Arthur Balfour became Prime Minister when his uncle stepped down. Within a year he found himself trapped between tariff reformers and Free Traders. Chamberlain split the Conservative party in 1903 as he had previously assisted in the break-up of the Liberal party. Ironically the separation which had been predicted in 1885 now took place – Chamberlain broke with Devonshire and Goschen – but it took place in the Conservative rather than the Liberal party. Chamberlain, the old Radical, succeeded in capturing the Conservative party and in driving out many who detested the Liberals but were unable to shake off their belief that English prosperity and Free Trade went hand in hand. The Colonial Secretary was genuinely concerned about unifying the empire and believed that a tariff would provide more employment as well as funds for a system of old-age pensions. But he soon found that many of his supporters were manufacturers and farmers whose major concern was the protection of the occupation they represented. The Fair Traders of the early 1880s had finally found a leader and if he insisted upon linking their demands for protection with his fuzzy ideas about unifying the empire, they would not complain – not so long as it meant the return of a protective tariff.

It seemed to Chamberlain that he could begin the move towards imperial preference by returning the registration duty on corn to the colonies while maintaining it with regard to all other states. This duty had not been regarded as protective and was not finally removed until the early 1870s. It had been reintroduced by Hicks Beach in his 1902 Budget to help pay for the Boer War. Goschen endorsed the registration duty on corn because it was not protective and would broaden the base of taxation. He denied that it was 'the thin end of the wedge' that would ultimately lead to a protective tariff.[1]

C. T. Ritchie succeeded Hicks Beach at the Exchequer in 1902. Despite Chamberlain's objections, the new Chancellor convinced the Cabinet that the corn tax should be removed. The Colonial Secretary decided to present his case to the public in a speech at Birmingham on 15 May 1903. Goschen was aghast and made immediate plans to oppose Chamberlain. It was imperative 'that the difficulties of Chamberlain's policy, and its possible consequences should be exhaustively examined before men commit themselves to one side or the other'. His speech would be 'one of elucidation' rather 'than of denunciation'.[2] Goschen approached Chamberlain's proposals from a financial point of view, while Chamberlain's ideas were coloured by his manufacturing background. Goschen demanded that the Cabinet state whether it approved the Colonial Secretary's startling proposals. He wanted positive proof that a tax on food would lead to higher wages for everyone and asked how the system of old-age pensions was to be established.[3] Goschen's argument was really on two levels. His emotional appeal was that the people's food should not be taxed but intellectually he feared that protection would be another step on the road to state socialism. Through manipulation of the tariff, the state would be able to determine the levels of production in all British industries. The unity of the empire would be damaged since it would be based on commercial bargains over the rate of the preferential tariff every few years.

Goschen helped in forming a Unionist Free Food League in July 1903 and played an active part in rebutting Chamberlain's arguments. He pressed Devonshire and the other Free Traders in the Cabinet to get Balfour to speak out against the tariff reformers. The Cabinet was hopelessly divided, with Balfour trying to employ his own version of Gladstone's umbrella. Chamberlain was prepared to resign in order to take his programme to the people. Balfour was moving in Chamberlain's

[1] *Hansard*, CX (3 July 1902), 652–62.
[2] DP, Goschen to Devonshire, 2 June 1903, 340.2913.
[3] *Hansard*, CXXIII (15 June 1903), 837–931.

direction though he did not yet regard the introduction of colonial preference as practical politics. He did, however, accept the principle of retaliatory tariffs. But if Chamberlain resigned, Balfour was determined to remove the most doctrinaire Free Traders in his Cabinet – Ritchie, Lord George Hamilton and Lord Balfour of Burleigh. He wanted to retain the Duke of Devonshire as a symbol for the moderate Free Traders while the Chamberlainites were to be placated by making Austen Chamberlain the new Chancellor of the Exchequer. By chopping off the two extremes, Balfour hoped that he might maintain a degree of party unity. The Prime Minister's plan seemed to be a success. The Duke of Devonshire agreed to stay after hearing that Chamberlain had resigned even though Ritchie and Balfour of Burleigh had been dismissed and Lord George Hamilton had also resigned. Goschen returned from Germany at this time and pronounced recent developments 'a nice kettle of fish'.[1] Devonshire was stung by accusations that he had not been faithful to Ritchie, Balfour of Burleigh and Lord George Hamilton and took the first opportunity to resign three weeks later. Arthur Elliot, Goschen's biographer and a Free Trader, resigned as Financial Secretary to the Treasury when Ritchie was sacked.

Once Devonshire had resigned from the Cabinet in early October of 1903, Goschen found himself playing the same role he had played to such perfection in 1885–6. The Duke would lead the battle against Chamberlain while Goschen supplied the ammunition.[2] Devonshire promptly replied that he was 'very unwilling' to command 'a new political movement'. He was 'getting old' and was 'disgusted' with politics. The fiscal question was 'difficult and complicated' and he had 'never given any special study to it'. It would be awkward for him to undertake the action proposed by Goschen since he had just left the government after much hesitation and did not wish to attack it. Devonshire also wanted to keep the Liberal Unionist organization together and feared that it would collapse if he entered the fray against Chamberlain. While the Liberal Unionist Association might not

---

[1] DP, Goschen to Devonshire, 20 September [1903], 340.2967.
[2] *Ibid.*, Goschen to Devonshire, 9 October [1903], 340.3008.

be 'of much value to anybody' at that moment, it was a barrier against Home Rule and had been one of the Duke's 'chief political' contributions.[1]

Goschen spurned Devonshire's plea. It was a serious national emergency. If Devonshire failed to act, it would damage the Free Trade Unionists and would seriously impair 'the degree to which they may hope to have any influence on the public mind'. The Duke had indicated that he was prepared to accept re-taliation and Goschen replied that this would not disqualify him from leading the Unionist Free Traders.

We would not lay down that retaliation should be absolutely barred on principle, only we don't see how it is to be applied till we have a concrete proposal: indeed *your* attitude. There are some who would not go so far, but not many and I think the League might officially publish its opinion in the above sense.

They had no desire to attack the government and were prepared to handle this issue 'delicately' since the Free Traders were basically 'an anti-Chamberlain body'. Goschen could under-stand the Duke's 'scruples' about the Liberal Unionist Association but he wondered how important that body really was 'in the present situation'. Balfour was sinking 'deeper and deeper into a bag of contradictions'. It appeared, unfortunately, that the ' "party" ' was 'too much in favour of the Chamberlain plan'.[2]

After some additional coaxing, Devonshire agreed to take the leadership. Chamberlain became so annoyed that he had the duke stripped of his power in the Liberal Unionist Association. On 1 December 1904, a new Unionist Free Trade Club was formed with the Duke of Devonshire as president. But before the triumph of securing Devonshire, there was one bitter defeat for the Goschen family. George Joachim Goschen, the younger, a Free Trader like his father, was rejected by his constituency party. A Chamberlainite was selected to replace him at the next general election.[3] George was eventually adopted by another

[1] *Ibid.*, copy, Devonshire to Goschen, 10 October 1903, 340.3009.
[2] *Ibid.*, Goschen to Devonshire, 11 October [1903], 340.3010.
[3] *Hansard*, CXXXV (18 May 1904), 258–62.

constituency but received a sound beating in the general election of 1906.

Goschen was disgusted with Balfour's obscure statements. On 22 July 1904 he remarked: 'There is now a state of greater doubt and uncertainty than I can ever remember during the whole of my political life.'[1] And when Devonshire moved that the House of Lords express its opposition to a general or penal tariff and a 'system of Colonial Preference based on the taxation of food', Goschen observed:

I feel certain that intellectually Mr Balfour has not surrendered. As regards his will and other portions of his character, I am not sure how far the fascination of a strong man may not have affected him to a certain extent. I do say, however, that Mr Balfour's silence when Mr Chamberlain desires to annex him, and when he has declared that they are both agreed in essentials, is significant, and it is in my judgment absolutely deplorable. It is a silence that has done immense harm to the Party and has led to much mystification and confusion in the country.

Balfour was 'too timid', 'too cautious', and 'too abstract'. Devonshire's motion which Goschen had supported was defeated 121 to 57.[2]

Goschen spoke many times on Free Trade platforms throughout the country. He pointed out that food and raw materials made up three-quarters of the imports into the United Kingdom. This left less than 25 per cent which could be called 'criminal alien' merchandise. 'On the other hand, some 80 per cent of *our* exports represent manufactured goods.' It was impossible to deny that Britain's industrial leadership had been lost but it was to be expected that other nations would attempt to build up their trade and commerce much as the British had done. There was no need to become 'hysterical' and rush to carry out 'sudden changes of a vast character'. Chamberlain's scheme would not bring unemployment to an end.

However much you may change the terms and the forms of employment, there will be in this country, as there has been in almost every country – as

[1] *Ibid.*, CXXXVIII (22 July 1904), 930–3.
[2] *Ibid.*, CL (27 July 1905), 541–51.

there is now in New York, and there is elsewhere – a large residuum of men whom all your efforts to secure increased employment will scarcely reach.[1]

Goschen agreed to investigate the consequences of a retaliatory tariff but he remained unalterably opposed to a general scientific tariff.

Balfour's majority in the House of Commons withered away as he refused to commit himself wholeheartedly to either Chamberlain or the Free Traders. He finally decided to resign on 4 December 1905 hoping that Liberal dissension might prevent them from forming a government. He was mistaken; Sir Henry Campbell-Bannerman successfully constructed a Cabinet. The Boer War, opposition to the Education Act of 1902, and strong support for Free Trade had restored Liberal unity. The Conservatives were now reduced to fighting over Balfour's body. Hoping to moderate the activities of Devonshire and Goschen, Balfour conjured up the spectre of a Radical electoral victory. Home Rule and many other 'violent' measures would be produced. Was it wise, the Prime Minister had asked, for Goschen and Devonshire to appear on the same platform with Radicals? Goschen replied that the 'Conservative organizations would never give us a platform or help us to have a meeting.'[2] A week later, Goschen condemned a Balfour speech as 'incorrigible... The Chamberlainites so far seem dissatisfied, but can we be satisfied? He expounded retaliation to a point, where it became so broad, that on his principles, it would have a very wide, not an exceptional application.'[3]

The expectation that Campbell-Bannerman would call for an immediate dissolution in January led both Chamberlainites and Unionist Free Traders to claim that the former Prime Minister supported their position. Goschen wanted Balfour to state his opposition to a general protective tariff.

My great desire is that you should make such declarations as would enable as large a group of Conservative anti-protectionists to remain within

---

[1] Goschen, 'Some Aspects of the Fiscal Controversy', speech delivered on 27 January 1905.
[2] DP, Goschen to Devonshire, 8 November 1905, 340.3156.
[3] Ibid., Goschen to Devonshire, 16 November [1905], 340.3159.

the party as possible under *your leadership* so that the Conservative party may not drift to Chamberlain as a whole, this not only for the sake of Free Trade, but for the sake of the highest interests of the country. I think it of the greatest importance *now* that Chamberlain should no longer claim you as substantially agreed with him. . . Give those who are really your followers, both retaliationists proper, and those who squeeze their conscience up to retaliation, a brief for their constituencies which will clearly free them from the charge of being protectionists in disguise.[1]

Chamberlain, however, was confident that the future belonged to him. But he expected the Unionists to receive a drubbing in the forthcoming election. All Goschen's hopes that something might be salvaged were destroyed when the Liberals scored a massive victory in the general election.

The appearance of more than 50 Labour members was even more significant than the Conservative debacle. Only 157 Unionists were elected and more than 100 were Chamberlain's supporters. Goschen was angry at the way the tariff reformers were 'gloating over every Unionist Free Trader who lost his seat'. He still wanted to hold the Unionist Party together if at all possible even though tariff reformers and Free Traders seemed more irreconcilable than ever. At first he had thought that Chamberlain would regard the election as a defeat for tariff reform but Goschen now realized that this was not the case. He confided to Devonshire:

I thought, and think, that in view of the extraordinary composition of the new parliament, all shades of Conservatism would be inclined to act as far as possible together to mitigate as far as possible the dangerous legislation which was sure to be proposed in every direction and that the fiscal controversy, after the smashing defeat of Protection would not be a welcome subject for the rank and file of the Unionist Party.

I have recognized by this time that I was mistaken. Chamberlain, his friends, and his press continue as truculent as possible, and I see that they are already angling for the Labour vote. They are determined that the Unionist party is to be exclusively a protectionist party.[2]

Balfour had lost his own seat in the election but was then returned for a vacancy in the City of London. In February 1906,

---

[1] BP, Add. Mss 49706, ff. 311–16.
[2] DP, Goschen to Devonshire, 28 January [1906], 340.3190.

he capitulated to Chamberlain in the 'Valentine letters'. Goschen complained at the release of this correspondence just prior to a meeting of the Unionist party and Balfour replied in an irritated tone:

> I am very weary of leading a Party which either cannot, or will not, understand what seem to me to be quite plain statements, and if it were not for the fact that to abandon my post now would be little short of desertion I would take my doctor's hard-pressed advice, and throw up the leading part in what is too petty to be called 'tragedy' and too dull to deserve the name of 'comedy'.[1]

Goschen expressed his distress over the 'Valentine letters' in the House of Lords a week later. In the past, Balfour had been 'anxious only to retaliate in those cases where retaliation was specially necessary' while Chamberlain 'wished to cover the whole country with a tariff which would rest upon trade as a whole instead of simply aiding parts that might be shown to be especially suffering'. The 'Valentine letters' seemed to prove that Chamberlain had won.[2]

Goschen had continued to keep a close eye on his beloved Admiralty and he became apprehensive at the aggressive re-forming policies of the First Sea Lord, Admiral Sir John Fisher. Fisher regarded Goschen as a prime enemy of his policies. He would certainly have been surprised by Goschen's advice to Balfour on 4 March 1905. Lord Selborne had resigned as First Lord of the Admiralty in order to go to South Africa as Governor-General in Milner's place.

> I am wondering (with much anxiety) whom you will send to the Admiralty. The boldest plan would be to make Fisher a peer, and First Lord; not unconstitutional, but, I fully admit, a course open to many objections.
> But it is equally, perhaps more objectional, to have the First *Sea* Lord practically a dictator, and the First Lord subordinate to him in fact, though of course only in fact; and the position of a new First Lord, *unless he is a very strong man*, might and probably will, be a difficult one, indeed a false one. Besides his own intellectual equipment, perfect knowledge and powers of plausible presentation of his views, Fisher has the whole press at his back and *the King in his pocket*. I think even Selborne's position was often not

[1] BP, copy, Balfour to Goschen, 15 February 1906, Add. Mss 49706, ff. 317–18.
[2] *Hansard*, CLII (22 February 1906), 477–81.

very comfortable. The Navy would dislike the appointment but there is much to be said for it, especially as I don't see the strong man whom you have got to send to the Admiralty, and if you have not a strong man, the position of the Civilian First Lord may be damaged to a degree which will change, who knows for how long, the relative position of the civilian and professional elements.[1]

Goschen's counsel was not accepted. Earl Cawdor, formerly chairman of the Great Western Railway, was sent to the Admiralty.

In early February 1903, Goschen informed Milner that the biography he had been writing of his grandfather – the publisher of Leipzig – had finally been published.

Out! out at last! I am so glad to be done with the book. I say in my preface that it has been a labour of love and so it has in a sense, but I am glad to have done. . .

Reviews out to-day; *Times* excellent: *Daily Telegraph* very good: *Daily Chronicle* intelligent, (hitting kindly enough at my diverging too much) but very appreciative: *Morning Post* thin, and *Standard* poor. But no jarring note.[2]

Milner was delighted with the news that the biography had been completed after so many years.[3] Goschen also had the task of defending his former secretary when the latter was denounced by the Bishop of Hereford for permitting Chinese indentured labourers to work in the gold mines of South Africa. A labour shortage in that war-torn area made their presence absolutely essential, Goschen argued, and Milner's plan would provide adequate protection for them. The House of Lords supported Milner by a majority of four to one.[4]

While Goschen was glad that Free Trade had been saved as a result of the general election of 1906, he discovered that he had called in the devil in order to cast out the devil. The Liberals were united behind their elderly Scottish Prime Minister and determined to carry out a programme of social reform. Home Rule for

[1] BP, Goschen to Balfour, Add. Mss 49706, ff. 306–7.
[2] MP, typed copy, Goschen to Milner, 6 February 1903, Box 85.
[3] *Ibid.*, Milner to Goschen, 28 February 1903, Box 28. A German translation had very little success. Goschen informed Lady Blennerhassett on 7 January 1906 (Blennerhassett Papers, Add. 7486/52) that only 99 out of 800 copies had been sold. 'Disastrous! The book was, I fancy, insufficiently pushed but *most* favourably reviewed and recommended.'
[4] *Hansard*, CXXXII (21 March 1904), pp. 129–33.

Ireland was put aside for the moment. One of the most important measures of the 1906 legislative session was a new Education Bill designed to remove some of the Nonconformist complaints over the Education Act of 1902. It was amended out of existence by the House of Lords which indicated that it was going to follow the same path of obstruction which it had pursued in 1892-5. Goschen had approved of the Education Act of 1902 though he did object to the degree of control which he felt local authorities would now be able to exercise over Church of England schools. He spoke as a manager of a 'humble parish school' who believed that the power of the school inspector was already 'thorough and despotic'. It seemed to Goschen that the bill went too far in weakening the school managers and in enlarging the influence of the local authority which could now add two members to the four who served at present on the boards of the voluntary schools.[1] Liberal proposals for amending Balfour's Act in 1906 were 'intolerable'. Goschen conceded there was room for improvement but he was convinced that the 'verdict of the country is in the main against secularism'. He agreed that the country 'insisted upon public control' but he wondered if the civic authority would be as effective 'as a local body which has been long in touch with the parents and children in the locality'.[2] The Conservative Lords had little difficulty in transforming the bill which the Liberals had passed in the Commons. Eventually the Liberals angrily decided not to pursue this issue. The Education Bill was dropped but not before Goschen delivered his last parliamentary speech. He defended the Lords' amendments and expressed his fear that the Liberals might try to do by administrative decree what they had failed to do by law.

The Church, at all events for the present, retains its 12,000 schools, and it will be the business of the Church, by increased exertion, by increased enthusiasm, and by increased sacrifices, if necessary, to see that she keeps the same position of respect and confidence which she has established in the country, so that when fresh attacks come it will be found that the Church

[1] *Hansard*, CXV (4 December 1902), 1266-78.
[2] DP, Goschen to Devonshire, 20 April [1906], 340.3241; *Hansard*, CLXIII (25 October 1906), 301-2.

has not been asleep, but has done its utmost, in these troublous times, to maintain the schools, which have been founded by the exertions of the past, and which will be continued by similar exertions in the future.[1]

Goschen was especially worried that the Gladstonian tradition for economy and the Radical dislike for armaments might lead to large defence cuts. On 30 July 1906 he again urged the retention of the two-power standard for the British navy. Germany's naval activities had aroused considerable concern in Britain and Goschen proceeded to analyse the actions of the kaiser and his associates. His assessment was balanced and moderate.

If there is an idea that Germany is arming against ourselves I think it a mistake; if it is thought that Germany is arming against France or Russia, or any particular Power I believe that is also a mistake. Why does Germany push on her naval expansion, which France will plead compels her to do the same? Not for aggression, but from a settled policy. She requires more territory for her teeming millions. She feels that she must have colonies, that she must expand, that she must have outlets for her commerce, and that she must have sea power like us to hold her own against every possible effort to limit her colonial expansion or paralyse her action. Her Ministers have no desire for war. But they have an Imperial German policy. Is it likely that anything that will happen at the Hague Conference will arrest what they consider to be their mission – what the Emperor considers to be a mission placed upon himself to expand the German power? Those who think so are living in a fool's paradise.[2]

Perhaps the most pleasant event of Goschen's final years was his selection, without opposition, as Chancellor of Oxford University in 1903 upon the death of Lord Salisbury. He took a very keen interest in the work and functions attached to his office.[3] Neither Goschen nor Devonshire was, as yet, greatly worried about a new Home Rule Bill. On 22 January 1907 Goschen wrote to the duke to inquire about Walter Long's attempt to form a Union Defence League in case it should be needed. Long had just asked Goschen to join the new body. The elderly statesman wondered

[1] *Hansard*, CLXVII (19 December 1906), 1407–11.
[2] *Hansard*, CLXII (30 July 1906), 313–18.
[3] Goschen Papers, Bodleian Library, Dep. C. 183. There are three packets of letters from Goschen to Percy Matheson, a tutor at New College who acted as Goschen's secretary. They cover the years from 1904 to 1907 and are concerned with the Chancellor's activities.

if Devonshire would join this group though he had recently declined the presidency. 'I should not like to act differently from you as to *joining*. *I* think the whole thing unnecessary, and don't care to put myself under Long's auspices, but I don't know quite what to say.'[1]

The duke's advice made little difference. In less than three weeks Lord Goschen died in his sleep. His will had been signed on 22 May 1905 and was probated on 24 May 1907. Goschen left over £141,000, which taxes reduced to £122,000.[2] Just after the funeral his daughter Beatrice wrote to Milner that

such a swift and peaceful passing away was indeed *merciful*. He had often talked to us about death and always *had* hoped it might be *sudden* and one feels his wish was granted him as a reward for his noble and good life – one could not bear to think of him having to withdraw from politics and other interests for when his physical prowess had failed one felt his heart and mind would still be in them.

She stressed the 'example of faithfulness, duty and courage in adversity' which her father had always represented to the family.[3]

John Morley commented on Goschen's death in his diary on 7 February 1907:

Everybody to-day is sorrowing at the death of Lord Goschen. He had been a good friend for many years: one of the very *cleverest* men, in the strict sense of the word, that I have ever known in my life. The papers are quoting to-day what I said about him in my book on Mr. Gladstone: that he had the large views of Liberal Oxford along with the practical energy of the City of London, added to a hard fibre given him by Nature – Poor man – I'm truly sorry he has gone.[4]

The Spectator concluded that 'No Englishman has done more to rescue politics from the charge of subordinating public interests to those either of persons or of parties.'[5]

Goschen's death in 1907 spared him the pain of witnessing the social turmoil of the period immediately prior to the First World

[1] DP, 340.3255.
[2] George Edward Cokayne, *The Complete Peerage* (London, 1910–59), vol. 6, p. 30.
[3] MP, Beatrice Goschen to Milner, 20 February [1907], Box 45.
[4] Lord John Morley, *Recollections* (London, 1917), vol. 2, pp. 201–2.
[5] XCVIII, (16 February 1907), 243–4.

War when Asquith's Cabinet rode the whirlwind of Irish, trade-union and feminist demands. While one must admire Goschen for his honesty and personal integrity, it is apparent that he was severely limited by a philosophy – *laissez-faire* liberalism – which had been only partly appropriate in the mid-Victorian period and which became increasingly obsolete with the passing of time. The achievements of nineteenth-century liberalism were, however, of considerable magnitude and significance. Goschen had been in the vanguard of the struggle to replace the aristocratic state with a liberal market society in which each individual would have equality of opportunity and all careers would be open to talent.

During the nineteenth century the middle class revolutionized the means of production and released the productive potential of the nation. The industrial revolution thoroughly altered class relationships in Great Britain, the first nation to endure the promise and agony of modernization. An aristocratic, parochial, agricultural society became democratic, urban and capitalist. But Adam Smith's *laissez-faire* utopia was never achieved, since other elements of society rushed to defend themselves against the destructive aspects of industrialization.

By the end of Gladstone's first ministry much of the British middle class was satisfied with the broad outlines of the new society it had constructed. It now became necessary for many Liberals to decide if their liberalism was a dynamic philosophy which must continually adjust to changing situations or whether it was nothing more than a specific programme designed to meet one particular set of problems. For the latter group it would be easy to move into the Conservative party in order to protect property of all types against the challenge of the non-propertied. *Laissez-faire* was under attack from democratic liberalism, radicalism and socialism.

The Liberal Unionist party was the vehicle that carried many Whigs and moderate Liberals into the Conservative party. This enabled the Liberal party to move decisively in a radical direction when it returned to office in 1905. But it was all to no avail as the once great Liberal party was displaced by the Labour movement.

The enduring values of liberalism have influenced, however, every corner of British life, including Conservative and Labour platforms.

Goschen's brand of nineteenth-century liberalism was shaped by a passionate belief in *laissez-faire* economics. His optimism about the future turned sour as he came to fear the implications of democracy. Writing in the middle of the Second World War, R. H. Tawney argued that 'freedom' must mean 'not the mere absence of restrictions, but the presence of conditions enabling all to participate according to their powers, in the treasures of civilization'. Goschen had been a splendid warrior in the battle to remove 'restrictions'. But he drew back from doing more, believing that constructive economic and social legislation would be harmful rather than beneficial. Democracy, Goschen feared, would lead to equality and equality would destroy the liberty for which the middle class had fought.

Goschen might very well have been thinking of himself when he described his grandfather as a 'moderate reformer'.

Though an idealist by temperament, he was no dreamer of dreams: his views were broad and practical. But no doubt a strong conservative vein ran through his character: his tastes inclined him to the keeping up of old manners and customs, especially if they were emblematical of some traditional sentiment. Generally, I apprehend, he was classed as old-fashioned.

The printer of Leipzig preferred to hold on 'to good old traditions, in contrast to a rising generation, who were anxious to impart an entirely new form and spirit to the book-trade'.[1]

The new 'form and spirit' of the twentieth century would stress state intervention, collectivism, equality and socialism. But it would owe a great deal to those liberals – like Goschen – who had transformed the aristocratic state, modernized the economy, and provided a climate for free and open discussion, even though it meant that their own ideas would also be revolutionized by an ever-changing environment.

[1] Goschen, *Georg Joachim Goschen*, vol. 2, pp. 458–9.

FINANCIAL INTERESTS OF THE GOSCHEN FAMILY

Three of Goschen's four brothers, Henry, Charles Hermann and Alexander Heun, were active in the firm of Fruhling and Goschen. Charles Hermann Goschen was the senior partner in the firm and also became a director of the Bank of England and a chairman of Lloyd's. The first issue of *The Directory of Directors* in 1880 listed some 2000 Joint-stock companies which had filed reports. This volume (pp. 97–8) indicates that George Joachim Goschen was a director of Alliance British and Foreign Life and Fire Assurance Co.; Alliance Marine Assurance Co.; and a governor of the Hudson's Bay Co. Henry Goschen was a director of the East and West India Dock Co.; London Assurance Corporation; London and San Francisco Bank Ltd.; and the Mexican Railway Co. Ltd. Charles Hermann Goschen was a director of the Bank of England; and the Royal Exchange Assurance Corporation. Alexander Heun Goschen was a director of the Dunaburg and Witepsk Railway Co. Ltd.; and the London Joint Stock Bank.

The Directory of Directors for the year 1890 shows (p. 222) that George Joachim no longer had any directorships (he was then Chancellor of the Exchequer) while the financial interests of his brothers remained substantially the same. Alexander Heun Goschen acquired two additional directorships: Indemnity Mutual Marine Assurance Co. Ltd.; and Northern Assurance Co. Henry Goschen was no longer on the board of directors of the East and West India Dock Co.

The Directory of Directors shows the same kinds of financial and insurance interests rather than industrial commitments in 1900 (pp. 315–16). George Joachim's nephews are now also included. They had been brought into the firm of Fruhling and Goschen and were acquiring directorships of their own. George Joachim Goschen, the younger, was a member of the London committee of the Bank of Roumania; and the Imperial Ottoman Bank. Goschen's other son, William Henry, was a director of the Alliance Marine and General Assurance Co. Ltd. and one of Goschen's nephews was a director of the Ocean Marine Insurance Co. Ltd.

The Directory of Directors for 1910 demonstrates that the new generation of Goschens' was following in their parents' footsteps. The second Viscount Goschen (George the younger) was a director of the Bank of Roumania Ltd.; and the Star Life Assurance Society. He was also chairman of the London County and Westminster Bank Ltd; and a member of the London Committee of the Imperial Ottoman Bank. His brother, William Henry Goschen, was a director of the Provincial Bank of Ireland Ltd.; the Sun Insurance Office; the Union Discount Co. of London Ltd.; and vice-chairman of the Sun Life Assurance Society. Their cousin, William Henry Neville Goschen, was a director of the Atlas Assurance Co. Ltd.; the Chartered Bank of India, Australia and China; and the National Provincial Bank of England Ltd.

The yearly edition of *Bradshaw's Railway Manual, Share-holders' Guide and Official Directory* is not of much importance with respect to the Goschen family since the only railways on which they served as directors were the Dunaburg (Riga) and Witepsk Railway Co. Ltd in Russia and the Mexican Railway Co. Ltd.

A letter from Cromer to Elliot commented upon Elliot's recently published biography of Goschen. Cromer, like Goschen, remained a Free Trader and was elected president of the Unionist Free Trade Club upon the death of the Duke of Devonshire in 1908. Parts of the letter of 2 May 1911 from Cromer to Elliot follow:

The book has interested me deeply; partly by reason of the very warm friendship I entertained for Goschen and partly because I have passed through very much the same transitions of political thought which he traversed.

During the years 1877–79 which were very critical years in Egyptian history I was practically serving under Goschen's orders, and had very excellent opportunities of forming an opinion of his character and abilities. Amongst other things I may say that I think he was certainly one of the shrewdest critics I ever came across. He was undoubtedly a strong man, and was not at all averse to decisive action when he saw his way clearly, but he was very cautious. His judicious, highly trained and very evenly balanced mind led him to foresee every possible difficulty that might occur when any proposal was laid before him. This rendered him critical, sometimes hypercritical. I had at times to act without waiting for any definite approval on his behalf, but looking back after a lapse of years I can well see now that the combination of Goschen, who was very cautious in London, and myself, being more inclined to make up my mind rapidly, in Cairo, was in many respects most useful. It enabled us eventually to get the Commission of Enquiry appointed, which led to the abdication of Ismail and gave the death-blow to the infamous system of government with which he was associated.

Goschen's prophecy (vol. 1, page 163) as regards the dethronement of political economy and advance of philanthropy is very remarkable, and has turned out to be absolutely true. I notice (page 281) that he rather modified his opinion subsequently, but in this case I confess I think his first thoughts were better than his second.

There is a typed copy of the above letter in the Cromer Papers, F.O. 633/20, which also contains a copy of Elliot's reply of 3 May 1911.

After commenting on Cromer's views about Egypt, Elliot wrote:

Your doubt as to whether Goschen was right in his advocacy of what is called 'broadening the basis of taxation' has always been present to me. My tendency is rather to agree with Gladstone's views, and it has rather strengthened me in so thinking, that Goschen himself in his half-dozen budgets, and in years of peace (though war did not seem very far off) never suggested *a means* for carrying out that policy – except indeed the abortive little 'veal and ham' business. . .

I shall put your letter in my special copy of 'Goschen' as a most interesting comment on his career. I took a great deal of pains in tracing out through letters and articles the general modification of his views, and the effect that experience had upon him in turning him *against* democracy. As you say, his distrust as to the working classes on matters where a *not* well-instructed sentiment might conflict with established conclusions of political economy is very *striking*. It is to me also striking that none of innumerable newspaper reviews on the book have alluded to this!

SELECT BIBLIOGRAPHY

The small collection of Goschen material at the Bodleian Library is but a tiny part of what must have been the Goschen Papers. Some letters were returned to various correspondents but the vast majority seem to have disappeared. Correspondence with members of the Goschen family failed to turn up anything of significance with the exception of the letters (mostly pertaining to South America) in the possession of Mr D. C. Goschen of Rusape, Rhodesia. Only those manuscripts, books and articles which were of particular importance in the writing of this biography have been listed below.

MANUSCRIPTS

First Earl St Aldwyn Papers (Sir Michael Hicks Beach), Williamstrip Park, Cirencester
First Earl of Balfour Papers, British Museum
Sir Rowland Blennerhassett Papers, Cambridge University Library
Edward Cardwell Papers, Public Record Office
First Viscount Chilston Papers (Aretas Akers-Douglas), Kent Archives Office, Maidstone
First Earl of Cranbrook Papers (Gathorne-Hardy), Ipswich and East Suffolk Record Office, Ipswich
Joseph Chamberlain Papers, University of Birmingham Library
First Earl of Cromer Papers, Public Record Office
Eighth Duke of Devonshire Papers, Chatsworth, Derbyshire
Sir Charles Dilke Papers, British Museum
First Marquess of Dufferin Papers, Public Record Office of Northern Ireland
Arthur R. D. Elliot Papers, Philpstoun House, Linlithgow, West Lothian, Scotland
William E. Gladstone Papers, British Museum
Second Earl Granville Papers, Public Record Office
Fourth Earl Grey Papers, University of Durham
Hambleden Papers (W. H. Smith), Strand House, London
Sir Edward Hamilton Papers, British Museum
First Earl of Iddesleigh Papers (Sir Stafford Northcote), British Museum
Viscount Milner Papers, Bodleian Library
First Marquess of Ripon Papers, British Museum
First Earl Russell Papers, Public Record Office
Third Marquess of Salisbury Papers, Christ Church, Oxford
Fifth Earl Spencer Papers, Althorp, Northamptonshire
Queen Victoria Papers, Royal Archives, Windsor
First Baron Welby Papers, London School of Economics

WRITINGS AND PUBLICATIONS OF
GEORGE JOACHIM GOSCHEN

The Rugby Miscellany, 14, in the British Museum contains a copy of 'The Celts'.

The Theory of the Foreign Exchanges. London, 1861. [Goschen revised the book slightly in 1863 and again in 1864.]

'The Leap in the Dark', *St. Paul's Magazine*, I (October 1867), 8–22.

'The New Electors, or Probable Effects of the Reform Bill on the Strength of Parties', *St. Paul's Magazine*, 1 (November 1867), 148–62.

Reports and Speeches on Local Taxation. London, 1872.

The Egyptian Debt: Daira Creditors. London, 1877.

Mental Training and Useful Knowledge. Bristol, 1879.

Addresses. Edinburgh, 1885. [This book contains Goschen's speeches of 31 January, 3 February and 11 February 1885.]

Addresses on Educational and Economical Subjects. Edinburgh, 1885.

'Hearing, Reading and Thinking', *Aspects of Modern Study*. London, 1894.

The Metallic Reserve. London, 1891.

The Cultivation and Use of Imagination. London, 1893.

International Prejudice. Birmingham, 1896.

The Life and Times of Georg Joachim Goschen, Publisher and Printer of Leipzig. 2 vols., London, 1903.

Essays and Addresses on Economic Questions, 1865–1893. London, 1905.

Some Aspects of the Fiscal Controversy. London, 1905.

Exports and Prosperity. London, 1905.

PARLIAMENTARY AND CABINET MATERIAL

List of Cabinet Papers 1880–1914, Public Record Office.

Photographic Copies of Cabinet Letters in the Royal Archives, Public Record Office.

Parliamentary Debates (Hansard).

AUTOBIOGRAPHIES, DIARIES, PRINTED
CORRESPONDENCE AND COLLECTED SPEECHES

Chamberlain, Joseph, *A Political Memoir 1880–1892*, ed. C. H. D. Howard. London, 1953.

Colson, Percy (ed.), *Lord Goschen and His Friends*. London, 1945.

Gathorne-Hardy, Alfred E. (ed.), *The Diary and Correspondence of the First Earl of Cranbrook*. 2 vols., London, 1910.

Gooch, G. P. (ed.), *The Later Correspondence of Lord John Russell 1840–1878*. 2 vols., London, 1925.

Hamilton, Lord George, *Parliamentary Reminiscences and Reflections*. London, 1916–22.

Headlam, Cecil (ed.), *The Milner Papers*. 2 vols., London, 1931–3.

Hutchinson, Horace G. (ed.), *The Private Diaries of Sir Algernon West*. London, 1922.

SELECT BIBLIOGRAPHY

Lowther, James W. (Viscount Ullswater), *A Speaker's Commentaries.* 2 vols., London, 1925.

Morley, Lord John, *Recollections.* 2 vols., London, 1917.

Paul, Herbert (ed.), *Letters of Lord Acton to Mary, Daughter of the Rt. Hon. W. E. Gladstone.* London, 1904.

Ramm, Agatha, *The Political Correspondence of Mr. Gladstone and Lord Granville 1868–1876.* 2 vols., London, 1952.

   The Political Correspondence of Mr. Gladstone and Lord Granville 1876–1886. 2 vols., Oxford, 1962.

St Helier, Lady (Mrs Mary Jeune), *Memories of Fifty Years.* London, 1909.

Selborne, Earl of (Roundell Palmer), *Memorials.* 4 vols., London, 1896–8.

Victoria, Queen, *Letters of Queen Victoria.* 9 vols., New York, 1907–32. [The first three volumes (1837–61) were edited by A. C. Benson and Viscount Esher and the final six (1862–1901) by George E. Buckle.]

West, Sir Algernon E., *Recollections 1832–1886.* London, 1899.

BIOGRAPHIES AND BIOGRAPHICAL STUDIES

Askwith, Lord George R., *Lord James of Hereford,* London, 1930.

Blake, Robert, *Disraeli.* London, 1966.

Cecil, Lady Gwendolen, *The Life of Robert, Marquess of Salisbury.* 4 vols., London, 1921–32.

Chilston, Viscount, *Chief Whip: The Political Life and Times of Aretas Akers-Douglas, 1st Viscount Chilston.* London, 1961.

   W. H. Smith, London, 1965.

Churchill, Sir Winston, *Lord Randolph Churchill.* London, 1951.

Elliot, Arthur R. D., *Life of George Joachim Goschen.* 2 vols., London, 1911.

Fitzmaurice, Lord Edmond, *Life of the Second Earl Granville.* 3rd edn., 2 vols., London, 1905.

Fraser, Peter, *Joseph Chamberlain.* London, 1966.

Gardiner, Alfred G., *Life of Sir William Harcourt.* 2 vols., London, 1923.

Garvin, J. L. and Amery, Julian, *Life of Joseph Chamberlain.* 6 vols., London, 1932–70.

Gooch, George P., *Life of Lord Courtney.* London, 1920.

Hamer, D. A., *John Morley.* Oxford, 1968.

Hammond, J. L. and Barbara, *James Stansfeld.* London, 1932.

Hicks Beach, Lady Victoria, *Life of Sir Michael Hicks Beach, Earl St. Aldwyn.* 2 vols., London, 1932.

Holland, Bernard, *Life of the Eighth Duke of Devonshire.* 2 vols., London, 1911.

James, Robert Rhodes, *Lord Randolph Churchill.* London, 1959.

Magnus, Philip, *Gladstone.* New York, 1954.

Monypenny, W. F. and George E. Buckle, *Life of Benjamin Disraeli.* 6 vols., London, 1910–20.

Morley, John, *Life of William E. Gladstone.* 3 vols., New York, 1903.

Ponsonby, Arthur, *Henry Ponsonby: Queen Victoria's Private Secretary.* London, 1942.

Reid, Sir T. Wemyss, *Life of William E. Forster.* 2 vols., London, 1898.

248

Memoirs and Correspondence of Lyon Playfair, First Lord Playfair of St. Andrew, 1818–1898. London, 1899.

Wolf, Lucien, *Life of the First Marquess of Ripon*, 2 vols., London, 1921.

Wrench, John Evelyn, *Alfred Lord Milner: The Man of No Illusions*. London, 1958.

Young, Kenneth, *Arthur James Balfour*. London, 1963.

Zetland, Marquess of, *Lord Cromer*. London, 1932.

SPECIAL STUDIES AND MONOGRAPHS

Ausubel, Herman, *In Hard Times: Reformers Among the Late Victorians*. New York, 1960.

Beer, Samuel, *British Politics in the Collectivist Age*. New York, 1967.

Brown, Benjamin H., *The Tariff Reform Movement in Great Britain 1881–1895*. New York, 1943.

Clapham, Sir John H., *The Bank of England*. 2 vols., Cambridge, 1944.

Dangerfield, George, *The Strange Death of Liberal England*. New York, 1935.

Ensor, R. C. K., *England 1870–1914*. Oxford, 1960.

Farrer, Sir Thomas H. F., *Mr. Goschen's Finance 1887–1890*. London, 1891.

Feuchtwanger, E. J., *Disraeli, Democracy and the Tory Party*. Oxford, 1968.

Gollin, A. M., *Balfour's Burden*. London, 1965.

Proconsul in Politics. London, 1964.

Gorst, Harold, *The Fourth Party*. London, 1906.

Hammond, J. L., *Gladstone and the Irish Nation*. London, 1938.

Hanham, H. J., *Elections and Party Management*. London, 1959.

Hardie, Frank, *The Political Influence of Queen Victoria 1861–1901*. Oxford, 1935.

Jenks, Leland H., *The Migration of British Capital to 1875*. New York, 1927.

The numerous works of that versatile journalist, Henry W. Lucy, provide many interesting insights into the political life of the times.

Lynd, Helen, *England in the Eighteen-Eighties*. New York, 1945.

Mallet, Bernard, *The British Budgets 1887–88 to 1912–13*. London, 1913.

Medlicott, W. N., *Bismarck, Gladstone and the Concert of Europe*. London, 1956.

O'Brien, Conor C., *Parnell and His Party 1880–1890*. Oxford, 1957.

Ostrogorski, Moisei, *Democracy and the Organization of Political Parties*. London, 1902.

Polanyi, Karl, *The Great Transformation*. Boston, 1957.

Reid, Sir T. Wemyss, *Politicians of Today*. London, 1880.

Robinson, Ronald and Gallagher, John, with Denny, Alice, *Africa and the Victorians*. New York, 1961.

Rostow, W. W., *British Economy of the Nineteenth Century*. Oxford, 1961.

Ruggiero, Guido de, *The History of European Liberalism*. Boston, 1959.

Schumpeter, Joseph, *Capitalism, Socialism and Democracy*. New York, 1962.

Smith, Paul, *Disraelian Conservatism and Social Reform*. London, 1967.

Southgate, Donald, *The Passing of the Whigs 1832–1886*. London, 1962.

Stansky, Peter, *Ambitions and Strategies*. Oxford, 1964.

Strauss, E., *Irish Nationalism and British Democracy*. London, 1951.

Thomas, J. Alun, *The House of Commons 1832–1901: A Study of its Economic and Functional Character*. Cardiff, 1939.

Vincent, John R., *The Formation of the Liberal Party 1857–1868*. London, 1966.

ARTICLES

Brebner, J. Bartlett, 'Laissez-faire and State Intervention in Nineteenth-century Britain', *The Journal of Economic History*, supplement, VIII (1948), 59–73.

Cornford, J., 'The Transformation of Conservatism in the Late Nineteenth Century', *Victorian Studies*, VII (1963–4), 35–66.

Ensor, R. C. K., 'Some Political and Economic Interactions in Later Victorian England', *Transactions of the Royal Historical Society*, 4th series, XXXI (1949), 17–28.

Fraser, P., 'The Liberal Unionist Alliance: Chamberlain, Hartington and the Conservatives 1886–1904', *The English Historical Review*, LXXVII (January 1962), 53–78.

Glickman, Harvey, 'The Toryness of English Conservatism', *The Journal of British Studies*, I (November 1961), 111–43.

Goodman, Gordon L., 'Liberal Unionism: The Revolt of the Whigs', *Victorian Studies*, II (December 1959), 173–89.

Harnetty, P., 'The Indian Cotton Duties Controversy, 1894–1896', *The English Historical Review*, LXXVII (October 1962), 684–702.

Howard, C. H. D., 'Joseph Chamberlain and the "Unauthorized Programme" ', *The English Historical Review*, LXV (October 1950), 477–91.

Milner, Viscount Alfred, 'George Joachim Goschen: Obituary', *Proceedings oj the British Academy 1907–1908*, 359–64.

Pressnell, L. S., 'Gold Reserves, Banking Reserves, and the Baring Crisis of 1890' in C. R. Whittlesey and J. S. G. Wilson (eds.), *Essays in Money and Banking*. Oxford, 1968.

Roach, John, 'Liberalism and the Victorian Intelligentsia', *The Cambridge Historical Journal*, XIII (1957), 58–81.

Spinner, Thomas J., jr., 'George Joachim Goschen: The Man Lord Randolph Churchill "Forgot" ', *The Journal of Modern History*, XXXIX (December 1967), 405–24.

Tholfsen, T. R., 'The Transition to Democracy in Victorian England', *International Review of Social History*, VI, pt 2 (1961), 226–48.

INDEX

Abdul Hamid II 67–71, 74f, 81, 199
Acton, Lord 65, 83f, 86
Admiralty: Goschen on 38f, 188f, 202f, 235; Goschen at 19, 35–42, 187, 224f, 235; Alabama claims 37; loss of troops at sea 38; reform 38f, 188f; Defence Committee 189, obstructive attitude to 193; conservatism of 189, 196; service estimates 202, 206, 211f, 218; policies, for Africa 203f, 206, 212, for Far East 204, 219–21, for confrontation with Russia 205f, with Germany 217, 220f; Spanish American war 206f; threat to Gibraltar 208–10; Fashoda incident 210; Boer War 214–17; aggressive policies of Admiral Fisher 235
Adullamite debates 30
Africa: Goschen on 161–4, 200, 203, 212; Ashanti punitive expedition 41f; Egypt the 'key' to Africa 105; confrontation with Germany in 160–3, 203; French presence 197, 'encroachment' 203f; British imperialism moves forward 164; Defence Committee on 191, 195; see also East Africa; South Africa
Agincourt, loss of 38
agriculture: Goschen on 86; depressed state of 184; suffrage of agricultural labourers 22, 25, 58f, 95, 172; rates relief for labourers 34; creation of small-holdings 116, 181; effects of Irish Land Purchase Bill 169, 172; poor relief 181; protective tariffs 228; effects of Industrial Revolution 240
Akers-Douglas, Aretas, see Chilston, Viscount
Alabama Claims 37
Albania 70, 77
Alexandria 89f
Algeciras 207–10

Alliance Fire Company 174
Alsace–Lorraine 35
Ambalema 6f, 174f
anti-semitism 1
Arabi, Colonel Ahmed 89
Arabs 160
Argentina 146, 147, 148, 174
Argyll, Duke of 85f, 100, 115
aristocracy ixf, 18, 29, 172, 188, 240
Aristotle 11
armament 36, 48, 206, 211, 218, 238
Armenia 68, 71f, 79, 197, 199, 202
Army: Goschen on 27, 98, 106, 137, 157, 194, 196; Goschen's grandfather declines to enter 1; flogging 27; purchase of commissions 29; economies 36, 42, 157, 197; loss of troops at sea 38; supplies 39, 186; Ashanti punitive expedition 41; troops in Malta 57; 'militarism' 64; military consuls 68; troops in Egypt 89f, 157f; service estimates 130, 143, 190, 192, 211; Defence Committee 188, 190–9; Algeciras crisis 207; Gibraltar 208; Fashoda incident 210f; Boer War 214–22
Arnold, Dr Matthew 3
Ashanti expedition 41f
Asquith, H. H. 240
Atcheson and Topeka Railroad 174
Athenaeum Club 133
Australia 23, 38, 106, 175, 184
Austria: Goschen on 159f; Austro-Prussian war 10, 22; aggression against Denmark 18; participates in Egyptian Commission of Public Debt 49, 51; Eastern Question 69, 76, 199; as British ally 197, in Mediterranean 159

Bagehot, Walter 10
Balfour, Arthur: Goschen on 155, 185, 231, 232, 233–4, 235; on

INDEX

Uganda 162–4
Ulster 95, 112, 120f, 123, 125
unemployment 11, 30, 170, 173, 226, 232f
Union Defence League 238f
Unionist Free Food League 229
Unionist Free Trade Club 231, 233, 244
United States 18, 23, 37f, 174, 199–202, 204, 206f, 212, 216f, 219; Goschen on 199f
University College, Oxford 1n, 4
university reform 30
Uruguay 174
utilitarianism 13f, 31

vagrancy 31
Valentine letters 235
Vancouver Island 199
Venezuela 199f
Victoria, Queen: relations, with Goschen 21, 38, 39f, 55, 71, 73, 83, 97, 112f, 124, 131, 134, 166, 171, 188, 233f, with Hartington 64, 110, 119, 122, 128, 137, with Salisbury 107, 112, 117, 128, with Rosebery 177, 186; horror of radicals 64f, 100, 112, 116f, 166f; approval of moderates 66, 100, 116–20, 122f, 127, 130, 131f; on foreign affairs 22, 73, 160, 162, 185, 199, 217; on electoral reform 95, 97; on home rule 123, 124f; on coinage 146; amendments to queen's speech 171, 182; Diamond Jubilee 213; dies 228

Wales 172
Wallace, Robert 127
Wallroth, Charles 7f
Warren, Sir Charles 170
War Office 21, 36f, 41, 88, 189–96, 208, 214, 218, 225
Webb, Sidney 181
Wei-hai-wei 205
Welby, R. E. 150, 175f
welfare, social x, 83, 171
West, Algernon 138, 175f
wheel and van tax 141, 153
Whigs 5, 22, 30, 43, 45, 46, 57, 83, 84, 89, 91, 92, 100, 107, 109, 110, 117, 118, 119, 121, 122, 123, 133, 240
Wilkinson, Spencer 188–90, 196
William II, Kaiser 1n, 197, 202, 215f, 220f, 238
Windsor Castle 130f
Wolff, Sir Henry Drummond 132f, 143, 157, 207
Wolseley, Sir Garnet 41, 90
workhouses 31
working class x, 17f, 22f, 25–8, 31, 43, 95, 102f, 108, 110, 172, 181

Yangtse valley 205, 220
Young, G. M. ix
Yukon, river 184

Zambesi, river 161
Zanzibar 160, 200, 203
Zetland, Marquess of 52